We Who Lived

We Who Lived

*Two Teenagers
in World War II Poland*

Hava Bromberg Ben-Zvi

Foreword by Justine M. Pas

McFarland & Company, Inc., Publishers
Jefferson, North Carolina

LIBRARY OF CONGRESS CATALOGUING-IN-PUBLICATION DATA

Names: Ben-Zvi, Hava, author. | Pas, Justine M, writer of foreword.
Title: We who lived : two teenagers in World War II Poland / Hava Bromberg Ben-Zvi ; foreword by Justine M. Pas.
Description: Jefferson, North Carolina : McFarland & Company, Inc., Publishers, 2018 | Includes bibliographical references and index.
Identifiers: LCCN 2017048118 | ISBN 9781476670089 (softcover : acid free paper) ∞
Subjects: LCSH: Ben-Zvi, Hava. | Ben-Zvi, Ephraim. | Holocaust, Jewish (1939–1945)—Poland—Warsaw—Personal narratives. | Jewish teenagers—Poland—Warsaw—Biography. | Jewish children in the Holocaust—Poland—Warsaw—Biography. | Warsaw (Poland)—Biography.
Classification: LCC D134.7 .B46 2018 | DDC 940.53/1809253509438 [B]—dc23
LC record available at https://lccn.loc.gov/2017048118

BRITISH LIBRARY CATALOGUING DATA ARE AVAILABLE

ISBN (print) 978-1-4766-7008-9
ISBN (ebook) 978-1-4766-3119-6

© 2018 Hava Bromberg Ben-Zvi. All rights reserved

No part of this book may be reproduced or transmitted in any form or by any means, electronic or mechanical, including photocopying or recording, or by any information storage and retrieval system, without permission in writing from the publisher.

Front cover photograph: Hava and Ephraim Ben-Zvi following their wedding, 1950 (author's collection)

Printed in the United States of America

McFarland & Company, Inc., Publishers
  Box 611, Jefferson, North Carolina 28640
    www.mcfarlandpub.com

To the memory of my husband, Dr. Ephraim Ben-Zvi,
for love and support everlasting.

In memory of my father, Herman Bromberg,
who perished in the Holocaust.

In memory of my mother, Dinah, my brother, Michael,
and all Holocaust martyrs.

For my son, Henry, my daughter-in-law, Molly, and my
grandchildren, Sarah, Daniel, and Michael.

Table of Contents

Acknowledgments   ix
Foreword by Justine M. Pas   1
Preface   5
Prologue: At the Gate   9

1. My Family   11
2. Life with Father   26
3. I Remember   39
4. War   47
5. Under the Germans   59
6. The Orphanage   70
7. On the Farm   80
8. Special Attentions   86
9. Our World in Europe at Peace   92
10. Displaced Persons (DP) Camp   101
11. Forging a New Future   110
12. A New Friend   115
13. The Event That Changed Their Lives   124
14. In the Kolkhoz   129
15. Siberia   133
16. Germany, Now a Common Enemy   137
17. Return to Poland   140
18. Building a New Life   144
19. The Rebirth of Israel   146

20. Newlyweds	155
21. New Horizons	166
22. End Matters: Love and Loss	179
Aftermath: Martyrs and Survivors	184
Postscript	200
Appendix Chronology, 1933–1945: Major Events of World War II with Emphasis on the Holocaust and the Events in Our Lives	205
Bibliographic Essay	209
Index	217

Acknowledgments

I owe a debt of gratitude to my first editor, Amy Donley, for her kindness, insight and hard work.

I express my deepest gratitude to individuals, publishers and organizations for their gracious permission to reprint their materials and use them in my book. They are:

"Ziselman of Honcharska Street," a memoir by Nina Luszczyk Ilienkowa, retold and translated by Hava Bromberg Ben-Zvi, used by permission of Anna Engelking and by Vallentine Mitchell. Previously published in Hava Bromberg Ben-Zvi, ed., *Portraits in Literature: The Jews of Poland: An Anthology*. London: Vallentine Mitchell, 2011, pp. 101–104, and also in Nina Luszczyk Ilienkowa, "Ziselman z Honczarskiej," *Warsaw Quarterly Regiony* 1, no. 96 (2000): 14–16. Pani (Mrs.) Nina, a member of a Polish-Belarus family, was born and resided in the capital of Polesie, Pinsk, in Belarus. She exemplifies the complex, mixed religious and ethnic makeup of the area, where Poles, Jews and other people of Belarus lived together.

The United States Holocaust Memorial Museum, Washington, D.C., for their cooperation and gracious permission to use many of their photographs.

"Four Days in August: A Family's Last Journey," a memoir by Irene Eber, used by permission of Irene Eber. Previously published in *Moment*, vol. II, no. 5 (May 1986): 37–46. Irene Eber is a Louis Frieberg Professor of East Asian Studies (emerita) at the Hebrew University of Jerusalem and a Senior Fellow at the Harry S Truman Research Institute. She is the author or editor of eight scholarly books on Chinese history and thought. Irene Eber's book, *The Choice: Poland, 1939–1945*, Schocken Books, 2004, is "a memoir about defeating deportation and death in wartime Poland's atmosphere of fear and desperate hope belongs to what is most poignant in the vast literature of the Holocaust." Comment by Elie Wiesel.

Yigael Yadin's letter (in Chapter 19), used by permission of Orly and

Littal Yadin, Yigael Yadin's children, and by permission of HarperCollins. Previously published in Martin Gilbert, *Israel: A History*. New York: William Morrow, 1998, p. 203.

"The Silver Platter," by Nathan Alternam, used by permission of ACUM, Israel, on behalf of the author's heir, Nathan Slor, and the University of Texas Press. Previously published in *No Rattling of Sabers: An Anthology of Israeli War Poetry*. Translation and introduction by Esther Raizen. Austin: University of Texas Press, 1995.

Carol Grimes, for her permission to reprint experts from her eulogy for Dr. Ephraim Ben-Zvi (in Chapter 22).

"Otynia" (Chapter 17) including the section on the destruction of the Jews of Otynia, published online at www.shtetlinks.jewishgen.org/Ottynia/ottynia.htm and used by permission of Philip Spiegel. This portion was translated by Spiegel from the *Encyclopedia of Jewish Communities* (*Pinkas Ha'Kehilot* in Hebrew), vol. II. Jerusalem: Yad Vashem, 1980. Spiegel's translation became the initial version of the information on the internet. He also translated into English a book by Mykhailo Khavlyuk: *Otyniya: Historical Essays*. Ukraine, 1998. Selected information from this book, pages 56–57, was consulted as one of the sources I have used for my present work. Spiegel is the author of *Triumph Over Tyranny: The Heroic Campaign That Saved 2,000,000 Soviet Jews*, 2008. See www.triumphovertyranny.com.

"The First Ottynier Young Men's Benevolent Society and Life in Otynia" (Chapter 18) appears online at www.shtetlinks.jewishgen.org/Ottynia/ottynia.htm used here by permission of Herbert Latner and Norman Latner.

Information about the Jewish National Fund and photographs of the Blue Box used by permission of Jodi Bodner.

I will always be grateful to my mentors and editors: Dr. Justine M. Pas of Lindenwood University; Irene McDermott of the Crowell Public Library, City of San Marino; Marti Tippens Murphy of Facing History and Ourselves; Jeanette Shelburne, a wonderful teacher and her entire Simon Wiesenthal Center Writing Class; and especially Madeleine Isenberg.

Sarah D. Ben-Zvi, my granddaughter, whose participation and contribution to my work will always warm my heart.

My niece, Shulamit Toledano, for her help and dedicated research.

My special thanks are due to Julek Sokal, Ephraim's brother, for all the information he has given me about their early life and about life in Otynia and Siberia.

Acknowledgments

To Linda Rourman and Alice Shulman for their assistance.

To Kay Haugaard and to my friends and assistants who were always there: Carolyn Coleman, Pearl Tyree and Giovanna Fradkin for their help and advice; Shlomo Leon, for much information; Bertha Marston; Marlena Pfeifer; Zygmund and Maryla Bromberg; all the members of the Arroyo Writers group; Hannah and Norman Ackerman; and Lisa Silverman of the Sinai Temple Library, Los Angeles.

To the staff of the Crowell San Marino Public Library, and particularly Jeff Plumley.

Brita Richardson, for her scholarship and patience.

I gratefully acknowledge the wonderful resources and support of the staff of the Hebrew Union College Library in Los Angeles: Dr. Yaffa Weisman, Sheryl Stahl and their entire crew. Jessica Phillips and Yukika Skorpil, the staff of the Pasadena Public Library, the Simon Wiesenthal Center Library.

And my deepest thanks for the help and support of my son, Henry Ben-Zvi, always.

Foreword
by Justine M. Pas

Writing about the past is never easy. For survivors of the Shoah, revisiting the past involves an emotionally grueling return to incredibly frightening and heartbreaking events that, as many survivors relate in their stories, they tried to forget. Hava Bromberg Ben-Zvi echoes this sense of wanting to forget, or at least not thinking about the past, when she recalls in her preface that she and her husband Ephraim rarely discussed their wartime ordeals. They needed to concentrate on the demands of the present, which, immediately after the founding of Israel, were far from easy. Having been children during the war who carried burdens of unbelievable enormity, both Hava and Ephraim became adults who created a family together and forged independent careers, all the while keeping the past at bay. As Hava explains in the preface, she wrote this book not because she felt the need to create order out of chaos, but because she felt compelled to build a textual memorial to each and every person who, as she reminds us, "faced death individually and alone."

Holocaust survivors' textual memorials like *We Who Lived: Two Teenagers in World War II Poland* add crucially important individual particularities to historical accounts. Every account of survival offers a glimpse into a single, unique human life. Each of them reminds us that every life matters because human beings, regardless of race, ethnicity, or religion, should never be expendable. As Hava herself affirms, individual accounts "illuminate the enormity of the crime," and the more stories we read, the more we become aware of "how different each story" is, even if all survived "the same murderous regime." In *We Who Lived*, Hava shares with us much information about her life before and after the war. She describes her family and marriage in Israel as well as her new family's immigrant life in America. Hava also includes a biography of her beloved husband,

Ephraim. As Hava told me, she wrote Ephraim's story, based on her conversations and correspondence with Ephraim's brother, because she wants to leave a record of her husband's life.

The sense of *We Who Lived* as a simultaneously autobiographical and biographical homage to the love of Hava's life helps readers navigate how the stories of their pasts, though presented in separate sections, blend together to form the background out of which Hava and Ephraim created their marriage and family. Moreover, the book's broader temporal scope is somewhat atypical because many accounts by Holocaust survivors stop short of describing the challenges they faced as displaced people and refugees who rebuilt lives in new countries, cultures, and languages. Hava grew up speaking Polish and hearing her parents speak Yiddish. She learned Russian during the war. After the war ended, she made yet another linguistic and cultural transition to learn Hebrew in Israel. Finally, as a wife and mother, she made a transition to learn English when she and Ephraim built their family life and future in California. Hava's book reminds us that people whose lives were indelibly marked by suffering and loss had to recreate their lives after the war in new languages and cultures.

Hava enjoyed an ordinary childhood in Warsaw, Poland, before the war. She recalls running to buy her father's favorite Yiddish newspaper, playing with dolls, and reading children's stories and fairy tales. Likewise, she describes Ephraim's life as a member of an ordinary middle-class Jewish family living in a small town in southeastern Poland. The outbreak of the war in 1939 irrevocably altered these ordinary lives. While Hava and Ephraim's paths to survival were very different—she passed as a Christian under the Nazi rule, while he lived with his mother and brother in abject poverty in Siberian exile—the very irrevocability with which the war permanently transformed their realities brought them together years later in Israel. "We understood each other," Hava writes as she introduces her story of Ephraim's survival. "Having a common Polish background, we instinctively shared each other's hopes, problems and motives." The couple needed to say little about the war: "Between us, few words were needed" because "we were lucky to have the opportunity to overcome the destruction and cruelties of war." No matter how difficult life in Israel may have been and no matter how alienated they might have felt upon their arrival in the United States, Hava and Ephraim worked together to create a future.

Many accounts of Holocaust survival share a similar writing style, and Hava, too, writes in a matter-of-fact narrative voice, almost entirely avoiding deeper affect, nostalgia, or tearfulness. She relates her stories in a very straightforward, chronological manner with little artifice. Hava's account, much like those of other survivors, reads not so much as an autobiographical rendering, which shapes the past into particular stories, but as a historical memory project to record facts. There is a sense of urgency here to ensure that the experiences of those who survived are preserved long after they are gone. She wants these largely unembellished memories to survive her, as they have already survived Ephraim, so that readers will continue to learn what happened between 1939 and 1945, not only from books written by historians, but also from those who were there and who endured.

Hava's candid rendition of her and Ephraim's past reminds me of conventional histories, where a recording of facts shows how individual persons survived against all odds. At the same time, I cannot help thinking that such a dispassionate recording of an unbelievably agonizing past kept the pain from resurfacing, helping Hava to focus on experiences, facts, and details instead of emotional reactions and feelings. But even without detailed descriptions of her emotional state and reactions, no reader can miss the pain beneath the tapestry of facts. This is powerfully evident in her description of when Germans began their occupation of the Soviet-controlled territory where Hava and her father found refuge. Hava tells us that her father had to report for what everyone assumed was a day of mandatory labor. Hava is twelve years old when she sees her father for the last time on the morning of his departure. Once the news of the real goal for her father's departure reaches her—Germans executed all adult Jewish men that day—Hava recalls her refusal to lose hope because "hope would help me cope with my pain and heartbreak." This is an extraordinarily poignant passage, yet Hava records this tremendous loss with little affect. She leaves her readers to imagine the loneliness and fear the child must have felt as Hava concludes simply: "I knew I could not feel or be a child any longer." The war stole her father and her childhood, plunging her into a world marked by death and destruction where, at the very young age of twelve, she "took [her] own life into [her] own hands, and accepted the risks and the consequences." Hava describes a war-torn world where children needed to become adults in order to survive, where they had to endure unbearable losses while pretending to be someone else. They hid in plain sight while disguising unthinkable and ever-present pain and fear.

Hava Bromberg Ben-Zvi did not shape *We Who Lived* into a moral lesson about human goodness. Rather, she documented her and Ephraim's lives to ensure that each of us recognizes the individuality and uniqueness of every person who survived the catastrophe. At the same time, like other Holocaust survivors, Hava recorded their lives to ensure that we remember where hatred and hunger for power lead. Hava's book is an important reminder about the rhetoric of hatred at a time when political rhetoric has turned virulent in an effort to divide and blind us to the humanity of those who look or pray in ways we do not recognize or sanction. I am unwilling to think about Hava and Ephraim's lives without seeing their stories' implications for today and for future generations. We must heed their stories to commemorate the lives of survivors and to pay our respects to those who perished. Not doing so means forgetting what survivors' stories compel us to always remember.

Justine M. Pas is an associate professor of English at Lindenwood University in St. Charles, Missouri. Her research and teaching interests include American literature and translation studies.

Preface

I never knew I was a Holocaust survivor until I wrote this memoir and visited a school to tell the students about my life and experiences during World War II. As I entered, the class greeted me with applause. I was speechless, never expecting any accolades. Then the teacher introduced me as a Holocaust survivor which, to me, felt like an entirely new label. Even the mere idea that my experiences shaped not only my past but also my identity was a foreign and near unfathomable concept. I never thought of myself as a survivor. In my mind, I was a woman, a daughter, a wife, a mother, a neighbor and a friend. My husband Ephraim and I faced the war's consequences, but never considered surviving it of any relevance to our newly rebuilt life. Instead of thinking about our past we got on with things: we went to high school, to college, and to work.

But of course, I was *a Holocaust survivor*. I always knew I had a story to tell and felt a duty and an obligation to tell what had happened to me. Six million is a number. A number does not represent a face and a life, and each of the victims faced death individually and alone. By presenting my story—the story of a real survivor—I believe I can help to illuminate the enormity of the crime. I read many memoirs by other youthful and adult survivors and it was striking how different each story was, even though they all happened within the same murderous regime. I knew my story, like the others, was one that needed to be told.

In 2004 I wrote and published the first version of my memoir: *Eva's Journey*. Students in my area's high schools could not wait to get their hands on it and read it. Years passed. I knew I needed to tell far more about myself, my husband, our life together, about the times, and address myself to an audience of adults in terms of facts and their descriptions.

I knew well what had happened to me, even though some details were blurry, but writing about my husband Ephraim presented a problem. He and I seldom—if ever—talked about his life before we met in 1947, about the war years and what he had been through. Never before did I wonder about the reasons for our silence. It was not because we tried to forget, but life after was hard and demanded all our time, attention, and efforts. We had a child to love and bring up in peace.

It wasn't that talk of our past lives was forbidden. It was mentioned in our home. It was never a secret to any of our friends. Our son knew we had lived through it, but we never wanted to traumatize a growing, hopeful child by describing the details of the horrors. Perhaps rarely mentioning the Holocaust was our way to cope. Or perhaps we needed the distance of time and security, before returning to the past.

I recall there was little interest and few memoirs were published immediately following the war. Did everyone try to forget it? We woke up approximately two decades later, in the 1970s and 1980s, to return to the war years, to tell our stories. By that time, I believe, America had recovered from the wounds and impact caused by the war, and was more receptive to hear our memoirs.

The stories differed in their locations, the ages of the rescued and the rescuers, the finances of all involved, the characters and motivation of the rescuers, the attitudes of neighbors and the prevailing community spirit and values. Many Righteous Gentiles in Poland were mortally afraid of being reported to the Germans by their neighbors. Each memoir was unique, and changed the lives of the rescuers and rescued forever.

My growing awareness of being a Holocaust survivor only strengthened my resolve. Like the others, I needed to record my tale. As I wrote it, I noted, for the first time, my own self-control as a child of twelve, strength, resilience, and, above all, hope. Sometimes I felt my tale lacked drama. In the quiet village, I learned to milk cows, to raise a generation of piglets, to care for chickens and geese. All these definitely lacked dramatic impact, but I lived day by day hoping that every new day would be as undramatic as the one before.

I knew that with the passage of time the facts may be forgotten, or even denied. We, the survivors, were getting older, and soon there would be no living witness. As genocide was, and still is, occurring in different parts of our world, I believed that the international intervention we had witnessed in selected areas, such as the former Yugoslavia, were the result of the lessons taught by the Holocaust, and the world's silence at that time.

But now I needed to know more about Ephraim's life and he was no longer with us. Julek Sokal, Ephraim's younger brother, who immigrated to Australia to become a lecturer in the department of Civil Engineering of the University of Queensland in Brisbane, was of immeasurable help to me. He and I knew each other well. Now, in memory of the brother he loved, he told me more than I ever knew about their family. He wrote to me about their home life, and he described the experience of growing up in a warm, close-knit family and community. I learned about their house, in the middle of the marketplace and the large extended family living in three separate apartments, but still together, nonetheless. I learned about the two bistros on the ground floor belonging to their two grandfathers, one of whom lived with Ephraim's family. I learned about their small town (shtetl), about its non–Jewish and Jewish population, about the social stratification and about the people's excessive respect for class and position. Julek told me about their father, Henryk Sokal, his education, occupation, marriage and place in the community.

I recalled Stasia (Sarah) Schreier, my mother in-law, while chatting in the kitchen together, mentioning to me the many kerosene lamps and the chamber pots required an army of maids. I gathered the family was wealthy—she mentioned a diamond ring, a Persian carpet.

I recalled Stasia once telling me about her father's scrutiny of a rug she had just purchased. "How much did you pay for this carpet?" he asked. Stasia replied, "100 zlotys" to her father, who responded, "To you, mud and money are one and the same thing." It was then that she revealed to me the rug actually cost four times that amount. Stasia loved Israel with all her heart, and appreciated the sacrifices and achievements permitting us to live there, yet enjoyed telling me about her former wealth and position in the community.

Stasia was proud of her observance of Jewish dietary laws (kashrut) in her home and told me about the two boys, Rysio (later Ephraim) and Julek, the differences in their characters, temperaments, and temper tantrums. The children tested Stasia's patience, and she frequently delegated their care to the nannies.

Stasia described their imprisonment, deportation and life in Siberia, her work there as a men's barber and the "animal-like" (her expression) anti–Semitism of the Polish women, her fellow deportees. I listened to the family's legend of the cow in the cellar.

One day Stasia heard from an eyewitness that her old mother, Malka, while driven to her death by the Germans, had her swollen feet wrapped in rags. She could no longer wear shoes. Even my hardened heart stopped beating. This was the new "normality" in Jewish family sagas.

In addition to piecing together Ephraim's history through family stories, I made friends with other Siberian deportees and heard about different work and conditions in different areas. Hunger was universal, and some deportees survived only by gathering wild fruits, mostly blueberries, in the forests.

I met with many other Holocaust survivors, trying to learn how much of their war experiences were shared with their children and each other. One son told me: "In our family all the roads lead to Auschwitz." Unlike his family, where most of the conversations revolved around the past, many other survivors, like Ephraim and I, kept their silence.

For political background and to fill the missing pieces I needed historical sources and used books, the Internet, and libraries and archives to provide context and other perspectives.

In *We Who Lived*, I describe my young years in the first person, from a young child's perspective. Maturing, my voice changed to that of a young adult, then a young woman.

I hope this work will serve as a modest gift to the martyrs to preserve their memory and a tribute to a caring, much loved man, my husband, Ephraim Ben-Zvi.

Prologue: At the Gate

Shivering, I stood looking up at the white mansion on the hill. Formerly the residence of a Polish nobleman, now an orphanage, its white columns spoke of wealth and security, and maybe safety. A frosty November wind blew and whistled through the trees.

I was twelve years old. I was Jewish, and the Jewish population was condemned to death in German-occupied Poland in 1941. Being accepted into the orphanage meant life. My Jewish identity had to be hidden.

I loosened my gray shawl. A shabby gray coat covered the schoolgirl navy blue dress I wore. I hoped that my blond hair, blue eyes and flawless Polish were in my favor. But would my story be believed?

I did not hesitate. There was nowhere else to go. Suppressing my fears, I clenched my fists and knocked on the door.

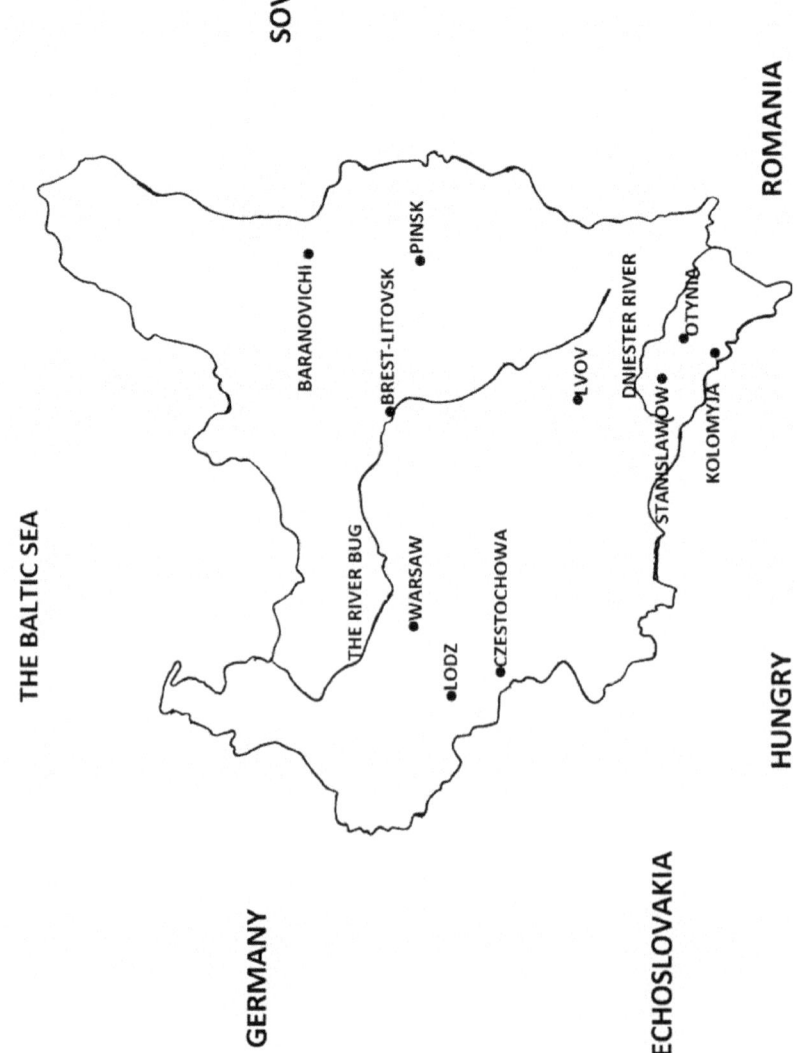

Chapter 1
My Family

The Catholic hospital of a monastic order in Warsaw, Poland, was in an uproar. All the bells were ringing: emergency! A young woman was brought in. She slipped on the ice and snow on a freezing winter night, suffering a serious fall in the seventh month of her pregnancy. Birth followed immediately.

The year was 1929. Dinah Lewartowska Bromberg gave birth to twin girls, but one of the babies did not survive Dinah's fall. The other one was alive and breathing, premature and very small.

One day my mother told me the story of my birth. When brought to her for the first time, I, Eva, had no nose, but just holes and a bone in my face. She was heartbroken. Concerned about her deep sorrow, the doctor explained that what she saw was the nose bone. The flesh would grow.

And he was right. By the time I was three months old I looked like a normal baby.

The nuns were very kind to her. When the time came to take me home, they dressed me and wrapped me in many blankets against the harsh Polish winter, exchanging sad glances, as if saying, "This baby will not survive."

As they said goodbye, they made a sign of the cross over my head and invoked the traditional blessing: "May you live to dress this baby for her wedding."

One day my father told me about the time they brought me home. Incubators had yet to be invented, and to keep me alive their apartment had to be kept unbearably hot. My mother was afraid to touch and harm this fragile little being. My father was then the one to bathe me, and I was small enough to be held in the palm of his hand. I listened quietly to his story. A bond had been formed from the moment I saw the light of day.

In a different world, in Warsaw, before the war, I once had a family. I lived with my mother, father and my older brother Michael.

My mother was short, blondish, pretty and elegant. At the time of

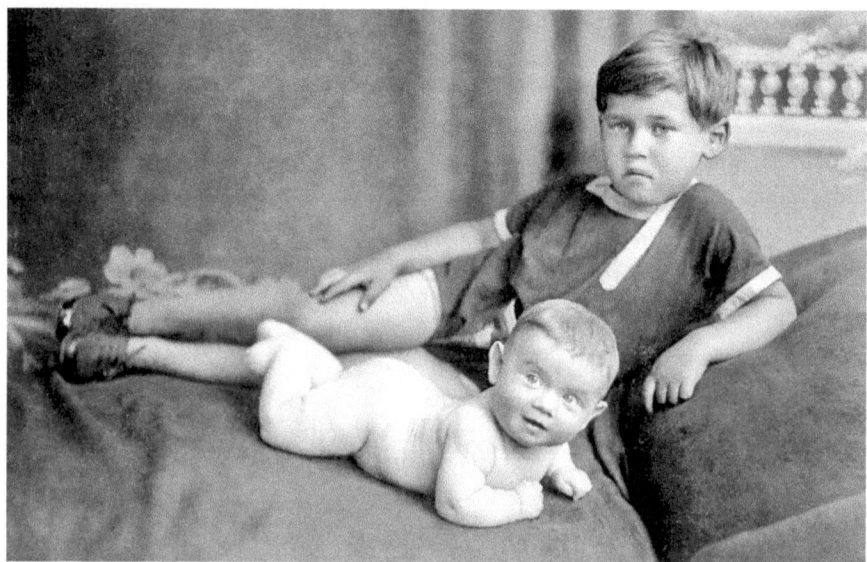

Top: **Eva's father, mother, brother and uncle, ca. 1928 (family collection).** *Bottom:* **Eva and Michael (family collection).**

my birth she was in her early thirties. Born in Siedlce, a small town near Warsaw, she came to Warsaw to study and later to teach. My father was in his early forties, taller, blue-eyed, dark-haired, handsome, and slightly overweight. Meticulous in his dress, he wore a pince-nez and a gold watch on a chain. I never heard him raise his voice in anger.

Eva's parents in Warsaw, 1930s (family collection).

My parents spoke excellent Polish, but sometimes slipped into Yiddish, usually about things we children were not expected to know. But Michael, my older brother, caught some words, and this was the extent of his poor Yiddish. I knew no Yiddish, and only later in life I heard enough Yiddish to gain a limited understanding of the language.

I don't recall any overt signs of love and affection between my parents, and sometimes there was a feeling of tension in the air.

When I was small, no more than three or four, I had a nanny. Nanny was an elderly woman, with her grey hair tied in a bun at the back of her head. I think my parents decided to call her Niania, nanny in Polish, because you could not possibly call an elderly person by her first name. The only alternative, in Polish, would be to address her as Pani, equivalent to Mrs. or Madam. But now I used to kneel on a chair by the kitchen table and watch Niania make dough, roll it out and cut it up thinly for noodles, cook soup and bake cookies. I was so small; I was even allowed to ride on the parquet floor polisher. I spent much time with Niania. Niania took me to church, told me about Pan (our Master) Jesus and taught me prayers. I learned to recite "Our Father, Who art in heaven, hallowed be Thy name. Thy kingdom come, Thy will be done on earth as it is in heaven. Give us our daily bread, and forgive our trespasses…." I also knew "Hail Mary full of grace, blessed be thou among women and blessed be the fruit of Thy womb, Jesus…." I think that no other Jewish child in Poland knew that. It was just a game to me. She also taught me to cross myself, and to kneel in church, following others. I didn't understand its meaning or significance. Jewish children knew nothing about Jesus. Little did I know that this religious background was to contribute to my chances of survival in the very near, frightful future.

Niania took me with her to church, then we would visit her relatives, who had already heard from her about tensions between my parents, and always asked: "Whom do you like better, Mommy or Daddy?" Niania taught me to reply diplomatically: "*Wszystko jedno*" (It is all the same to me). We visited the grand store of the Jabłkowski Brothers in Warsaw to look at the Christmas displays in their windows of Nativity and fairy tales. While together in the kitchen, Niania told me more about Pan Jesus. She even showed me a thorny twig, and told me it was a part of His crown of thorns, and told me that the Jews caused his death. I understood it must have been painful, for which I felt vaguely responsible. This was a secret between Niania and me.

One day Niana's granddaughter, who was to be a flower girl in a church procession, was ill. Niania, a Roman Catholic, did not hesitate. She dressed me in a white dress and put a wreath of flowers on my head. A basket of flower petals was hung by ribbon around my neck and I was taught to walk in a procession: take a few steps forward, scatter some flowers, turn around and fold my hands as if in prayer.

I understood that my Jewish parents were not to be told about it. I followed Ninia's instructions, enjoyed the experience and never breathed a word about it to anyone.

I spent much time with Niania. She treated me, small as I was, like a grown-up friend and companion sometimes. She showed me the clothes she had prepared for her own death: a long skirt and a long-sleeved shirt, all in black. She told me that the Capuchin monks bury their dead in a crypt under their church. This talk of death upset me. I imagined a dark, airless crypt in the earth. I was afraid I was the one to be buried there. Normally, I wasn't afraid of the dark, but this was different. I would be unable to escape, unable to breathe. I was frightened and locked myself in the bathroom, weeping. I must have been about five years old.

My mother, very upset, knocked loudly, ordering me to open the door. Afterward Mother seated me on the sofa, asking why I was crying.

I told her I wanted to be the last in the world to die. I already understood that death was inevitable. Mother did not hesitate at all. Fine, she replied, and rushed back to her work. I would have liked her to stay with me longer.

I had a vague feeling my mother could not keep her promise. There were powers beyond Mother's control, things I did not understand.

One day I asked my mom what twins meant. She understood I must have been listening to family gossip, and explained that I, Eva, was one of twins: two girls born at the same time. One of them did not survive the birth. I, the twin whom they later named Eva, was very much alive and very well.

I wanted to know my twin's name. To me at that young age a name meant her identity, and I wanted to know her. But Mother replied they did not yet name her. She was not ready to be born. I sat at my mother's side, silently contemplating what I had just heard. She hugged me, whispering they were very happy with me, expecting only one child to be born.

Michael, my brother, sometimes good-naturally, referred to me as *przybłęda*. I had a vague feeling it meant, in Polish, a stray dog or cat, finding its way to this (his) family by chance. It did not bother me. Michael and I were somewhat separated by our ages, by future events, and, primarily, by his imminent journey to Palestine.

Niania's son, who served in the Polish army, visited his mother one

Michael and Eva, ca. 1932 (family collection).

time wearing his military uniform and a four-square hat with the Polish eagle. He told his mother about boot camp and battles, preparations for war. I looked at him, heard him, and I knew what to do. There and then I made a decision to protect my unborn family: my children will all be girls rather than boys. Girls did not go to war.

I seemed to set the course of my life at the age of seven. One day in the spring both parents picked me up at school. I walked between my parents, holding them by their hands, feeling the tension between them, and noticing their chilly glances at each other. My parents sometimes spoke in angry voices to each other, but their words were beyond my comprehension. I understood this was part of family life. I knew something was expected of me, without quite knowing what. My mother squeezed my hand and pulled me to her lightly. My father's hand was warm. I recalled my father sometimes sitting alone in a darkened room, with a handkerchief in his hands. Was he crying? Did daddies cry? I was often by his side. There was a bond between us.

We walked in silence along a tree-shaded street in Warsaw. Then, for reasons I cannot explain, I said: I want to be with *Tata* (Daddy).

I never knew what came between my parents and why they had to part. I would have been too young understand it at that time, and I lost both of them too soon. I asked no questions, and raised no objections. I knew little of my parents' lives before they married. I knew only that they were both teachers and met at the teachers union in Warsaw.

My maternal grandfather was the only grandparent I knew, but he and I were not close. He was handsome, with his long white beard, and wore the traditional Jewish Orthodox garb: a long, black coat and a black hat. I knew he only came to see our mother and had little contact with me. I remember my mother crying one day. Her father had died.

Shortly afterward, my parents separated and I came to live in a rented room with Father, while my older brother, Michael, remained with our mother. It seemed that Michael and I had made the decision of choosing a parent. Nothing had been said. Without being manipulated by our parents, we subconsciously knew and did what our parents wanted. In retrospect, I think this decision was a burden we were too young to bear. My father believed he could care for and provide for all my needs. All too soon, he lived to regret it.

Father enrolled me in a nearby Jewish school. All the children were Jewish, and I believe so were most of the teachers. The language of instruction was Polish. I did not know it at the time, but one of the reasons for separate schools might have been that more often than not, Jewish children

Eva and father walking hand in hand in Warsaw, ca. 1936 (family collection).

were abused in public schools. Anti-Semitism was an accepted part of the culture in which we lived, definitely tolerated and practiced even by some of the teachers in public schools. It was necessary to find ways to protect us. These Jewish schools also taught religion, in this case Biblical history. I remember the special teacher. He was short, kind, never raised his voice and I felt comfortable listening to his stories. I was deeply impressed by vivid pictures of the flood, of Samson breaking the pillars of the Philistine edifice and of King Salomon's raised sword in judgment to threaten to cut the baby in half. Even though my parents were not observant of Jewish religious customs, I had an olive-wood box with the word "Jerusalem" on it, and I kept my treasures in it. I had no clue about our preservation of memory of this ancestral land, but evidence of it existed in our lives.

We went to school Mondays through Fridays and on Sundays, but not on Saturdays, the Sabbath. This exposed us to attacks by young Polish hooligans, who might have called us names, taunted or ridiculed us as Jews, thrown stones at us, and might even beat us up. My father always walked me to school on Sundays.

But Saturdays were spent with Mother. I enjoyed these visits immensely, and was never bored. Mother and I started the day with a visit to the Wedel candy store on the corner, buying a bag of candies, and going to the cinema. We saw films we both enjoyed, not children's films. I remember *Halka*, a film based on a love story, to the music by a Polish composer, Stanisław Moniuszko.

Halka was a peasant girl in the Carpathian Mountains. She was seduced and fell in love with the son of a local nobleman. Halka fell off a cliff on the day her lover married another girl, a member of the aristocracy. We shared our sorrow at her misfortune, shedding copious tears.

Mother was usually very busy. She established a small shop producing ladies' luxurious, expensive lingerie. She purchased especially lovely silks, organza and other fabrics, and cut them according to the patterns she made. The pieces were then sewn together by her girl assistants. A special assistant did the finishing parts, such as buttonholes, embroidery and trim. I watched all this with great interest.

At other times Mother taught me to use a sewing machine and to make buttonholes and silk flowers with which to decorate our nightdresses. I also remember a coral-colored dress with a lace collar my mother had sewn for me, and I loved it.

My father, who understood a boy's wardrobe better, usually dressed me as a boy. I was about eight at that time I came to live with him. He had no idea how to dress a little girl. Now, we went to a bazaar. I selected the fabrics I liked, and using my mother's coral dress as a pattern, Father ordered several dresses for me. But all winter I wore the same black sweater and a torn, black coat to school. My truly loving and perceptive father was obviously blind to some facts. Even after their separation, tensions continued between my parents, sometimes taking a tangible form. My school sponsored a masked ball, and my mother had promised to make me a costume of a Dutch girl with a big white cap and a long dress. I was looking forward to it, but for unknown reasons was not allowed to take part in it. It was a sad moment.

In 1937, not long before World War II started in Europe, my mother revealed to my father and me that she had plans for Michael, who was by then fifteen years old. Michael will leave for Palestine (present-day Israel), and stay with her sister Zipporah. She will follow Michael, and Father and I will follow them later.

My father's face was doubtful. He seemed unconvinced. This would end Michael's visits with my father.

Mother deeply believed that we must leave Poland to rebuild our homeland in Palestine, and create a safe haven for Jews to prevent their persecution. The idea of rebuilding an independent Jewish National Home in Palestine was not new. Due to centuries of oppression and abuse as a minority in foreign lands the Jews dreamed about returning to their homeland in Palestine, or the Land of Israel, sometimes referred to poetically as "Zion." They preserved the memory of Zion in their prayers, their studies and literature, since the Roman conquest, their forced dispersion 2000 years ago, and even earlier, following their defeat and exile to Babylonia in the sixth century BCE.

Mother's family and she herself felt very strongly about it. Mother was very proud of her family's drive and hopes. In modern times the movement called "Zionism" (return to Zion) was reborn and many, mostly young people responded to it, even though it required hardships and sacrifices. Persecution in Poland contributed and resulted in increased Jewish immigration and the building of villages, schools and collective settlements in Palestine. Mother's brother Kalman and her two sisters had lived there for years, since the 1920s. My aunt Sarah had left a secure and comfortable life in Poland to be a nurse and take care of babies in our old-new land, and my uncle Kalman Bar-Lev was one of the founders and writers for the newly-established newspaper *Davar*, or *The Word* in Hebrew. I listened, and thought I almost knew them. My mother hoped to join them soon.

I recalled my mother discussing Palestine with her friends, who used to visit our home in the evenings. They used words like pioneers, malaria,

Mother and Michael in Warsaw, ca. 1937 (family collection).

swamps, eucalyptus trees, anopheles, and orange groves. These words were a mystery to me, and I asked what they meant. Mother told me that pioneers are those who come first to a country or village; that Palestine was a far-away land to be rebuilt; that swamps were soil full of water and needed to be drained. She told me that anopheles was a mosquito, an insect living in swamps and causing a disease called malaria; and that eucalyptus trees needed much water and were planted in the swamps to drain them. The "Blue Box" of the Jewish National Fund was in our and

The Blue Box for the purchase and development of land in Palestine (courtesy Jewish National Fund).

every Jewish home, Orthodox or not, to save coins, no matter how small, for the purchase of land in Palestine and its development. Honoring people by planting a tree in their name in Palestine was and still is a time-sanctioned tradition.

Michael acted very grown-up about it, and bragged to me that he was going to be a pioneer in Palestine. It all seemed very important to me.

Michael working the land in Palestine (family collection).

I remembered saying good-bye to Michael at the teeming train station. Michael was going to Palestine alone to work on a farm and help prepare a place for us. There I would meet the family I never knew before, my aunts Sarah and Zipporah, my uncle Kalman and their children, my cousins.

Michael and Father embraced. Was that a tear in my father's eye? Mother put her arms around Michael and me, and held us close. I was sadly silent, comprehending something very important was taking place. I did not cry.

A few months after Michael's departure my mother called at midnight. She was to sail for Palestine in a few hours, in secret and illegally, because at that time the British who governed Palestine did not allow Jews to enter the land. She could take only very few things. She took my photograph with her.

I did not realize it at the time, but my mother was embarking on a dangerous journey.

In 1922 the League of Nations granted Britain a Mandate for Palestine, a commission to administer the government of Palestine. Britain was to follow a momentous 1917 declaration by Lord Balfour, British Foreign

Pioneers in Palestine pose on a sandy plot where they hope to erect a new kibbutz, a collective settlement (courtesy U.S. Holocaust Memorial Museum, photograph number 59776).

Secretary, stating, in part: "His Majesty's Government view with favor the establishment in Palestine of a National Home for the Jewish people, and will use their best endeavors to facilitate the achievement of this object." This formal recognition of the historic right of the Jewish people to re-establish their ancient homeland was met with joy and hope.

But in spite of international intent and their promises, British authorities repudiated their obligations, and, under Arab pressure, severely limited Jewish immigration, while permitting Arab immigration from the north and east, even when the Jewish immigrants were escaping certain death in later years, during World War II. Jews were turned away and not permitted to enter their "National Home."

In the summer of 1938, my mother was well aware of the British blockade and the dangers of Jewish underground immigration, but like many others before her, accepted the risks. She was fortunate: her unseaworthy, old Greek boat reached Palestine without incident. They were not caught by the British. The Jews of Palestine met them in the darkness of night and, since many of them could not swim, literally, carried the immigrants to shore on their shoulders. As soon as they arrived in the kibbutzim (Jewish collective settlements) nearby, their clothes were changed and the British could never tell who was a newcomer and who a longtime resident.

The captains of these boats, Greek, Italian and others, endangered their lives and their ships to bring these pioneers and later refugees home to Palestine. They could have been intercepted by British patrols, they could have been attacked and fired on, injured, killed or drowned. They were loved, praised, honored and extolled in tales, songs and poems.

> We lift our hearts in a toast to you, Captain.
> Your fragile, small boat
> and your paths in the sea
> so hidden and unknown today,
> will remain for all time
> in the Annals of Israel,
> and many a captain, in the days to come,
> will envy, our Captain, your glory.

In spite of the danger, due to increasing persecution in Germany and discrimination in Poland, this underground immigration increased.

The crews of the rescue boats were the boys from kibbutzim (collective settlements) nearby, and included Christian volunteers from other lands, inspired by the need and desperation of these passengers.

Chapter 2
Life with Father

My father liked to take me for walks along Warsaw's streets and gardens. He noticed my longing glances at the store windows, and bought me a blue velvet dress, with a white lace collar. I wore it at every opportunity. I think today that as a child I seemed to have had a sense of color and style. I dreamed about how I was going to furnish my future home. I planned the furniture arrangements and imagined myself wearing a long velvet dress. I was eight years old and boys or husbands had no place in my world.

I enjoyed films for children and never forgot *Sleeping Beauty* and even the name Walt Disney was familiar to me. Father and I once went to the theater to see a play. I loved the music and the songs, the actors in costumes, but had no idea what the play was about. It was in Yiddish, *Die Makhsheyfe* (*The Witch*).

Father was very fond of classical music and frequently whistled snatches of his favorite musical pieces, mostly by famous composers, such as Brahms and Liszt.

One day he suggested that instead of calling me, he will whistle a tune, a tune I liked, and asked me what I liked. I loved Schubert's Serenade, and from then on I always ran home from the courtyard whenever I heard him whistle that tune.

My father had two brothers living in Warsaw, Romek and Victor, and a younger sister, Lusia, who was a physical education teacher, and recently married. I remember Victor's wedding in the big synagogue on Tłomackie Street in Warsaw. I was very impressed with the ceremony, and saw myself as a bride, in a white gown and veil. Another of my father's brothers, Buziak, according to family legend, instead of following his father's wishes to become a rabbi, ran away to America and became a prospector during the Gold Rush years in Alaska.

2. Life with Father

Father was close to his older brother in Częstochowa and was in contact with him. The Częstochowa branch of our family counted three children, Zygmund, Ignas and Hanechka, all older than me. We were also close to the Reichmans in Częstochowa, whose mother sent us her special cake, a kind of fruitcake, called *keks*.

Father also corresponded from time to time with the father of our relatives in Mielec, south of Warsaw. This was of great interest to me because they had two daughters, and the younger one, Irena, was close to me in age. With time, I learned that Irena wrote poetry, and I remember her father sending us her poem about birds. I became even more curious when I learned Irena loved books. This was something we definitely had in common, and I hoped to meet her one day.

Father and I were not given to hugging and kissing or any such displays of affection. Instead, Father would tell me a joke or a story, such as the folk tale of the princess and Rabbi Joshua.

> Rabbi Joshua was very wise, but ugly to look upon. One day he met the emperor's daughter.
> The princess wondered how God could put so much wisdom in such an ugly vessel.
> The rabbi inquired: "Where does her father keep his wine?"
> The princess replied: "In earthen jars, of course."
> The rabbi advised: "He should keep his wine in gold or silver vessels, as befits a king."
> The king ordered some of his wine transferred to gold vessels, but found it soured.
> The soured wine caused the princess to complain that Rabbi Joshua had given her bad advice.
> The rabbi replied: "So you have learned that wine keeps better in simple vessels. So does wisdom."
> The princess countered: "But some people are both, wise and handsome."
> "Yes," said the rabbi, "but they might have been even wiser, were they less handsome."

I silently wondered if the story had anything to do with me and my love of pretty clothes. Did I put too much value on unimportant things?

Father liked to talk with me. He treated me sometimes as an adult, occasionally making critical comments about the people we knew. He trusted me to use discretion and keep silent when needed. Did he miss my mother and her company? I silently mused.

Ten-year-old Andrew was our neighbor. Andrew and his mother used to brag so about his skates and toy trains. Father considered her a very thoughtless woman, and shared his thoughts with me, that some parents could not afford such luxuries. Father trusted my judgment not to repeat everything he said and thought. I listened and took note of his comments.

For my birthday party, presents were not allowed or expected. They were too expensive for some children, and my entire class was invited to the party, to make certain all children came and were welcome. I understood my father and never expected any gifts, and to this day obligatory presents cause me some discomfort. But he gave me a gift: a lovely blonde doll who could stand by herself and a blue, doll-sized real baby carriage. I liked it, but I much preferred to play with my old rag doll whose clothes I could change by sticking pins into her.

One rainy day, while peeking into my father's drawers, I discovered a packet of photographs. Inquisitive and nosy, I asked about the people in the pictures, the children and the babies. I think I was about ten at the time, and he told me then about his family.

Our family has lived in Poland for generations, long before the 1800s. Father lost his mother, Hannah, when very young, and was frequently sent to stay with his grandmother in Ostrów Mazowiecki, a small town near Warsaw.

I asked about his grandmother's name, and learned it was Feiga Zisl. She was married to Reb (a title of honor) Itzhak Bromberg, and became a widow at a young age, with eight young children, six boys and two girls. To support her family, she now concentrated fully on her business. I was curious about the business, but Father did not remember the details. It might have been connected with forests and grain. He knew, however, that she was successful and soon became one of the wealthiest women in town, wise and charitable. Every Sabbath and holiday her house was wide open to all who were hungry.

Eva's maternal grandfather, Akiba Lewartowski (family collection).

There were many poor Jews

2. Life with Father

in town who ate at her table, and especially the yeshivah (religious seminary) students. Their poor parents sent them to study, because learning and scholarship were very important, even more important than earning a living and helping the family, and being a scholar was the highest achievement and honor. These young men and boys (girls did not attend a yeshivah) were always hungry. They frequently slept in the yeshivah on hard benches, by the stove, covered only with their coats, and depended on the community for their eating days (*essen teg* in Yiddish).

Eating days was something I never heard about before, and asked about it.

The students ate each day with a different family. I imagine that this must have been a harsh experience for them. But on Mondays and Thursdays, he remembered, all the students ate at his grandmother's house. Knowing they were hungry, she served them a sumptuous meal: chicken soup with noodles (*lokshen*), roast or boiled chicken, potatoes and *tsimes* (sweet carrot stew) and a desert of stewed prunes. Father loved those days. He enjoyed the students' attention, the food and the religious chants and prayers. Needless to say, he was doted over, and very soon, at the age of four, he became a student himself, and began his religious education. His grandmother also contributed funds to build a magnificent yeshivah, and rebuild it when it burned down. Fires were frequent in the wood-built communities. I listened and felt my father's pride in his grandmother, my great-grandmother. Will I follow in her footsteps and be as wise and charitable as she was? I wanted to be.

But that was not all. According to family tradition, Feiga Zisl's grandfather, Rabbi Dan Landau met with Napoleon Bonaparte, the Emperor of France.

I wondered how this could have happened.

Father related that in 1812 Napoleon, who at that time ruled Poland, embarked on a campaign against Russia, the enemy of Poland, and his army passed through Plock, where Rabbi Dan lived. No one in town spoke French, except Rabbi Dan, who became the Emperor's contact and interpreter.

The Emperor Napoleon was a hero to the Jewish population. Following the ideas and rules of the French Revolution, he freed them of restrictions previously limiting their rights of residence, choice of professions and freedom of worship. Now he needed funds to finance his war, and Rabbi Dan, my great-great-great-great grandfather, loaned him ten thousand gold thalers (coins), receiving a receipt signed by the Emperor. Napoleon lost his campaign in Russia, as well as his throne.

Two generations later there was a new government in France, sympathetic to Napoleon. My grandmother, Feiga Zisl, hired a lawyer, gave him the receipt signed by the Emperor, and sent him to Paris to claim the debt to her grandfather. She lost her case. The new government in France did not honor his debts. Rabbi Dan lost all his wealth and became an employee of the community, to support his family. Napoleon's debt has never been repaid.

Feiga Zisl's sons were known for their scholarship, and she married all her children into prominent Jewish families, known for scholarship and wealth. My curiosity was boundless, and I learned my great grandmother's children's names.

Dan was her eldest son. Then came Chaim Mordechai, Jakob, Zeev Wolf, Zvi Hersz and Natan. Zeev Wolf was my grandfather. I still wanted to know the names of her daughters. Father did not remember. These girls' names have not been preserved in the family's memory, and were lost forever.

I would have liked to know their names, I thought, pensively. My father would not have omitted my name. I moved closer to my father.

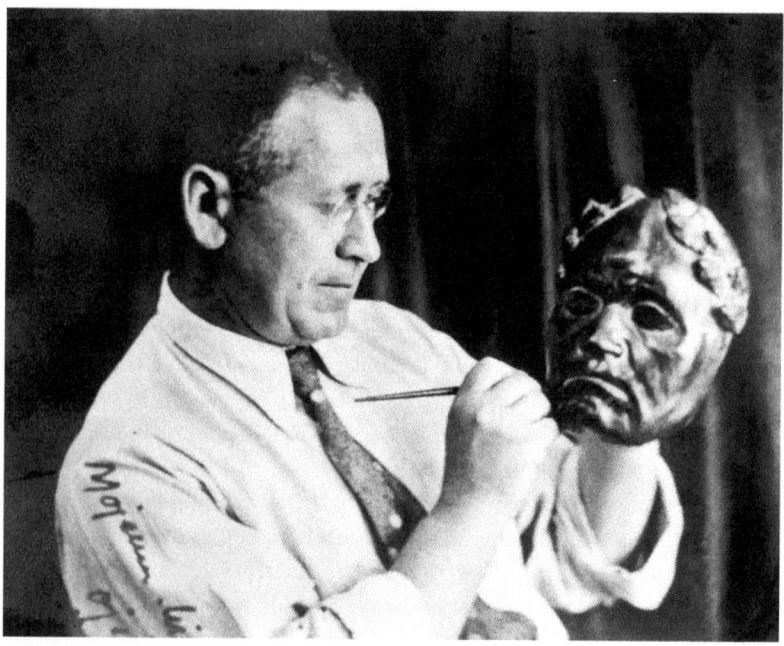

Eva's father, Herman Bromberg, with a postmortem mask of Beethoven in his last photograph, 1941 (family collection).

Eva's maternal grandmother, Chawa Lewartowska (family collection).

Most of Feiga Zisl's children later moved to Warsaw, and so did she. My parents always lived in Warsaw. That is where I was born. That was where my father and mother met, both members of the teachers union.

I liked these talks. They put my father and me on the same level. We understood each other and were good friends. I didn't comprehend it at the time, but we were a family, a family of two. But father was the only family I grew up with. There were no others to hear or see, no conflicts

Eva's mother, Dinah, the eldest, with her sisters, Zipporah (left) and Sarah (family collection).

or friendships to listen to, understand and learn from. Every day after school, around four in the afternoon I would meet my father in a restaurant for dinner. My father never cooked. I understood we were an unusual family, but did not question it.

Sometimes we visited a pastry shop. Father ate nothing, attempting to control his weight, while I enjoyed my favorite napoleons. Father used

Eva's mother, Dinah Lewartowska Bromberg (family collection).

to be a teacher before I was born, but in the 1930s, I believe, he worked as a business representative. I overheard him tell a friend that he was among the founders of the first Jewish public schools in Warsaw. But now he worked fewer hours, and spent time with me.

Sometimes he took me along to a Jewish commercial section of Warsaw, on Nalewki Street, where many of his friends and clients had stores and lived. It was a crowded, busy and noisy area, with Yiddish heard everywhere. In Yiddish, they also talked about me, commenting on my intelligence, to please my father. Even though I knew no Yiddish, I noticed their gestures and expressions, but pretended to have no idea of what was being said. While attending to business, they shared their private experiences, thoughts and gossip.

There was much poverty among the Jews of Poland, and in this section of the city many small shopkeepers barely managed to keep abreast of their debts and expenses.

One day the shops were buzzing with exciting news about Ziselman, a shopkeeper from Pinsk. Everyone asked if we had heard about him.

Father looked askance.

Ziselman was, we were told, a small Jewish shopkeeper in Pinsk, northeast of Warsaw, not unlike many of them. The story was brought, circulated and retold in Warsaw.

Dinah's last photograph, ca. 1960 (family collection).

In it, Pani (Mrs.) Nina Luszczyk Ilienkowa, a distinguished lady, a member of a non–Jewish, Polish-Belarus family, related the story of her own family's experience. Years ago her parents had suffered a grievous loss: their three-year-old Lidia, born with a heart defect, had died. The poor stricken family had no funds to bury their child. Nina, Lidia's younger sister was told about it, remembered it, and Ziselman, their neighbor, for the rest of her life. The story was now on everyone's lips. Like Nina Luszczyk Ilienkowa, I never forgot that tale. Nina grew up to be a storyteller, and later in life wrote about it. I will now retell Pani Nina's story I heard that day, years ago, and read again, later, as an adult.

"Ziselman of Honcharska Street"
by Nina Luszczyk Ilienkowa
Retold by Hava Bromberg Ben-Zvi

Short was the life of her sister Lidia. Three years older than Nina, she was a beautiful child, with an angel's face, who started early to talk and sing. But her little heart was sick from birth, and she died at the age of three. Their parents, Nina's older sister Valentyna and brother Vitaliush were disconsolate in their despair. In addition, the family found itself in dire financial need. Their father was employed by the state, but expenditures on doctors and medicines greatly reduced the family's means. Their father expected no aid from their family in the Novogrodek area, and their mama's entire family was in the Soviet Union. Her parents never were in debt before, buying nothing on credit or installment.

They faced, therefore, a dreadful fact: there was no money to bury the deceased child. Having consulted his ill and distressed wife, her father went to the church on Miodowa Street, to see the Reverend, with his painful request to bury his child, and the debt would be repaid in the near future.

And this was a grave error and a frightful, moral, life-changing experience for her father, a man of religious principles, brought up in a godly family. Her grandfather Prokop, a village teacher, taught the little ones religion along with the alphabet, and her grandma Emilia, even though not Orthodox Christian but Protestant, equaled her husband in devoutness, and so brought up their five children.

Until his death Nina's father did not forget the day he stepped into the office of the Reverend. He took off his railroad engineer's hat with an eagle, and, his voice choking with emotion, asked: "In God's name, bury my poor child."

The Reverend, surprised, gazed at her father: always clean-shaven, with lovely, fluffy hair and eyes as blue as heaven, he did not appear poor. Her father never forgot the words he heard:

"What?" the Reverend roared. "What? Will I do you a burial on credit? And he calls himself a railroad engineer! It is for you to pay, and if not you, who else?" Her father, still in the posture of a supplicant, his work-worn hands clasping the brim of his hat, didn't believe he was denied. Denied a prayer and a last service on earth to a dead child? The clergyman's words hit her father like a whip, his eyes dimmed by tears.

"Close the door on the other side and bring money, then we will bury, do hear, you filthy railway-man! Do you hear? Away from here, pretending to be poor!"

Her father closed the door, stepped down the porch and went away as a beaten dog, reviled by a man of the clergy, through no fault of his own, because of the death of his little daughter. And why was he abused so? Why? He did not neglect his Orthodox Christian Church and his wife, Marfusha, with her fine, rare for a woman alto voice, sang in the choir, and read the Slavonic language psaltyr. And the Church, in the person of its spiritual leader, denied them? Her father, passing from one street to another, knew not where he was going, as if pierced through the heart by a hot iron. My God, what shall he do? How can he tell his wife? No, no, she should not know it, he thought. His fingers clutched the fence, and he wept.

Old Ziselman sitting in front of his store, saw him, and alarmed, asked what the matter was. What had happened to him, and why such distress? And the storekeeper from Honcharska Street, Ziselman, led her father to his room, seated him, and holding in his palms the hand of the battered man, attempted to calm him down. Nina's father told him about the death of his little daughter, and about his financial straits.

Ziselman told him to be of good hope. Even though his little girl died, soon his wife will bear another daughter. And as soon as Ziselman grows a long beard, she will come and bring from her little garden the green small onions that Ziselman loves. And she will not fear the old Jew, for her parents will not teach her so. And about the money for the Holy Father.... Here Ziselman got up, opened his small chest, taking out a leather bag. Asking not how much was needed he counted enough to pay for all rites, and for the family to live on until her father's payday.

Asking no warranty of her father, this was not a wealthy man who rescued her family at that painful time. Ziselman, in addition, restored her father's faith in the goodness and decency of man. God, the Father of all men, did not forsake her parents, and again, showed man where goodness dwelled. And spiritual positions, when occupied by evil and greedy men, harm religion. Did God forgive the Holy Father? She did not know. Her family forgave him.

Ziselman remained a good friend for the rest of their lives. His prediction regarding the birth of a daughter was fulfilled to the letter. A girl was born, very small, but by the time she was one year old, she walked and talked. Nina. And at three she knew the good man Ziselman and feared not his long beard, his black kapota, nor his yarmulke. She loved him and dutifully brought him onions.

The money borrowed in an hour of need was repaid. And Nina, with this true story wished to leave a remembrance and respect for a good and God-fearing man, who foresaw her birth, spiritually contributed to it, and lit, in the heart of a little girl, a candle of goodness and love for all people. She will carry this memory through her life, to write in her old age this story and to tell people: Be good. Only thus will we save our God-given world.

Her story ended, and silently, deep in thought, Father and I walked home, I holding my father's hand.

Dr. Anna Engelking, a professor at the Institute of Slavic Studies, Polish Academy of Sciences and Nina Luszczyk Ilienkowa's friend and advocate, kindly permitted me to retell Pani Nina's memoir, and wrote to me.

Pani Nina till the end of her life suffered because of what the Germans and their helpers of all nations did to the Jews. She told me about her sleepless nights, "quarreling with God Almighty." She quarreled on behalf of her friends, Sonia and Ester, and all the others. Her mother, Marfa Kuzminiczna, did not survive the annihilation of the Jews of Pinsk. She could not stand and endure what was happening in town. It drove her to insanity, and she died a few days or weeks later.

I see before my eyes—from Pani Nina's words—an image of her mother, sitting on the steps of their house, shrieking, weeping, in utter desperation, and letting no one approach her....

Nina was then about thirteen years old.

2. Life with Father

Warsaw was a thriving city. In the years just preceding the outbreak of World War II approximately 380,000 Jews lived in Warsaw, a third of the total population, and before their destruction, were prominent in medicine, law, literature and the arts. But in particular, Jews played an important role in commerce, and many of them were small shopkeepers in towns and villages.

Warsaw, with its many synagogues, Jewish theaters, libraries, newspapers and schools was the world center of Jewish life, second only to New York, fluent in Yiddish, Polish and Hebrew. This civilization, existing and thriving in Poland for about one thousand years, was annihilated by the Germans between 1939 and 1945 through starvation, disease, torture and deportation to death camps. But all this was still in the mists of a future unknown, albeit around the corner. Today, in 1938, Father and I enjoyed friendships, camaraderie and laughter with our friends and business partners.

Father also enjoyed drawing and sculpture, and one of his first projects was the sculpture of a postmortem mask of Beethoven. Then he drew a portrait of me. His many friends, men and women, visited us to talk and to play chess.

I was often ill, with a slightly elevated temperature of unknown causes. Could the separation from my mother have been the cause? Several months before my family separated I was sent to the Medem Sanatorium in Miedzeszyn, near Warsaw. I had developed a nervous cough. I was very miserable there, where I had been sent to recover. We children spent most of our days resting on reclining chairs, some of us following surgery. Stories were read and told to us in Yiddish, a language I did not understand. I remember a boy who arrived with his head heavily bandaged and heard rumors he was a victim of a pogrom in Kielce, a city in Poland. The word "pogrom" was unknown to me, but strangely frightening. I learned later that it meant an attack on Jews. Another boy had an epileptic seizure, shaking and falling to the ground. We children were told never to mention it, especially to him, and no one ever breathed a word about it. I remember a girl with a red ribbon in her hair tied in a bow on the top of her head. To me it signified love and care and I envied her, feeling lonely and unloved. I saw the difference between us, two girls, and wanted to be pampered and cared for, like that girl with a ribbon in her hair. This feeling was magnified by the fact that every morning, while dressing, the teacher had to search for clothes for me. I was sent to the sanatorium without sufficient clothing, and each morning the teacher had to find something for me to wear. The rift between my parents might have contributed to it, especially that Mother stayed away and never visited me. Was she distracted by her impending journey to Palestine? I suffered insomnia and hardly slept at nights. The nurse checked on me several times during the long nights, always finding me awake. Even though my father visited me often, I never complained. I just did not know I could complain. I must have been about seven years old, and stayed in the sanatorium probably not longer than a few weeks.

It was 1938, before the outbreak of the war. I stayed in bed when ill, often reading my father's poetry books, mostly by prominent Polish poets, such as Mickiewicz and Słowacki, in the absence of children's books. I must have been about eight. We were yet to discover children's literature in libraries. Father stayed home evenings, not to leave me alone. It did not occur to me to question our way of life, even though I knew this was not the usual way families lived. I was happy, but I needed and missed my mother and brother. I was in no way prepared for the events to come.

I learned later that 250 children, patients of the Medem Sanatorium, shared the fate of all other Jewish children in Poland. The Germans surrounded the sanatorium and told the staff to leave. Most of them refused to abandon their small charges and were shot together with the children. It was reported and described by the Jewish Underground Movement in Poland. (See *The Black Book of Polish Jewry*, 1943, p. 132.)

Chapter 3

I Remember

I recall the scent of lilacs in Warsaw, the city of my birth.

In 1939 the city had many public gardens and monuments of Polish heroes. I ran freely through the neighborhoods, visiting my friends. I could always ask a policeman for directions.

Mina, my best friend and I were nine years old. In the Saski Park the chestnut trees spread their leafy shade. We loved to gallop through the streets to play chestnuts in the park, or play in the swimming pool in the hot days of summer. We spent much time in front of a toy shop window, dreaming. A candy store window was another point of great attraction to us. Sometimes we bought ice cream cones or warm crispy bagels from a vendor on the street corner. In a flower shop the kind owner permitted us to smell the flowers. But first we had to go to the library.

Mina and I shared a love of books. I liked stories about girls and their adventures in boarding school. I dreamed of living in a girl's boarding school. Their lives and crises seemed so exciting! I remember *The Adventures of Little Magdusia* and *King Matia the First* by Janusz Korczak, a well-known author. In *King Matia the First*, Janusz Korczak created an imaginary country, governed by children. King Matia appointed a children's Parliament, and I never forgot it. They debated the foods children should eat (never the hated fish oil) and other important issues. I paid little attention to my dolls. The local library was my favorite place and very important to me.

I always asked the smiling blond librarian for new books.

She thought I needed to be transferred to a new library. I already read all the children books in this small branch.

Life was happy and carefree. I was dimly aware of, but unconcerned with, the events occurring a short distance away, in Germany. I heard about Germany occupying Austria, and then Czechoslovakia. Our class wrote a letter to the Czech children in Prague, whose country lost its independence.

Janusz Korczak (center) poses with children and younger staff members of his orphanage (courtesy U.S. Holocaust Memorial Museum, photograph number 05323/74101).

Everyone listened to the radio, to the loud, shrieking speeches of the Chancellor of Germany, Adolf Hitler.

My father and his friends discussed the political events of the day, and worried that Poland may be attacked, but they believed that Poland was safe.

"No, Poland is too strong," I heard some opinions. I did not feel threatened and it was of no interest to me.

As my parents separated, Father and I moved to No. 1 Kilińskiego Street, a quiet corner of Warsaw, not Jewish, into a large, airy room, with light pouring through its enormous window.

I remember Father telling the landlady that his daughter liked the room. I noted his words and they remained with me. His daughter was important. Our room was part of a large apartment, with an enormous living room and four other rooms. The landladies were three spinster sisters. They occupied the living room, which served also as their bedroom at night. A long, heavy curtain went down every evening, screening their sleeping quarters on chairs, which were put together to form beds at night. Two of the sisters, Marta and Halina were quiet, self-effacing women, but Bronka, the manager, was tall, bony and rude in speech and manner. She was often unkind to me and the children visiting me. The four other rooms were rented to different families, mostly couples. We all shared a big bathroom with a tub and an enormous kitchen.

Our room was warm, sunny and friendly, my home. My father's bed with its shiny, copper headboard and its pink, satin bedspread occupied one corner of the room. I slept on the sofa. Each night, before falling asleep, I gazed at a portrait on the wall above me of a mother nursing an infant. This, I told all my friends, was a picture of my mother and of me. But one day a friend saw the portrait in a museum, and I lost some of my credibility.

I do not recall being unduly upset about it. I did know the difference between fact and fiction. I just did not know I could not say anything I liked. Did I, perhaps, miss my mother, and needed a proof of her presence, at least, in a picture?

A shiny, walnut colored cupboard, with a glass door stood against one wall. My friends and I, curious and hopeful, frequently found pineapple jam, sweet smelling vanilla cookies and peanuts in it. We spread newspapers on the floor, shelled the peanuts and ate them. My friends loved to visit me.

My father's large, walnut colored ornate desk was piled high with his books, magazines and newspapers, which Ola, our maid, tried to put to order each day. Almost every day I ran to buy for Father the Yiddish newspaper he loved, *Haint* (*Today*). My blond doll Lusia rested ignored in her elaborate, blue baby carriage, while Mina and I spent our time reading girl's stories and fairy tales. One of our favorites were also the tales by Hans Christian Andersen. I never forgot "The Little Girl with Matches" and "The Ugly Duckling." We loved them and took them at face value. The sociological messages went entirely over our heads. We also loved Robinson Crusoe, imagined and wished to be like Robinson, on a deserted island.

We examined our faces in the mirror, examining our good and mediocre features. I had nice teeth, curly blond hair, and a nice smile. Mina was unhappy with her hair (mousy), but very pleased with her green eyes. We created new songs by adapting well-known tunes to our favorite poems, and sang popular songs, such as "Forward, Brothers" and "By the Fireside." I was unspeakably jealous of Andrew downstairs for having a bicycle. I did not know or think I could ask my father to buy me a bike.

There was something about life, I thought: it was what it was, and it did not occur to me to attempt changing it.

I did my homework lying on my stomach on the parquet floor under the tulle-draped window. Lifting my eyes, I could see the trees in the courtyard's small garden. A green-fringed tablecloth covered an oval table in the middle of the room. The table and six brown leather upholstered chairs were the center of activity. We entertained our friends, ate, played checkers and dominoes and read by the light of the chandelier above. My world consisted of my father, school, friends, and books.

I was in third grade. Our teacher, Mr. Goldberg, was short, bald, and frequently angry with us, and we were mortally afraid of him. He was a good organizer. He created a notebook which each of us had, called *Łącznik*, a Polish word meaning a connector between school and home. For every act of good behavior we received a good stamp, and for everything bad a bad stamp. Our parents were expected to sign each time. These stamps were later counted into points to determine our grades in behavior and deportment. Mr. Goldberg used to hit the boys in their backs and to squeeze the chins of the girls for bad behavior. He never touched me. He and my father did not like each other, and I think our teacher was afraid of Father. I remember one of the parent-teacher conferences. We all sat together, parents and children, while our teacher introduced and discussed each child, in public, to all of us in attendance.

He introduced one of the girls as "a round orphan," meaning she had neither father nor mother. I remember feeling something was wrong, even though I could not say what it was, and the teacher's expression bothered me then and now. We always shared our lunches with this girl. She had red hair and was quiet and never had anything to say. Mr. Goldberg then discussed me, saying that I was forcefully pulled up beyond my years by reading books far too advanced for me. My father never guided me in my reading, and let me read whatever I wanted. Our teacher continued by clarifying the function of the Connector between school and home, and how each stamp affects the final grade and thus changes the value of the child. My father, from the back benches, corrected calmly that it changes only the value of the grade. The teacher quickly agreed with him. No other parent commented on anything presented. Perhaps, at that time the teacher's image as an authority figure silenced other parents' doubts or comments. The following year I was transferred to a different Jewish school in the neighborhood.

Father had many friends who visited us often. One of his friends used to regale us with popular songs:

> I have a date tonight at nine,
> and I long for her so.
> My chief will give me an advance
> for a bouquet of roses.

That room on Kilińskiego Street was to be my last home in Warsaw. I recall the childish feeling of trust, confidence and security I had felt. And yet, I had experienced anti-Semitism, an unfounded hatred of Jews. Being a child, I didn't know that rejection of Jews was a time-honored tradition in Poland, deeply embedded in the culture.

Some of his close friends had lost their jobs, Father told me one day, especially those in government positions, and Poles were hired instead. They very seriously consider emigrating to Palestine.

Anti-Jewish feelings were strongly felt. A comment by a neighbor's child, "We don't buy from Jews," left me confused. I was not conscious of being Jewish, but I had a distinct feeling that something was wrong, and that it concerned me, and bothered me. Yiddish was mocked by children in the courtyard. Expressions I heard, such as *"parszywy Zyd"* (dirty Jew) and "beat the Jews" were common and well known to me, a fearful part of my life. In a puzzling way, I realized these words related to me and they disturbed me.

Even in 1935, and very young, I remember a vague sense of fear while watching a procession pass by, the funeral of Józef Piłsudski, a Polish political leader. It was a state funeral, with horses and banners. I stood on the sidewalk on Marszałkowska Street, in front of our building, among a crowd of people, but in a mysterious way, I did not belong and felt I was in danger, even though my family had lived in Poland for at least several hundred years. I was afraid of the crowd.

I remember Alex, a new boy in school, whose family had recently been expelled from Germany as Polish Jews. Father donated some of his suits to help these refugees from Germany. Alex reported that the new government in Germany was declaring a war against the Jews, led by its leader, Adolf Hitler. Our teacher showed us ominous pictures even on a children's book, warning them not to trust Jews. Father told me that laws were passed in Germany (the Nuremberg Laws, 1935) denying Jews the right to work and other citizenship rights, imprisoning them in concentration camps. I know today that ultimately, a few years later, all those prisoners would be condemned to death, every Jew, man, woman, and child. My father discussed the Nuremberg Laws with his friends. Both the Nuremberg Laws and the term "citizenship" were a mystery to me. Only in later years I understood their meaning and the danger of denying these rights to Jews. At that time however I already felt that threats against Jews were threats to me. My peaceful childhood and way of life were coming to an abrupt and frightful end.

Everyone listened to the radio most of the time. While I listened to the many merry marching songs spreading encouragement and lifting our spirits, I thought about war as something almost splendid. Was this the intention? We heard nothing from the important Polish leaders.

Panel from a 1944 exhibit in London, England, entitled "Germany—the Evidence," showing Adolf Hitler. The exhibit panel reads, "The Evil We Fight" (courtesy U.S. Holocaust Memorial Museum, photograph number 55571).

Haß ohne Maske

In seiner maßlosen Wut hat der Jude noch immer die größten Fehler begangen. Der größte Fehler, welcher ihm in unserer Zeit unterläuft, ist der, daß er seinen Haß gegen alles Nichtjüdische so offen zur Schau trägt.

Caricature on the front page of the Nazi publication *Der Stürmer* depicting the Jew as the hater of all non-Jews. The caption reads: "Unmasked hatred. In his unbounded rape the Jew has once again committed a grave error which in our time has undercut him, (and that error is) that he so often displays his hatred against all non-Jews" (courtesy U.S. Holocaust Memorial Museum, photograph number 37857A).

I remember the name "Hitler" frequently mentioned, and watched my father as he listened to the radio transmissions of Hitler's loud, shrieking voice and long speeches. We heard about crowds cheering and supporting their Fuhrer, their leader, Hitler. I heard frequently the term "Kristallnacht" as something very sad. I later learned what it meant: The Night of the Broken Glass. Synagogues, Jewish stores and homes were vandalized and burned on November 9, 1938. Many people were killed, and 330,000 Jewish men were arrested and sent to German concentration camps. A great many of them never returned. Our friends discussed later

Page from the anti-Semitic German children's book *Der Giftpilz* (The Poisonous Mushroom). The text reads, "Just as it is often very difficult to tell the poisonous from the edible mushrooms, it is often very difficult to recognize Jews as thieves and criminals" (courtesy U.S. Holocaust Memorial Museum, photograph number 40005).

that the Jews were ordered to clean up the streets after the Kristallnacht, and to pay for the damages caused by this attack. In 1938, however, I knew that this was in Germany, while we were safely in Poland. I noticed Father's concentration and worried expression, but he did not share with me his thoughts and fears of the impending danger.

Chapter 4
War

In September 1939 Germany attacked Poland with continuous air raids on Warsaw. The general population of the city was not prepared for a sudden attack. I was awakened by the sharp whistles preceding the "boom" of falling bombs. Explosions were heard everywhere. I felt our big building shake and heard the noise of broken glass of the windows. The air was full of dust and smoke. The neighbors alerted us to hurry and run down to the cellar under the building. There were no other shelters. Fearfully, everyone rushed down the stairs to reach the cellar as soon as we could. Families unused to emergencies helped each other. Father and I dressed quickly and followed our neighbors.

The dark dusty cellar served as storage area to discarded furniture and equipment and as a nest to rats now scurrying away under our feet. Each one of us tried to find a corner to sit down. We all sat in silence listening and feeling the falling bombs, while our own building shook dangerously, expecting to be hit and die any moment. The radio described the air raid, advising us to reinforce our windows with strips of paper and keep our apartments completely dark at night. In contrast to our feelings the radio continued transmitting cheerful military music, marches and love songs related to war, and even glorifying war.

> Oh little war, little war,
> what a mistress are you!
> Your followers, your followers,
> are all handsome, selected boys.

We were expecting it, but there were no broadcasts by any known Polish leaders.

Coming out of our cellar-shelter after the raid we saw multi-storied buildings collapsed burying thousands of people. We saw buildings with collapsed walls, with some of the inside apartments and furniture still visible.

Many attempted to seek shelter in cellars, but the cellars under the destroyed buildings, we learned, frequently became their graves. Some of the Jewish tenants of our building did not hide in these cellars but remained in their apartments.

A Jewish family, the neighbors on the ground floor we did not even know before, permitted everyone to use their apartment as shelter. We gathered there. This location could be even more dangerous if a bomb fell nearby. Father thought that it was still better than remaining on the second floor.

Father and I were so glad we found some shelter, even though that shelter was still dangerous. We could not have stayed in our second floor apartment. And we felt fortunate to have bought some bread, jam, sardines, and candles, since there was neither food nor water, and no electricity or gas. I was hungry but said nothing, knowing everyone was as hungry as I.

The bombs reduced most of the graceful city to ruins. Mrs. Tomkiewicz, next door, was weeping. Her son, Benjamin, a lawyer, along with many others defending Warsaw, went to dig anti-tank trenches, and was among the missing and the dead.

Mr. Goldman tried to escape Warsaw, but returned. He came to the ground-floor apartment where we took shelter now. He reported the roads were full of refugees trying to escape Warsaw, women and children, and many of them killed by low flying German airplanes, using their machine guns on them, civilians. I learned later that a relative was killed in those raids.

The bombardment of Warsaw continued for approximately a month. One day I noticed a crowd gathered around a recently killed man trying to learn his name and address. They were debating what to do, and how to contact his family. Holding my father's hand we walked through the devastated neighborhood. Father felt I had seen enough, and we briskly started walking back.

I saw the German army as it invaded Warsaw at the end of September 1939. The Poles did not welcome the Germans. People wept on the almost deserted, silent streets. Nothing was heard but the German automobiles' ominous roar. The Germans, many of whom wore glasses, looked calm and in control, victorious.

Father told me that now in 1939 while the Germans invaded western Poland, the Russians encroached from the east. They have followed a mutual, secret at that time non-aggression pact between Germany and the Soviet Union (Russia), dividing Poland between them. Western Poland was to be part of Germany, while eastern Poland part of the Soviet Union. Poland, Father explained, had a sad history of invasion and oppression by its neighbors, Germany and Russia. It was free and independent between 1919 and 1939, and now, once again, has lost its freedom. Holding my father's hand, I watched the motorized German army drive slowly by. The future was as yet unknown. I sensed the sadness and the danger and wondered what would happen to us. Father didn't know, but he recalled that during World War I the Germans did not persecute the Jews. But he expected hard times.

After the German army occupied Warsaw, in October 1939, the Jewish population was singled out for oppression and abuse. Jewish properties were confiscated, Jewish schools closed, and soon a Judenrat (Jewish Council) was established, for the sole purpose of implementing German orders. There was even a rumor about being forced to wear armbands, identifying us as Jews. I watched a German soldier point a pistol at my father. Father, my only protector, was himself helplessly in danger. A neighbor whispered to my father to move quickly back into the shelter of the gate. I saw two German soldiers beating an old, bearded Jew, pulling and cutting off his beard. He was bleeding. To my astonished eyes, they were laughing.

Father and I waited in the line of a soup kitchen. Father tucked his hand under the arm of a neighbor woman, to look as if we belonged together.

"*Jude?*" (Jew) asked a German soldier. We left the line.

Jews, my father and I among them, were banished from soup kitchens. Many were beaten and humiliated in the streets. Father seemed very pensive and silent one evening, his face grave. He could hardly speak. He heard the Germans rounded up all the Jews of Falenica (a small town near Warsaw) and drove them into a pond.

I asked if they let them drown.

"Yes." No further words were needed.

I froze in fear and my heart hurt. My aunt and uncle lived there, with their two little girls, Lilka and Rysia. In my terror, I could not even cry. I was always afraid of water.

Father shared his thoughts and plans with me. He told me that we would try to escape Warsaw and the Germans. We will go into Eastern Poland, now occupied by the Soviet Union. We would cross the river Bug, even though the borders have been closed, and it was illegal now. We knew we would be shot if caught by the Germans.

A few days before our escape from Warsaw my 24-year-old cousin

Zygmund, from Częstochowa, a city in central Poland, south of Warsaw, came to Warsaw to say goodbye. Zygmund was dark-haired and tall. He paid scant attention to me. That night Zygmund and Father slept together in my father's bed. They thought I was asleep, but I listened to their whispers at night.

I heard Zygmund's voice tell that on Bloody Monday, on the 4th of September, the Germans arrested and shot over 160 Jews in Częstochowa. Rosh Hashanah, the Jewish New Year was on September 14th. That was the time the Germans arrested a great number of Jews. All Jewish businesses and industries had been confiscated and transferred to non-Jewish owners. This happened to Zygmund's factory as well. Nearly one thousand young men were sent to a forced labor camp, under inhuman conditions. We heard that many of them died. All Jewish schools had been closed, homes looted, and Jewish money and valuables confiscated.

I heard Zygmund continue.

The Jewish community of Częstochowa was forced to submit a list of industrialists, professors, lawyers and other wealthy and influential people. They had been arrested. His own father, Leib Bromberg was on that list. They were then ordered to form a Judenrat, a Jewish Council, and his father became one of its members.

Its duties were to carry out and enforce German policies and orders: extortion of money and lists of people for forced labor, or worse. His father was in agony about it. He felt they had been forced to cooperate with the Germans. I heard, sometime later, that his father suffered a heart attack and died during one of the Council's meetings. Zygmund had to return to his family tomorrow, to assist them these days.

A few days later, at dawn, taking with us only some clothes and a few valuables we could carry, such as money and jewelry, we left our home embarking on a dangerous journey. Our Polish neighbors, father and son, accompanied us to the train station for protection and carried our light luggage. Jews were thrown off trains. Whenever within earshot of German soldiers, they addressed me as Elsa, a German name. This train would take us to the new border between Germany and Russia. Walking slowly not to attract attention, we reached the train station.

Alone now on the train, we expected and feared a German patrol or a conductor asking for tickets, and of being recognized as Jews. But none of these things happened and we left Warsaw unnoticed.

Then on a cold, dark autumn night, in a small boat and in total silence, we rowed across the river Bug, separating the German zone of Poland from the Russian occupied area. The river was wide, and our progress so slow. I feared we would be drowned in the cold water, and breathed a sigh of relief at the sight of trees on the riverbank. Freedom was so close, I thought as we approached the shore. We anticipated and feared soldiers, deaths, arrests, violence and perhaps being sent back to Germany. But the area was dark and deserted. It was in the vicinity of Brest Litovsk. I breathed a sigh of relief at not being caught.

I asked if we could sing the "Internationale" now. The communist anthem was prohibited in Poland. My father only laughed.

Stepping upon Russian soil, we hoped to start a new life. The new authorities discouraged the use of the term "Russia." We all used instead: U.S.S.R., or the Union of Soviet Socialist Republics. The U.S.S.R. at that time did not single out Jews for persecution.

We have lost all our possessions, but we were free, and Father was lucky to find work as a teacher. Father used to teach math in the past. He told me that I would be enrolled in a Russian school when possible.

I did not care about other possessions, but I missed my books, especially my favorites. However, being with my father, I felt secure. My father set about finding a place to live, while I stayed in a hotel.

Father complained he was having some trouble finding a room for rent. They didn't want children but he found a place for us. A few weeks later the landlady confided in me.

She didn't want to rent to families with children, but I was not a child, she said. I was ten years old. Noticing how lonely I was, she introduced me to several Jewish girls my age. They spoke Yiddish, and their Polish was poor, but they spoke Polish with me, and we understood each other.

Everyone always treated me as if I were a hundred years old. Staying in my room and reading, I behaved like an adult. Having so few friends, I spent my time in our room, reading everything I could find. The books I found were for adults, but I loved them and understood them, probably on my level, at ten. Once I found an old, falling-apart copy of Jewish tales. I enjoyed them immensely and one of the tales remained with me.

Once there was a woman who loved gossip. But not any kind of gossip. She spread evil words from house to house, about people she knew. Autumn came, and with it the Day of Atonement or Yom Kippur, in Hebrew. On that day Jewish people are obligated by their faith to ask for forgiveness of all those they might have hurt. She felt guilty and went to the rabbi to ask for his advice.

The rabbi, a wise man, told her to go to the market and buy a goose, and bring it to him, and on her way to his house to pluck all its feathers. When the woman objected, the rabbi said sternly: "Do as I say."

She followed the rabbi's command and brought back the plucked goose.

"Now," said the rabbi, "go back, collect the feathers and bring them all to me."

The woman did as she was told. Coming back to the rabbi, she said: "I could only find these two feathers."

"Yes," said the rabbi. "Words are like feathers. Once said they can never be retrieved again. Let this be a lesson to you." I sat quietly, in my solitude, contemplating the rabbi's words. I waited and hoped to go to a Russian school when established by the new Soviet authorities.

We lived now under the Soviet regime surrounded by Soviet propaganda. Pictures of Stalin, Lenin, Marx and Engels, the contemporary and ideological Soviet leaders, were everywhere. We had to be careful with our speech and opinions, worried about being reported to the Soviet authorities. Russian military and civilian families were among us, and listened. But remembering our experiences under the Germans, we still felt fortunate to have escaped. No one persecuted us as Jews now.

The Russians among us insisted their communist system was the best way to live. But they were buying all kinds of articles of daily life, still available in stores. A watch was a rare and highly valued possession. Russian women bought luxuries they never knew before, delicate soaps, perfumes and cosmetics. One day, Father, returning from a teacher's conference reported that all the Russian ladies made their appearance in nightgowns. They loved the silks and laces and believed these were evening dresses. This caused much amusement among the other teachers, the refugees from western Poland. Young people were expected to join the Pioneers, or young communist party members. I did not join, and never wore the red scarf of the Pioneers.

In the meantime, Father taught me the Yiddish alphabet, beginning to dictate simple phrases. It was easy, since Yiddish was a phonetic language, meaning that you read exactly what you write, clearly pronouncing every letter. We wrote to Mother and Michael in Palestine, so they would know where we were. We thought we would join them after the war. My heart was singing. Our family would be together.

In September 1940 a Russian school opened. Learning Russian was so easy for me. I told Father I liked Russian poems and stories. I also liked one of the new Russian teachers, and I had a new friend, Alicia. She was tall, dark-eyed, and pretty. They lived in their own house, so they could even have a cat. Alicia, who was soon to play a vital role in my survival, was Catholic and my friendship with her, while very natural to me, was viewed as strange by my Jewish girlfriends, who had no Polish friends. But we were refugees from Warsaw, rather than local residents, and might have had different ideas about human relationships and suitable friendships.

Alicia and I became best friends. We drew, painted watercolor flowers, decorated our notebooks with cut-outs and crayons and played games. We learned and sang popular Russian army songs. "Katiusha" was one of the favorites:

> While the apple trees were blooming
> and the clouds drifted above
> on the banks of the river, Katiusha sang her tearful song.
> She sang of her beloved,
> she sang of keeping faith...

Alicia and I spoke Polish, even though we attended the Russian school so recently established by the new authorities. I was a better student, excelling in Russian and literature, but Alicia was taller, prettier, and had some interest in other things, such as using cosmetics.

One day she announced that her brother let her use his bike. I was envious, but she promised to teach me to ride it. And she did, holding me up each time I was about to fall off the big men's bike. Moshe, our landlady's youngest son, was our classmate and friend. My grades were always higher than his, to the constant annoyance of his mother. But my native language was Polish and learning Russian, a similar Slavic language, was easy and natural for me, while Moshe spoke Yiddish. Russian, to him, was a strange and unfamiliar tongue.

Now and then Father received letters from his brothers in Warsaw and from his friends. Knowing that the letters would be censored, the friend wrote us that death has lost much of its romance in the streets, and that they missed their children Ruthie and David.

The message was clear to us. By that time, we understood the worst: their children were dead. People in the Warsaw ghetto were dying of starvation and disease in the streets.

We learned later that the streets were full of dying people and starving children. Food was smuggled into the ghetto, and most of the smugglers were young children. They were small, and could more easily crawl through the cracks made in the ghetto walls at night. Hundreds of them were caught by the Germans and shot. About thirty Jewish children trying to get out of the ghetto were caught and openly drowned in the water of the lime pits of Okopowa Street. This was reported by a Pole who escaped Poland in 1942. (See *The Black Book of Polish Jewry*, 1943, p. 48.)

A Polish-American, Adam Sokolski, who returned to the United

A small boy begs on the sidewalk in the Warsaw ghetto. Heinrich Joest, a German army sergeant who photographed this scene, originally wrote: "They all expected nothing from me, the small beggars like this barefoot youngster with his hat on the street" (courtesy U.S. Holocaust Memorial Museum, photograph number 32325).

States in 1942, reported that he saw the death of an eight-year-old Jewish boy smuggling food into the ghetto. He was caught by a tall, manly German soldier who shot the boy, smiled and continued walking with his head raised high. No one in the crowd dared to intervene. Adam Sokolski also reported that compassionate Poles frequently supported the starving, begging children and gave them something to eat. (See *The Black Book of Polish Jewry*, 1943, p. 48.)

A woman and her ill child on a rickshaw in the Warsaw ghetto. Joest's caption reads: "Where would this rickshaw driver take this child who was obviously sick with Typhus? Was there still a hospital for Jews? No one among my German comrades could tell me" (courtesy U.S. Holocaust Memorial Museum, photograph number 32329).

And a few months later came a letter from Zygmund: "We have changed our address." We understood there was a ghetto in Częstochowa.

My father worried and felt he must send them a package of food. But we had so little. We needed all the money he had earned. We ate most of our meals in a restaurant. Father had no idea about housekeeping, and I, at twelve, was too young to understand and to remedy it. I had a feeling of impending danger, but our lives, I thought, were safe at that time.

The refugees (*bézhentsy* in Russian) from western Poland sometimes

Two destitute children sit on the cobblestone pavement in a square in the Warsaw ghetto (courtesy U.S. Holocaust Memorial Museum, photograph number 08156).

met in the evenings in their rooms or apartments, drinking tea and sharing their hopes and worries, primarily about the progress of the war and, in the 1940s, the seemingly unstoppable advances of the German forces across many European countries. Our safety and future were our main concerns. We also shared our backgrounds, and especially our distress about the families most of us left behind.

My mother and brother were in Palestine, and we believed safely out of Germany's reach. But Father had a young sister and two brothers still in Warsaw. Among us was a young man whose wife had recently given birth to an infant boy. He longed so to hold his new born son in his arms and worried about the mother and child who remained in western Poland. He left them because at that time everyone believed only men were in danger.

A young couple had left their aging parents behind, and it did not help that the parents themselves urged them to leave and attempt to escape the Germans. We were close to Naomi, a fellow teacher in the Russian school. She and her brother were determined to escape and survive together. I quietly sat by my father's side and listened.

One of the young women among us related she was formerly a teacher

4. War

A destitute child sleeps on the pavement in the Warsaw ghetto (courtesy U.S. Holocaust Memorial Museum, photograph number 08154).

in the Janusz Korczak Jewish Orphanage in Warsaw. The name Janusz Korczak, a pseudonym for a well-known radio personality, was familiar to many in our group, but few knew he was also a physician and a director of an orphanage in Warsaw.

I, Eva, was immediately alerted. I had read and loved Dr. Korczak's story, *King Matia the First*, and never forgot his kingdom ruled by children. I learned now that in his real orphanage, Dr. Korczak created a children's parliament and many special interest circles, including a published newspaper, *The Little Review and a Court of Law*. I wanted to hear more and more. The young teacher continued telling us that the doctor was born into an educated Jewish family. The family was impoverished by his father's sudden death, and their young son, Henryk Goldszmit, later Janusz Korczak, helped support the family by tutoring. He graduated from medical school, served in the Polish army during World War I and later worked with children. He believed in and promoted the rights of children.

She told us now about his kind, soft hands, noticed and appreciated by each new orphan admitted to the orphanage and examined by its director. We heard about the rows of clean, small, white beds in the boys' and girls' bedrooms and about her reading to them stories after bedtime. She missed Dr. Korczak and the children and hoped for their survival.

Many years later I learned that on August 5 or 6, 1942, German soldiers surrounded the orphanage ordering the children to line up outside. The children were told they were going on a suburban outing to the wooded area around the city. There were eyewitnesses who saw and described the procession of orphans, in their best clothes, each child carrying a blue knapsack with their favorite book or toy, toward the Umschlagplatz, the gathering and departure place near the railroad tracks, leading to the death camp, Treblinka. Guarded by German soldiers, the children proceeded to their destination in the August heat, with SS men leading the way, and Dr. Korczak with them.

According to memoirs, Dr. Korczak was offered the option to leave. He refused to abandon his children and boarded the train taking them to their death. He became a legend. His staff followed his example.

But this was still in the future, unknown. Now, in the late months of the 1940s, the civilian population and we, the Jewish refugees, not knowing what the Germans' plans for us were, still hoped to live through these times.

Chapter 5

Under the Germans

Father and I as well as other refugees lived in constant tension and fear, aware we were just across the river from the dangerous German forces, alert to any news about their progress, ardently hoping for their defeat.

Unexpectedly, on June 22, 1941, Germany attacked Russia, and Hitler's army invaded the zone of Poland where we were, until now occupied by the Russians.

Soon we watched Russian officials' families leaving in government-provided trucks. I knew some of these families: their children, Natasha among them, were in my class at school. They left at night, in darkness, in silence and haste. There were no goodbyes.

Father decided: we also must escape the advancing German forces and go east, away from the Germans, into the heart of Russia, even though we must travel by foot. We will join other, mostly Jewish families. For us there was no transportation of any kind.

Trudging slowly along country roads, carrying rucksacks on our backs and smaller baggage in our hands, we saw peasants approaching, armed with scythes and long sticks.

I saw Father whispering, *Oh my God*. He took my hand and kept me close. I thought they might kill us, and fearfully clung to my father.

The peasants grabbed suitcases from our hands and from the rented horse-driven cart. One of the women with us struggled with them, holding onto her suitcase.

She screamed that she worked hard for it, the same as they. They took her suitcase anyway. We were robbed of our poor possessions, but otherwise unharmed and proceeded slowly east. We soon heard the unmistakable sounds of automobiles, saw clouds of dust and heard German voices along the main road. Clearly, we were overtaken by the motorized German army. A decision had to be made: to proceed even though it seemed hopeless, or to return and submit to our fate at the hands of the Germans. Father in his fifties and I, age twelve, were unable to proceed on foot any longer into Russia, and had to return to the small town–village we lived in, Lachowicze. Now, again, we were under German rule. Father and I gave up, but others, mostly young people, our friend from the orphanage among them, decided to continue the difficult travel, hoping for escape and freedom. Many of them broke through the German lines, reached the Russian interior, escaped the Germans, the Holocaust, and survived the war.

For us who remained life had changed radically. German soldiers roamed the street, looting and shooting Jews at random. Their loud, brutal, barking orders, "*Juden raus!*" (Jews out) were heard everywhere. Seeing a German soldier could easily mean death. The Germans always walked in pairs, for their own security. They looked arrogant and superior to me. Our lives were in their hands. In dreadful terror, Father and I often hid, sometimes in attics of kind Polish strangers. While hiding in the attic we could sometimes see through the small windows the German soldiers and hear their loud, assured, cruel voices. They barged into Jewish homes, beating, sometimes shooting and taking anything they wanted.

While hiding one day, I met my friend, Frieda, also Jewish, who used to be in my class in the Russian school. She was heartbroken. She told us that her brother Leibl and another eighteen-year-old boy were ordered by German soldiers to dig a grave. Then they were shot by German soldiers and buried in it. I felt numb, fearful and speechless. I imagined the boys' fear and terror. I remembered Leibl with the dark mole over his eyebrow, the least handsome of his brothers. Yaakov, the eldest, who sang in a choir. And Hayim, the middle son, dark and handsome, once took me on a bike ride. And Leibl, I thought, was as tragically unlucky in death as he was in life.

And our friend Reva, I learned, in a nearby village, came home from vacation to find her parents and brother dead. Remembering Reva and her family, my eyes watered. I couldn't breathe. I once spent a vacation with them.

One day, two German soldiers barged into the home I lived in, with my father.

"Money, jewelry!" they shouted in German at the old landlady. She gave them what she had.

"My dear friends, that is all I have," she said, her voice trembling. The soldier slapped her face.

"I am not your dear friend!" I watched, standing in the doorway of our room, in paralyzed silence. They left, fortunately, paying no attention to me.

There were rumors of whole Jewish communities being killed, but these rumors were too terrible to be believed. We thought there must have been a reason. Perhaps the Germans thought they were aiding the Russian partisans in the forests, we tried to calm ourselves. Everyone hoped to live through these terrible times. This was 1941 and mass murder of entire communities was still unthinkable to us. "They cannot just murder women and children," I heard our landlady comment to her neighbors. All this came about very soon after the German invasion, and in this area of eastern Poland there was no starvation so far, and no deportations to ghettos and death camps. All that was waiting for us were mass graves, but we were still in the dark about it. We were to follow the fate of other Jewish communities.

In the meantime, all Jews, ages twelve and older were ordered to wear white armbands with a blue Star of David on it. I was twelve, but pretending to be younger, I did not wear it. "We should be proud of it," I overheard our landlord saying. I did not understand it, but it remained in my memory.

"How old are you?" A German officer stopped me in the street, glancing at my arm, and, generally, appraising me. I had heard about German soldiers assaulting Jewish girls. I did not understand how lucky I was because of my youth not to qualify as "a girl." "Ten," I said, sensing instinctively it was safer to be younger.

Father revealed to me one day he thought about placing me in a convent for the duration of the war. He heard some Catholic convents were hiding Jewish children, especially girls. My father tried to protect me. We both knew I was all he had, but even at that early date, in July 1941, we understood we had to separate. Alone, I had a better chance of survival.

Alarmed, I asked what would happen to him. He told me he would survive. We didn't know, at the time, what the German plans were for us all. We hoped to survive. I knew all this was happening to us because we were Jews, but never asked "Why?" I already knew, even at that age, that a reason was not needed.

There was no school for Jewish children. I was still reading, sometimes under a tree, in a field behind the house, and still felt protected by my father's presence.

I remember reading, *In Desert and Wilderness* by Henryk Sienkiewicz, a Polish writer, and *Born on One Soil*, in Polish, by an author I didn't recall. But some of the words and thoughts in that book remained with

A priest and several nuns pose with a group of children at a Franciscan convent school in Lomna, Poland, where Jewish children were hidden during the German occupation. Among those pictured are Tereska, a Jewish girl who remained at the convent after the liberation when no one came to claim her (front row, center); Sister Blanka Pigowska (second row, far right); Sister Tekla Budnowska (second row, third from the right); and Sister Zofia Olszewska (second row, far left) (courtesy U.S. Holocaust Memorial Museum, photograph number 44909).

me to this day, especially about a heart bleeding at separation from those we loved.

The next morning my father said good-bye: he was ordered by the Germans to report for what we thought would be a day of compulsory labor along with a group of about fifty other Jews. Against all evidence, we believed them and parted calmly. By evening, he still did not return.

I waited and waited alone all night, sleepless and full of fear and foreboding, but still hopeful. In the morning a young man came to see me.

The youth was among those taken yesterday with my father, and was the only one the Germans let out. He was only seventeen, and not a community leader. My father asked him to see me. I was to contact Mr. Korygin. He might help me and my father.

This was my father's last message to me, his last good-bye. I flew to

A priest poses with six young girls on the occasion of their first communion. Standing from the left are Halina Wroncberg (a Jewish girl), Basia, and Ala Chormanskie; others unknown (courtesy U.S. Holocaust Memorial Museum, photograph number 63665).

the Korygins who were Catholic, teachers and friends of my father. They promised to help. Later in the day Mr. and Mrs. Korygin came to see me.

They told me my father and his group were driven out of the city. They were no longer here. The Korygins were helpless. They had no influence outside of this town.

A few days later I heard a rumor that my father and the other men taken away with him were shot. The pain was unbearable, overwhelming. I grieved and wept in silence and alone. There was no safe, sympathetic ear to ease my agony. My mother and brother were in Palestine. I was totally alone.

I knew that my father was lost, but didn't permit myself to believe it or see my father in my mind's eye. Even in the face of evidence to the contrary, I maintained some hope, knowing that, for the time being, hope would help me cope with my pain and heartbreak. But, of course, he never came back.

I learned, much later, that the Germans followed an established system in all areas of their occupation: one of their first steps was to eliminate from the Jewish community all potential leaders to prevent escape, revolt and other forms of resistance. The Germans had a list of those they were to destroy, and my father was in that group of about fifty men.

But now I was alone. I knew I could not feel or be a child any longer. I alone was responsible for my life. My fate was in my hands. But I did not weep for myself. I wept only for my father. I did not think about myself as an orphan and gave no thought to my own condition at that time.

I stayed with the family we rented a room from. One day my landlady ordered me to go to the local Jewish Council, asking for exemption for her family from compulsory labor, due to my presence in their home. I did, but was told later by the landlady that my presentation of their problems was stupid and did not accomplish its aim. And before that, she thought I was smart. I think today that I, a child, was sent on an errand requiring maturity and experience.

I overheard the landlord calling me "*di heldin*," in Yiddish, the heroine, and "*treyf kishke*," referring to my not helping her in the kitchen and to my eating with my father in an un-kosher restaurant. His wife defended me by saying she did not ask me to help. She was, essentially, a kind woman. My agony and grief for my father were, however, so deep, that these words were nothing in comparison to my pain. Nobody and nothing could hurt me more. I did not permit myself to think about it, but the hurtful words remained with me to this day. At that time my heart seemed frozen and immune to further pain and remained so for many years, until the birth of my own baby, many years later.

In my loneliness and despair, I visited nineteen-year-old Adela, who lived with her mother. Their son and brother Emanuel had shared my father's doom.

Adela bitterly complained that her landlady didn't let her use the kitchen. Yesterday she locked the door and Adela couldn't even enter her room. Adela told me she was so unhappy, so miserable.

I, at twelve, silently mused that Adela at least had her mother, and that all Jews were unhappy and miserable at this time. I hoped my mother, in Palestine, was safe, but didn't think about her much. I understood that engaging in dreams would be useless. All my energies were needed for survival. At that time, however nobody knew that even the children were destined to be killed.

I loved and was very close to my father. In the absence of my mother, brother or any other family member, he was all I had. Without him now,

I visited his friends, who told me how inordinately proud of me he was, shamelessly bragging about me to anyone.

Mr. Zimmerman told me that my father used to tell everyone about me, and that he would have bent heavens for me. He was one of the teachers and Father's friend. I knew how my father loved and respected me, and was determined to be brave and to deserve it.

The Zimmermans, both he and his wife, were now in charge of a kindergarten, and invited me to visit them. I saw the children at their games and heard their songs. They sang in Russian a song to Commissar Voroshilov, an army commander now at the front.

> Klimu Voroshilovu pismo ya napisal
> "To Comrade Vorishilov, I wrote a letter:
> Comrade Voroshilov, national Commissar:
> If my beloved brother is lost in the war
> write for me as soon as you can."

Even kindergarten children were mobilized to fight the war for their motherland.

Now my father was gone. I was alone, completely alone. Staying with our landlady and her family, I could neither eat nor sleep. Being used to the sorrow and misfortune of being a Jew, I endured my agony silently, grieving for him, knowing I was in his last thoughts. This blow was too much to bear, and yet I knew I had to face it. I did not worry about myself. Not knowing what was to come, I didn't see myself as a child, alone, without a hope of survival, in a land torn by cruelty and war. My tears were only for my father.

I tried to talk to my friend Frieda, and share my pain. *My father...,* I began, but got no further.

"Oh, Eva," was the somewhat impatient reply. I felt even more alone. I understood no one wished to listen to a tale of sorrow, and I never spoke of it again. I remembered the phrase I had recently read in *Born on One Soil*: "Don't let your heart grow close, so it won't bleed at separation." I understood it now. As bad as it had become, neither other Jews nor I fully realized the impending danger to our own lives. But I dreamt about German cars and soldiers gathering in the marketplace, surrounding us. Even in my dreams I was frightened and anticipated our very near future.

The next day, in early morning, I noticed an unusual activity by German soldiers in town. There were too many German cars, too many soldiers in the street.

"They are going to shoot us all," a rumor quickly spread from person to person.

Come with us, Mrs. Jelinek, the landlady, urged me, as she gathered her children, hoping to escape through the fields. I did not respond. I knew the farmers were not friendly to the Jews. Instinctively I knew I had a better chance of survival alone. Quickly and quietly I slipped out of the house and made my way for the home of my Christian friend, Alicia.

It was cold. I took nothing with me but my coat. I knew that from that moment on I was not a Jewish but a Polish Catholic girl. I knew I would have to invent a last name and a story about my missing parents. If caught by the Germans and questioned, any object such as a photograph or a letter may betray me.

It seems to me today that even at the young age of twelve, I did not permit circumstances to determine my fate. Rather, I took my life into my own hands, and accepted the risks and the consequences.

On my way I saw my Jewish friend, Symka, who ran out of her house, crying loudly. I knew Symka could not pass for a Christian girl. Her recognizable "Jewish" features, such as dark hair and eyes, and especially her Yiddish accent would betray her. And she was a member of a large family, with younger siblings. She could not leave, as I could. Despair and tears were her only response.

I thought about my father, and how his death paved a way to my possible survival. Alone, I had a chance to pass for a Polish girl. I understood well and felt Symka's horror, but could not permit myself to dwell on it. By an act of will I suppressed my emotions and terror. My own life was in danger. They would soon come after me too. Unable to help, I kept walking.

Arriving at Alicia's house I was silently welcomed and permitted to stay. There was no need for words. Alicia's house, like other houses in the area, had only one room and a big kitchen, a common gathering place. Alicia's father was gravely ill. I sat on a bed in the kitchen, holding a cat in my lap. The cat purred and I hoped I looked as if I belonged there. Mrs. Kamińska, a neighbor, came in, noticing me.

She reported that Lithuanian soldiers were assisting the Germans. They went from house to house rounding up the Jews, driving them to an area outside of town for execution. Her husband and other Christian men were ordered to dig ditches to bury the bodies. Alicia jokingly held two fingers to her head, showing how a Jew is shot. I knew well what was happening, yet did not permit myself to see it clearly in my mind. Staying in Alicia's house, I heard no screams, no cries. We were too far removed from the area of the massacre, outside of town and from other houses.

5. Under the Germans

A group of German and Lithuanian soldiers in their gray-green military uniforms and heavy boots suddenly burst into Alicia's house, searching for hidden Jews.

One of the soldiers looked at me.

"And is this not a Jewess?" asked a soldier loudly, in Polish, pointing his revolver at me. I held my breath and remained calm pretending to be unconcerned. I did not let horror overcome me. I showed no fear, and my face reflected nothing but calm and indifference. Any sign of emotion would give me away. I knew that if caught, you could not ask for mercy. I allowed myself no feelings of fear nor anguish, suppressing them and submerging them in hope.

"No, she is ours," replied Alicia's mother, her tone slightly bored and ordinary, as if this information were of no great import.

A Jewish doctor and a priest were attending to Alicia's dying father in a room next to the kitchen. I knew the doctor. He was one of the refugees from western Poland. The priest administered the last rites to the dying man. The soldiers took the doctor away. He was led out past me at gunpoint. I knew he would not betray me. A shot rang out. The doctor fell on the sidewalk, right outside the house. More shots were heard. Other Christian neighbors came in, taking note of my presence.

"Has Eva left?" asked Alicia's father, concerned about the safety of his wife and daughter. Alicia's mother looked through the window.

"In a little while," she said soothingly, to gain a little time for me, who was grateful to them and understood their fears. I knew that in Poland sheltering a Jew could be punishable by death. I took anti-Semitism for granted and knew I was condemned to death. Controlling my fear and tension at that moment, I concentrated on my survival.

By nightfall I knew that I must leave, not to endanger my friend's family any longer. Too many people saw me in their home. My next challenge was to get out of town.

I asked Alicia to please give me her grey coat and shawl to cover my head. It would attract less attention.

Alicia gave me her cross, on a sliver chain. She thought that if anyone stopped me, it may help. I put it under my clothing. It would have been too obvious to wear it outside. Carefully looking both ways for German soldiers, I stepped out of Alicia's house.

The streets were deserted and strangely silent. I noticed a gang of local boys, and thought these boys were helping the Germans by leading them to places Jews were likely to hide. Some of these boys were my age and might have seen me in school. They would recognize me. I quickly avoided them, turning the corner, resisting the urge to run. Trying to stay off the streets, I stopped by the house of my friend Roma, a schoolteacher.

"They took Roma away," her landlady said tearfully. Her husband was one of the men ordered to dig the graves. Roma's mother and sister worked in a village nearby, perhaps sewing clothes. They were the only Jews in the village, and the Germans came and shot them. The farmers buried them together in one grave, and they showed Roma their grave. Roma gave her a letter to give to Roma's husband, who was in Harkov, Russia.

I left and continued on my way, away from the doomed town.

Cold and soaked by rain I found shelter that night in the home of a girl I knew from school. After that I wandered from village to village, pretending to be a Christian, and hoping someone will allow me to stay. I was fed by the farmers who might have kept me, at least for a while, but were suspicious and afraid. Their lives would be in danger. They fed and sheltered me for the night, but in the morning I had to leave. I felt no hunger, even though I usually had no food all day. Fear of betrayal and hope of survival dominated my thoughts. While staying for the night, I tried to help, usually with children and babies. I played with them, rocked them to sleep and held them if they cried.

In my wanderings I met Aaron, a Jewish youth I knew of about eighteen, who was also trying to escape and find a place to stay. As we stood on the road that cold November night, a farmer was passing by. There was no use pretending. The farmer understood who we were: two Jewish children condemned to death. The red haired youth spoke Polish with a recognizable Yiddish accent. He was also a refugee from another area of Poland.

The farmer advised the boy to change his speech, trying to be helpful. "To Russian? I can," said the youth. He didn't know his accent gave him away. I knew he had no chance of passing as a Christian. He had no chance to live, and seemed to feel it and knew he would be caught. His eyes reflected no hope but resignation. We parted with a sad good-bye. I never saw him again. We were at crossroads.

The friendly farmer told me not to go to the next village. The people there were bad.

His words of kindness almost brought me to tears. Almost, but not quite. This was no time for tears. I nodded my thanks to the man and turned to go in another direction.

As night was falling, I tried my luck by knocking on a farmhouse door. They let me stay and fed me bread and milk. In the morning, I tried to help by holding and calming their crying baby. A tall, burly militiaman in a sheepskin coat walked in. I learned he was a policeman, and the farmer's wife had probably brought him in to ask for his advice. Sitting down, he put his rifle between his knees and silently observed me, while talking casually and softly with the farmer's wife. I rocked the baby in its cradle, trying to be useful and crooning softly a Polish lullaby. The man listened. I sang a bit louder, knowing my Polish accent was perfect. Other Jews in this area spoke Polish with a Yiddish accent.

The policeman told me there is an orphanage nearby. They might accept me, he finally said, because I was an orphan. He told the farmer's wife she could get me later, if she wanted me to stay with her.

I breathed easier. I had escaped immediate danger, and there was new hope. The orphanage might be a safe place to stay, at least for a little while, if I could only be accepted as a Christian and admitted.

At the time I thought the policeman believed my story of being a Christian girl. As years passed, I wondered why he asked me no questions about my parents, my family and home. He asked no questions at all. Perhaps he didn't want to know.

Chapter 6

The Orphanage

Controlling my fear and even my awareness of the danger I walked slowly toward the graceful, beckoning white mansion on the hill. This was my only chance of survival. There was nowhere else to go. I avoided the front door and walked around the back door of the building, breathed deeply and knocked.

A plump, blond, blue-eyed young woman wearing an apron opened the back door. I asked if they needed any help, pretending I was looking for employment. She told me her name was Lonia, and asked me to come in. The kitchen was warm and the smell of potato soup inviting. Girls my age were busy in the kitchen peeling potatoes, washing dishes and slicing bread. I understood bread was scarce.

I followed Lonia into the director's room. They whispered for a few seconds, most probably about me.

Alexander Petrovich, the director, and his beautiful, blond wife Anita were eating supper. The director asked me to come in, and sit down. He knew my name was Eva. Lonia must have told him. I nodded, and quickly picked a Polish last name. Sharing their meal with me, they asked questions about my name, how I happened to be there, and where were my parents. They were friendly and curious.

I told them my parents and I were from Moscow (the Russian capital seemed distant enough to tell lies about). My parents were killed in an air raid by the Germans, I continued. We always spoke Polish at home. I came here because we had relatives in Warsaw, but it is so far away. I would like to stay here through the winter. I was asked to tell them about myself.

They listened quietly, and wanted me to tell them more and more about myself. I mentioned that my mother and father were teachers. I liked to read. They even wanted to know what I was reading. *Robinson Crusoe, Aesop's Fables, Children of the Underground* (a Russian novel), *King*

6. The Orphanage

Mathia the First.... I remembered my father, who took me to the library, just down the street from our apartment in Warsaw.

They wanted to know if I had been traveling a long time. I replied: yes, for several months. Alexander Petrovich wanted to know if I had seen what was happening in the towns and villages around us.

I replied that yes, they have been rounding up Jews everywhere, and shooting them. I spoke as evenly as I could, as if it did not concern me much.

They inquired what I thought about it. A fleeting image of my father, recently killed by the Germans, crossed my mind, but I kept my calm. I knew I was being tested, to see my reaction and responses.

I calmly replied that I thought they should not kill the children. They are innocent, venturing a safe, commonly known sentiment.

The director pronounced: "You may take a wolf cub and bring it up. But it will always return to the forest." I said nothing. His response was predictable. I had heard it before.

Alexander Petrovich was younger than my father, perhaps in his forties. His Polish, to my ears was impressive, bespeaking education and culture. He spoke like my father, bestowing, in spite of his words, a feeling of familiarity and, perhaps, trust. I felt his wife Anita's charm and kindness, in spite of the ugly, woolen knit cap she wore covering her ears for warmth.

After supper she led me to the girls' dormitory, assigning me a bed in a long row of small white beds. Everyone was asleep. I fell asleep, worried by the director's comments about the Jews, but hopeful.

In the morning no one was surprised to find a new girl among them. It had happened before. The girls washed, using a basin and pitchers. There was no running water.

Valia, tall, blue-eyed and pretty, carefully combed her honey blond hair, studying her image in a small, hand-held mirror. Valia mentioned her older sister in a nearby village. Dark-haired, slanty-eyed Sonia lovingly helped her five-year-old little brother, Volodya, with his washing and dressing. She combed his hair. Sonia's features, dark coloring and slanted eyes bespoke a Tartar background, not uncommon in this area of Poland. Curly-haired, green-eyed Tania talked about her recent visit with her older brother, who lived in town with his wife.

I silently noted the contacts between the orphanage and the city. The more contacts, the more danger, I knew.

Fania, a tall heavy-set girl, took care of three-year-old Romcio, blond and loveable, hugging and kissing him. I quietly washed and dressed. The girls, used to newcomers, asked no questions. I was glad.

At breakfast I heard complaints about this potato soup, again! I was silent, grateful for having even a temporary shelter, paying scant attention to the taste of the soup.

After breakfast I was called to the director's office. Alexander Petrovich was direct. He was an educated, intelligent adult, and understood who I was. He informed me that the story I told them yesterday was not true. That I did not grow up in Russia—my Polish was far better than my Russian. And my clothes showed no evidence of my traveling by foot for months. My clothes were not worn out enough, nor were my shoes. I could not have been traveling, homeless, for months. He concluded, correctly that I must be Jewish and had escaped the carnage around us.

He continued to say that I would remain here, in the orphanage. He would register me, but not now. As long as the Jews were being killed in the area, he could not reveal the presence of a new child. The Germans would question him about this child, and her identity. Registration could be done later.

Meanwhile my story must be more believable. He gave me some suggestions: My language is Polish and I am a Pole, not a child brought up in Russia. I must be careful and not trust anyone. And make no friends. He followed this with a curious request to report to him any sexual activities. I had no clue as to what "sexual" meant, and never had anything to report, but using my instincts, I understood it had something to do with relationships between men and women. I was, I believed, advanced beyond my age in some areas, but in everything pertaining to sex I was amazingly naïve. Growing up with my father, without women around me, I never heard any women talk, or gossip. All my information came from talking with friends my own age, who knew little more than I.

I needed friends and knew close relationships would increase my security, but understood the need to be always on guard, revealing nothing of my former life.

I was silent, studying the man carefully. Trusting him was my only option. There was nothing to say.

The next morning Anita instructed me: I will join the older girls, in cleaning the orphanage's rooms, washing the floors, doing everyone's laundry and helping in the kitchen. A few days later a barber cut my shoulder length hair very short, and I cried.

I heard Anita's hissing in my ear and catching my eye that my curly hair looked Jewish. Then she announced loudly that I would now look like a Parisienne, known for their charm.

No one questioned my presence, except one. Fifteen-year-old Valia,

6. The Orphanage

a village girl who had been one of the first girls to talk to me, spread the rumor that I was Jewish. I understood, and so did everyone else how dangerous such rumors were, and yet she did not hesitate to spread them. I controlled my fears and tensions, never responding, pretending to know nothing about it. I knew I could not confront her, and that a truly Polish girl would probably ignore these rumors. I never understood why Valia persisted in returning to the subject. Could it have been the difference in our way of speech that alerted her? The orphanage was in a rural area, populated by farmers. I definitely noticed the difference in the use of language between myself and other children. My Polish was correct, that of a city child, and a well read one at that. Their language was "rural," mostly White Russian, reflecting a lack of education and literary use and experience. Valia, never having heard any one speaking the way I did, might have sensed the difference in our backgrounds, and divined (unerringly) that I was Jewish.

Time flew quietly in the orphanage. I made friends with Lonia, the cook, and with others, both teachers and children. As months passed, I wondered about the duties of the teachers, since there were no activities of any kind. One of the teachers was an old lady, who spent her time warming herself by the oven and arguing with Lonia about better food for herself. Lonia shared this information with me. I appreciated her confidence in me, and kept silent. Fourteen-year-old Vanka the Fool shared his bread with me. Vanka was different from the others, perhaps slow-witted. He was bigger, his shirt was never buttoned right and hung out of his pants. He somehow had more food than the rest of us, and I asked no questions. I ate the bread. It would have been dangerous to refuse it, and I needed all the support I could get, even Vanka's.

Marysia, an eighteen-year-old orphanage employee who helped in the kitchen, was pregnant, and there was talk about her soon-to-be celebrated wedding to one of the teachers, Mr. Zborowski. There were whispers she had Alexander Petrovich, the director, to thank for this hasty wedding. Valia and Fania were convulsed with laughter. I had no idea why they found this so funny.

Lonia the cook was a pleasant young woman. She never had a watch before, but Anita thought she needed it in the kitchen, and gave her one. I taught her to tell time, always careful not to betray my background in word or deed, and saying nothing in response to her hints about the rumors of my being Jewish. Silence was safer. I fully understood how dangerous these rumors were. I remembered how the Germans sent two soldiers to a remote village to kill two women, my friend Roma's mother and sister. Nothing was more significant to them than the destruction of the Jews, and nothing too minor to ignore. I knew what my fate would be if the rumors about my being Jewish ever reached the German authorities.

Would a Polish Catholic girl respond to such rumors and try to prove them false, or would she ignore them, secure in her Catholic identity? In any case, I had no options but ignore them. Any investigation would be fatal to me. Every contact with the world outside the orphanage was dangerous.

The girls were very friendly. One night Wanda crawled into my bed.

She suggested we say our prayers together. Having had a Christian nanny, I began: Our Father who art in heaven, hallowed be Thy name, Thy kingdom come.... Hail Mary, full of grace, I continued next, whispering the unknown parts inaudibly. Not knowing the rest of the prayers, I had to pray in silence, I explained. My nanny's "education" had proved helpful.

I was given used orphanage clothing now, and was very pleased with my "transformation." I no longer looked like a Warsaw schoolgirl in a navy blue dress with a white collar. I thought I blended into the crowd of children and felt almost invisible. Every morning we all went to school, bundled up warmly against the freezing weather in felt boots and galoshes. The girls and I liked the blue "orphanage" bonnets and our warm maroon coats. On the way through the town I kept my face carefully down so as not to be recognized by anyone. At school I spoke little and kept close to other orphanage girls.

In a required German class all students had trouble pronouncing German words. Everyone stammered dreadfully. I stammered also: "*Der erweiter-ter-ter-ter satz*" (the enlarged or extended sentence), adding more syllables so as not to be different and to sound like all the other children.

One day an Eastern Orthodox priest visited the orphanage, dressed in long, dark clerical robes, a tall black hat and a gold cross on his breast. We children stood in line in the main hall. One by one we approached the priest, crossed ourselves, and he put his hands on our heads and blessed us.

I piously crossed myself, left to right, as taught by my Roman Catholic nanny, unaware that all the other children crossed themselves right to left. The priest noticed how I crossed myself, and mentioned it to the director, who stood by: she is Roman Catholic?

Yes, she is Roman Catholic, hastily confirmed the director. His wife, Anita was suspiciously pale. She knew that discovering I was Jewish would put their lives at risk.

6. The Orphanage

Whispers about my being Jewish persisted. I also overheard one day Anita saying: She has papers to prove it! The conversation must have been about me. Anita, the director's wife lied to protect me. There was also some gossip that seven-year-old Valentin was a Jew. Valentin came to the orphanage with a transport of orphaned children from Russia, boys and girls of various ages. The older girls had bundles of their clothes with them which, for reasons unknown to us, they were not allowed to use. We all had to wear the same orphanage clothing, while their own clothes were put in storage. This caused them much anxiety, since some of them were older than I, and quite aware of their appearance. At that time, about twelve years old, I was not aware of my looks. I, of course, was concerned primarily with my survival and gave no thought to the director's reasons and motives. I thought about little Valentin, and silently hoped that these rumors about him and me would not spread beyond the walls of the orphanage. I kept saying nothing, knowing that if caught, there would be no escape, and I would be shot. You would not ask the Germans for mercy, any more than you would ask a machine, a lion, or a serpent for pity.

Food was scarce, but not to the point of starvation. Occasionally farmers brought some potatoes to feed the orphans, and we all waited hopefully for the farmer's wagons to arrive.

Eight-year-old Tania complained that she was so hungry, and wished we had something else to eat, instead of this potato soup, thickened with flour and flavored with fried onions. Even the bread was rationed.

I did not complain. Silent and hopeful, I lived day by day. Every hour was a victory.

One evening an inspector visited the orphanage. The children paid scant attention to him. I was alert, and later I was called to the director's room.

"The inspector wants to speak with you," I was told by Anita, obviously nervous and worried. I was the only one the inspector wished to question. I knew, to my distress, that I somehow differed from the other children. I was a blond, blue-eyed girl and thought I was not different at all. Perhaps my being a Catholic among the other Eastern Orthodox children triggered his interest.

The inspector kindly asked what happened to me and why am I in the orphanage. Although frightened and always on my guard, I calmly related the revised fictitious story of my life as suggested by the director.

I was Polish, my parents were killed in a bombing raid. Himself a Roman Catholic, the inspector looked at this small, blond girl who talked like an adult, and made a decision. He and his wife would like to adopt me.

I asked the inspector if they had children of their own. They had three. Moved, but knowing it was too dangerous to leave the orphanage, I sweetly replied that I was afraid I would always feel the difference of not being their own child. The next day Alexander Petrovich, the director, heard about the inspector's offer.

He was glad I understood my chances of survival were better in the orphanage, within a group of children, than as an individual, in new surroundings, he explained. I had no idea what the word "individual" meant, but I understood its meaning: alone. Alexander Petrovich frequently overestimated what I understood and what I knew.

Rachel, a dressmaker, and Shlomo, a shoemaker, Jews from a nearby ghetto came to the orphanage often to sew and to repair shoes. That ghetto was an area fenced in by barbed wire and guarded, where Jews were forced to live. Both Rachel and Shlomo were thin, hungry, and subdued. Rachel was pregnant. I learned later that she had given birth to a lovely little girl. "Like a little doll," Shlomo told me. I spent much time sitting at Shlomo's side, while he repaired my snow shoes, since we had no other shoes. Shlomo was short, dark and had a long, hooked nose. I felt Shlomo and Rachel suspected who I was, but asked no questions. I felt safe in their presence. These people were not going to betray me. Everyone knew there was safety in silence, and asked no questions. I felt I had a better chance of survival alone in the orphanage than they had, in the ghetto, and that you cannot reveal what you don't know.

The director warned me I was spending far too much time having my shoes repaired. He understood why I chose to sit at Shlomo's side, and worried I might reveal who I was. I knew better, but the time I spent waiting for my shoes to be repaired were the only times I relaxed and felt no fear. Shlomo was not going to talk thoughtlessly and endanger my survival.

The Jews in the ghetto were starving, and traded clothes for food. It was easy to carry clothes out of the ghetto by wearing several layers of them, but difficult to carry food into the guarded ghetto area. It was prohibited in Poland, under penalty of death, to help the Jews in any way. Getting out of the ghetto to work in the orphanage, Rachel and Shlomo had an opportunity to get some food, but it was too little for their families.

One day Anita asked if I would help her smuggle a basket of food into the ghetto. You had to be careful of militiamen. If caught, I knew they would investigate who I was.

I was ready to go. Anita and I, looking like any mother and daughter,

6. The Orphanage

walked down the street, observing the marching militiaman guarding the ghetto. Behind his turned back I quickly pushed the basket through a pre-arranged hole in the barbed wire fence and continued walking as if nothing had happened.

Anita laughed, breathing with relief, and joked she was more afraid of Alexander Petrovich for risking her life and mine, than of the guards.

We older girls kept the entire orphanage clean by washing the wooden floors, and once a month we washed everyone's clothes. The washing day began by heating huge cauldrons of water in a separate house, now part of the grounds of the orphanage. The house had previously belonged to a Jewish family, and Maria, who had served them as a maid for many years supervised us. Lazer, the son of that family, now lived in the ghetto but came to work in the orphanage each day and served as a handy man, helping by stocking the stove with wood, bringing water from the well and moving the heavy cauldrons of boiling water. Lazer was young, perhaps in his twenties, and handsome. I realized we were now occupying the house formerly belonging to his family and kept silent, keeping my reflections to myself, and so did he.

The clothes were boiled first. Then we girls, standing in a row at a long wooden table, took one garment at a time, applied soap and rubbed it by hand on both sides. We had no other implements or equipment, not even a wooden washboard for washing clothes. The garments were boiled again, soaped and rubbed by hand a second time, then rinsed in cold water and hung out to dry. Later, after the destruction of the ghetto by fire, I learned that Lazer was found among the many other charred bodies.

While working, we girls sang in Russian and Polish about love, death and war. We sang in Polish:

> "Ty pójdziesz górą"
> You will walk through mountains,
> I will walk through valleys.
> You will bloom like a rose
> while I wilt in grief.
> You will be a maiden in a glorious court
> and I a monk in monastery dark.

A Russian song about lovers parting and going to war was very popular with us:

> "Na positsiu dievushka"
> A girl escorted her lover
> to the front.

> In the dark of night
> they said good-bye,
> and all through the night
> the young warrior
> could see
> a candle in her window.

Maria was kind to me. Stirring the laundry she sighed heavily and told me that Valia talked about my being Jewish. I said nothing, neither protesting nor acknowledging it even by a nod. Maria understood and didn't expect a response. On a washing day, in Valia's absence, Fania and Marysia gossiped: Two years ago Valia was brought to the orphanage by her older sister, who said she could not keep her. Their parents had died. Valia was accepted and given clothes and shoes. After a few months she ran away, taking all her clothing with her. And now, two years later, her sister brought her again, and Alexander Petrovich accepted her. I quietly listened. A few months later Valia approached me suggesting running away together.

As if I didn't know, I inquired where would we go: "To my sister, of course," replied Valia.

I wondered aloud if she would accept us, pretending to consider this seriously. A firm "no" would reveal my fears as a Jew. Valia tried to tempt me by promising that we could take all our clothes and shoes with us.

A few weeks later Valia ran away again. I worried about the rumors Valia might have spread about me, but she was not heard from again.

The gossip about my being a Jew was persistent in the orphanage, and dangerous. In the spring of 1942 I was sent by horse and buggy, in broad daylight, to live with a farmer's family that was told of my true identity. Alexander Petrovich knew them and hoped they would not betray me. I was about thirteen by that time.

It was a warm, sunny day, but fear was always there, submerged in everyday behavior. I wore a blue and white dress, a blue beret and hoped to attract no attention. Being discovered as a Jew meant death, but I never permitted myself to think about death, nor to forget about it.

Traveling along the country road, the world seemed peaceful, but for me, deceptively so. Memories… Intertwined, random images appeared and vanished. I watched out for any German vehicles patrolling the area. Death was always only a step away.

On my way to live with a new, completely unknown family, I felt both fear and hope. I knew that fear, if allowed to be felt, would debilitate me. I permitted myself no such feelings. Even hope, which motivated me, was subdued and not allowed to fly high, to prevent any disappointment later. No rosy dreams about the future. Just silent survival, day by day. I knew I had gained a small measure of safety, being now a ward of the orphanage with "papers" to prove it. I knew those papers could not withstand a close investigation, but it might never come to that. Changing location from the orphanage to a farm may stop the rumors there about my being Jewish and afford me some safety, at least for a while.

The horse plodded slowly forward as the sun sank on the pink and mauve horizon. I knew that on the farm and in the nearby village there would be curious and suspicious people to meet. I knew that every word, gesture and impression was important. My life was still at stake. The tired horse trudged wearily on our way to the farm.

Chapter 7

On the Farm

The farmhouse kitchen was small and dark, dominated by a wide and high clay oven in the center. There was a small window, a table and a chair, a board for dishes, a pallet to sleep on. The one large room adjacent to the kitchen contained beds, a cupboard, table and chairs. The wooden floor was painted a shiny red. But this parlor was seldom used. Life was lived in the kitchen.

The oven was used to bake bread, to cook food and to sleep on its wide, flat top surface during cold winter nights. Only the lady of the house slept in that warm place. In winter, I slept on a pallet by the oven, but in summer, spring and fall I slept in the barn, on its bare floor, wrapped only in an old blanket, and, except in summers, very cold. Potatoes and beets were stored under the pallet in the kitchen. A bucket of clear water, drawn from a well every day, and a cup was at the kitchen entry, for everyone to use.

Food was home grown: wheat; oats and rye for bread; milk; and vegetables such as beans, cabbage, potatoes, beets, onions and carrots. Sour milk was used to make cheese, its cream skimmed for butter. The butter and cheese was sent to the owner's grown children. The village knew no hunger.

The family consisted of an old couple. Their children were grown and gone. The lady of the house, Teresa, was in her fifties; her husband, Vladislav, in his seventies. Teresa was tall, dark haired and described herself as beautiful when young, and married at sixteen. Vladislav was thin, with a reddish-blond mustache. I learned later he was nicknamed in the village "Thin Ass." Everyone, including me, wore old, unwashed, lice-infested clothes. Vladislav ate at the table with a single chair, Teresa sat on the oven, and I sat on the doorstep. There was no conversation.

The day began before sunrise with feeding, watering and milking the cows. These were my duties. The black and white one was gracious and

7. On the Farm

cooperative. The brown one would kick and spill the bucket of milk. In cold winter nights the cows' udders, frequently dirty, had to be cleaned with usually frozen water. No one ever suggested bringing some warm water to clean the udders, and I was too young and inexperienced to know it. One of my daily duties was also to add new, clean straw to the cows' bedding. Feeding newborn piglets required careful care and attention. I mixed cooked potato peels, leftover food, flour and warm water and carried the pail to the sty. The piglets' food had to be warm, never hot. Next to feed were the chickens, and before letting them out of the coop, I had to check each hen for an egg. This was tested by feeling each hen's anus. If an egg was to be laid, the hen was left in the coop until then. Geese, hissing and stretching their long necks to bite me, were fed each day and brought to water. One of my duties was also to water the huge chestnut horse. Each one of us attended to our work in silence. A similar routine was followed in late afternoons, at end of day. In winter days were short, and it was dark as early as 4 p.m., so the daily routine of feeding, cleaning and watering the animals began very early. The seasons changed, and in the spring we planted a new vegetable garden, in summer harvested the wheat, rye and oats, and in the fall we all picked potatoes. Garden vegetables ripened all through the summers. Long winter nights I spent tearing feathers: removing the sharp stems from geese and chicken feathers, preparing the stuffing for pillows and featherbeds. I knew that girls in the village usually met on winter nights to spin cotton into threads, sing and gossip. My farmer grew no cotton, so this activity had never been mentioned. I thought that, for me, it was for the best.

Lighting the oven and cooking breakfast came after feeding, cleaning and watering the animals. Vladislav frequently did that, while the lady of the house, covering her head with a black shawl, went visiting her friends in the village, sharing gossip in general, and telling stories about her husband and the new orphanage girl, Eva, in particular. She then reported loudly about these conversations at home, and about Vladislav's bad reputation in the village, all to humiliate him. I was not spared her wrath and abuse. These accusations were not entirely in her imagination. Vladislav was always too close to me, "accidentally" touching my back and arms. I, in my innocence, thought nothing about it, but Teresa recognized these overtures for what they were and reacted to them by loathing her husband and resenting me. My anxiety about her gossip knew no bounds, but I could do nothing about it. I just hoped no one would wonder about the reasons for the girl's remaining with them.

One day a village boy came in to chat, and offered a cigarette to

Teresa. I was unaware that these were the first steps in courting me. These overtures stopped following Teresa's gossip in the village.

Sometimes the family made comments about the Jews. Looking disdainfully at me, they stated that Jews were supposed to be smart. I attempted to defend my people, by pointing out that many Jews were much wiser than I, and feeling very inadequate. It was understood that I was not smart and I accepted their verdict. Neighbors were curious. In the village, while trying to pass unnoticed, I inadvertently caused a sensation, and questions were raised.

In the freezing weather I reverted to my childhood habit of wearing pants I had found in the attic. *The girl is wearing pants!* The rumors quickly spread. For a girl to wear pants was clearly indicative that something was wrong with her.

After my first public appearance in pants, I had no chance for friends in the village, but this might have been for the best. I always wore a kerchief on my head, to cover my blond, curly, cut-short "Jewish" hair. Three village girls came to the barn while I cut potatoes for the cows. They asked questions about my name, where I came from, stealthily eyeing me, wearing pants. The common verdict was not flattering to me. I overheard: A big fourteen-year-old girl, and she can't milk a cow. I learned fast. Other comments: She reads books! She finds them in the attic. The books, mostly textbooks and magazines, belonged to Teresa and Vladislav's grown children.

An occasional peek into the old textbooks in the attic was my only respite. I was given special tasks to do on Sundays, just to keep me from reading, I think: unraveling tangled threads, washing the red painted floor of the parlor. I worked with harvesters in the hot days of summer, noticing the sunsets, pink, orange, blue and mauve. I was aware of the trees and the beauty surrounding us, but knew it was of no importance. My people were being destroyed, and could easily be shot on days as lovely as these.

When the harvest was good Vladislav sold grain to other farmers. Helping him measure the grain into the sacks and lifting heavy loads, I listened: Vladislav bragged to his buyers about his niece's husband, suggesting that he was a very important man. According to Vladislav, the husband was a spy. I stood silently by, with a feeling that something was wrong, and that this conversation should not have happened. It was not clear for whom the niece's husband was spying, but he was later shot in his home by Russian partisans. There were partisans in the forests nearby, fighting the Germans. One night we were awakened by them, a group of armed men and a woman. They took food: bread, lard, potatoes, and generally helped themselves to whatever they wanted. The previous day, while

7. On the Farm

cleaning the room, I had left Teresa's ring on the counter. The woman-partisan took it. "A Jew gave to a Jew," commented Teresa. Evidently, the woman looked Jewish to her. Such behavior of the partisans was common, and even violence was accepted with resignation, as life went on.

Little by little I learned how to care for various animals and enjoyed milking the cows and washing their udders before milking. I fed and watered the chickens, geese, pigs and horse. Piglets were carefully tended as they grew. Dealing with the horse was frightening. The horse used to bite me, and Vladislav's favorite joke was that the horse bit me because he knew I was a Jew.

A newly bought young chestnut horse ran away when I took it to pasture. I ran after it, trying unsuccessfully to catch it, but each time I came near, it swished its tail in my face and continued on its way. If I could only get on its back, I could bring it home, I thought, and tried to climb on its back, but I was too small and the horse much too tall. I tried again, fell and scraped my nose. Lifting my eyes, I saw old Vladislav approaching from afar.

Vladislav wondered what in God's name was I trying to do. He asked, shaking his head in wonder, why was I trying to climb on the back of this huge animal? He told me to let it go. A horse always returns to its former home. Tomorrow he will go and get it.

In the spring Vladislav plowed the fields and sowed wheat, oats and rye. Teresa and I planted the vegetable garden: alternate rows of carrots, onions and beets. Cabbages, cucumbers, beans and potatoes were planted separately. In the fall the produce was harvested and stored in a deep underground cellar to last throughout the year.

A black and white calf I named Lucifer was born one freezing January day and was taken home from the cold barn to help it survive. I fed it through the winter, by dipping my finger in milk and letting him suck it. There were no bottles or nipples to feed it. Lucifer followed me everywhere. He thought I was his mother.

Sometimes I was ordered to cut the throats of chickens, and I did it, in a flood of tears. Teresa concluded that I was crying because I was a Jew—this kind of killing was not kosher. She had heard about the special Jewish way of slaughter, and asked me how Jews slaughtered animals. Because my family was not Orthodox, I knew little about it. I had heard animals were supposed to be slaughtered by one blow across the jugular vein, with an unblemished knife, to cause them the least pain. But I could not do that to these chickens. I could only cut their necks and chop off their heads.

One of the best cows died, and a needle was found in its intestines. The cow probably ate the needle while on pasture. A young calf choked on a beet left in the garden. I felt guilty about it. I should not have left the beets in the garden. Cutting the calf's throat, Vladislav remarked that I wasn't worth as much as this female calf, born of a good cow.

A dog, Azor, was always chained to the barn, and a small cat was never fed nor allowed indoors. It fed on mice in the barn. It needed no help, providing for its own needs. Vladislav cursed that even a cat knows when it is not wanted! I wished I could be as independent as the cat, but I could not remain outdoors in the barn. Along time ago I had heard about Jews trying to join the partisans living in forests, but Polish partisans sometimes betrayed their Jewish comrades to the Germans. In any case, I had no contact with anyone, except the farm family, and had only myself to depend on for my survival.

I gradually became more like a farm girl, but never learned to walk barefoot across a prickly, newly harvested field.

Village girls, myself included, were sent to harvest plums on a local estate of a Polish landowner. We harvested the ripe, sweet plums and enjoyed eating them. The landowner's old mother, beautifully dressed in a silk dress and pearls, sat in an armchair in the orchard, listening to our songs and talking with us village girls. While all the girls spoke White Russian, she discovered I spoke Polish. A few days later the landowner came to our farm. While I was busy drawing water from the well for the cows, the landowner started a conversation with Vladislav about the girl who speaks Polish so well that his mother had seen and talked with. Vladislav, knowing full well who I was mumbled something.

"She speaks Polish so nicely," continued the landowner.

"Hmm…" muttered Vladislav.

The landowner did not give up easily. He explained that his mother wants to adopt this girl. She would like a companion like that.

Vladislav continued mumbling while I pretended to be unaware of the subject of their discussion. In spite of all this give and take, the adoption never took place. I understand today that just by being myself, and speaking as usual, I was giving myself away. I was not a village girl. But at that time I could do nothing else.

Work was hard, but not unbearably so. Cutting straw for animal feed every day was backbreaking, especially with an ill-functioning cutting machine, but harder to bear was the loneliness and the fear of exposure. I never cried nor asked for sympathy. I understood that the Jews were a despised people, and at this time, condemned to death. And yet, I did not believe we were inferior to others. I fully realized that luck alone brought me to where I was, and the Christian family I was with was helping me survive, but at night, as I lay exhausted on my pallet, I felt their unkindness to me was only matched by their unkindness to each other. It was hard to bear, day by day. I did not permit myself to dream, to lessen the misery, or to think about the past. All my attention was needed to stay alive and out of danger. And yet, occasionally, I wondered if I would ever see my mother or my brother again. Or would I ever meet Irena, the relative who wrote poetry, and was so close to me in age and spirit?

The language used by Teresa and Vladislav was White Russian, a cross between Polish and Russian, but on Sundays the language spoken was Polish. Curses in White Russian and Polish were common, continuously in use and adaptable to the need and the occasion.

For example: "Girl, open the door, may your head split open!" "Wash the pots, may you be washed out!"

They addressed one another by such common expressions as "evil spirit" and other similar, "ordinary" terms, rather than by their names. I, "the girl," was the most frequent target of such everyday terminology, and the atmosphere of enmity resembled a war zone. Teresa frequently called me "Jewess" in the front yard. Fortunately, their house was on the outskirts of the village, isolated from other houses, and no one heard. I wondered about the villagers' thoughts and possible suspicions, but obviously, this was never reported to the German authorities.

In private, remembering my father and the fate of all other friends and neighbors, tears almost came, and I knew that the unborn were luckier than the born, and decided to have no children. But more sorrow was yet in store.

Chapter 8

Special Attentions

Soon after my arrival on the farm old Vladislav began to pay particular attention to me. In addition to being far too close to me at all times and touching and bumping into me as if by accident, one day, while working in the fields, he grabbed me and kissed my neck. I moved away, intending to ignore it and almost forgot about it. But Teresa, the lady of the house, felt and noticed these attentions and insistently questioned me about it. Under a barrage of questions, I told her what had happened, not comprehending its import to her, and to me as well. I was just fourteen.

Being brought up by my father alone, removed from contacts with any other family member, I grew up deprived of usual interchanges between family members, visiting relatives and neighbors. I might have been advanced in other areas, but it might also explain my inexperience and ignorance in areas such as sex.

Teresa did not let this pass. She confronted Vladislav with shrieks, abusive names and ridicule. Obscenity was part of her attack, but it all went over my head. I had no idea at all what these words meant, even though I knew these were not compliments.

Teresa decided that I should relate this to their sons when they come to visit, in their father's presence. I was mortified. Teresa insisted on it, and proceeded to coach and drill me specifically in the words and expressions to use. I was expected to tell how Pan (Master, meaning Vladislav) kissed my neck, how I concluded by myself that Pan *"chciał mnie zgubić"* (tried to ruin me) and how I ran away. I mournfully pointed out that I did not run away, for where could I run? I understood none of it. Why was this so important?

But Teresa insisted that this is what I should say. The fateful day arrived when the two sons came to visit.

After supper, with everyone gathered in the kitchen, I washed the dishes and heartbrokenly hid in my corner, on the doorstep. Teresa sat up straight on the oven, giving me a signal to begin. There was no escape. I began.

"I have something to tell you. Pan kissed my neck. I concluded by myself that Pan *chciał mnie zgubić* and I ran away."

The sons were silent, then laughed and talked about other things. Teresa felt victorious in shaming her husband. Vladislav said nothing at all and went to sleep. Before sleep, as he did every night, Vladislav knelt by his bed, reciting his long daily prayers: Our Father who art in heaven, hallowed be Thy name.... Hail Mary full of grace....

I remained wounded and humiliated. I did, indeed, feel ruined, even though Vladislav never repeated his advances. He knew, by now, that Teresa would find out about it. I blamed myself, without knowing what I was guilty of. And day by day, I was the target of a barrage of hurtful terms by Teresa.

Teresa reminded old Vladislav every day, loudly, of all his trespasses and infidelities since the day they were married, and there was much to talk about. She described in vivid detail and colors their first encounter following their wedding, and her total innocence and naiveté. His betrayals of their marriage vows began soon after.

Vladislav, for his part, did not remain silent. According to him, she was no saint. He reminded her of the time he was a prisoner of war and away from home, during World War I. He mentioned, one by one, a long list of what I thought were her lovers. I later found out these were venereal diseases, such as syphilis and gonorrhea, which she had contracted at that time. There never was a kind or even a civil word exchanged between them. Teresa made her husband's life unbearable. I was not spared. She demanded that I prove every day that I did not want anyone's (meaning her husband's) attention. She used unmentionable, obscene terms liberally, freely, and specifically, about body parts and sexual activities. Of course I did not know what they meant or what was I accused of, but I learned. Teresa had her own purposes. In desperation, I told her that had I been interested in someone, it would have been her young and handsome son. She was aghast, never having suspected that. It was true.

Upon my arrival at the farm, her young son tried to seduce me. I never agreed. We were alone in the house, but it never occurred to me I could have been raped. But I was not. I was fourteen and unbelievably naïve. He was probably about twenty, but obviously, we were both good and honorable kids. Now, his mother, upset, warned me never to tell anyone about it, and, of course, I never did. At a later time, the young man saw me on the farm while visiting his parents. "You were different then," he commented quietly one day. I was changed beyond recognition. Emotionally tortured day by day, of course I looked differently than before: in rags, with my head always covered to hide my blond, curly "Jewish" hair. The young man was killed a few years later by Russian partisans fighting the Germans. He was in the wrong place at the wrong time. My words of self-defense had no effect and did not prevent his mother, Teresa, from tormenting me every day, as usual. I wanted her to stop, and only in retrospect am I grateful that she did not look the other way. It effectively stopped any of Vladislav's overtures. This was my introduction to marriage, sex and family life.

A rash over my body caused by nervous stress made me feel "untouchable." I thought no one would ever want to come close to me. I was nearsighted and needed glasses, but did not know it, and questioned my own abilities, judgment and reason. I was referred to as "blind."

One day I was sent to a neighbor's house to return a borrowed pot. I entered a large kitchen, full of light. The father of the family was busy feeding their three-year-old daughter, while the mother cooked, talked and smiled at her husband, baby and me. Returning the pot, I thanked them and left. But I had glimpsed another world of almost forgotten civility in the family. Despite the temporary solace and the temporary return to the normality of day-to-day family life, the war was still being fought, and I had to remember that.

There was no news from the front, since possessing a radio was punishable by death. A neighbor stepped on a land mine and was severely injured, but otherwise the war was far away.

There was a German camp nearby, with imprisoned men and women. Some village girls we assigned to weed its gardens, I among them. I was curious who the prisoners were, but was afraid to ask. We were surrounded by gardens, and I saw no buildings nearby and no prisoners, except Krakowski, who, in spite of being a prisoner, was in charge of the gardens. Krakowski seemed to me to be a Jew. He was dark, thin, polite and spoke good Polish. At lunchtime I sat alone and not with the other village girls. Krakowski sat down beside me. He commented that I was a nice girl, and offered me some of his bread.

I felt like crying. These were the first kind words I had heard in years, but a display of emotion would have been too dangerous. I restrained myself and didn't cry. I noted, with trepidation, that there must have been something about me setting me apart from the other cheerful, gossiping girls. Perhaps my sitting apart; my ragged, neglected clothes; my covered head, blond (Jewish) curls escaping; and a general suppressed spirit drew his attention.

One day I was sent to the German camp alone. I could have refused to go, but did not recognize the danger of appearing alone. Two police guards approached me. They asked where I was from. I mentioned the name of the village, in my best White Russian. They continued asking why I was the only one. I replied that I was the only one the village elder sent. They left me without comments and investigated no further. I did not permit myself to dwell upon it, but exposure and death were so near. I believed my flawless White Russian accent saved me.

There was no encouragement from any quarter, and hope had to be sustained in silence that the Germans would lose the war. And sometimes, at night, I thought of what I might become after the war. I believed I could be a teacher, like my parents were.

I had been at the farm for approximately two years. Although I did not know it, as I had lost track of time, the war was drawing to an end.

One day a neighbor stopped by the barn where Vladislav and I were cutting straw to feed the animals. Teresa was sorting potatoes rotted by frost to feed the cows. He told us that the war was nearly over. Since possessing a radio was forbidden and there were no other sources of information, this was news indeed.

The neighbor told us, weeping, that the Germans had executed all the prisoners of the concentration camp. They were found with their hands tied behind their backs with barbed wire, and gunshot wounds. His girlfriend was among the dead.

I had no tears left. I was silent, too numb and too cautious to feel anything, even joy at the Germans' imminent defeat. I closed my eyes, remembering my father. Deliverance had come too late for him.

Liberation by the Soviet army came to our village on an April day in 1944. I saw a German soldier on horseback, riding away fast from the village, never to return. *The war is over*, rumors now spread throughout the village, but life continued pretty much as before. The farmers' lives were never threatened, and growing their own food, they never knew hunger. The end of German rule was anticipated but there was no great celebration of freedom. Instead, all waited for the Soviet army to occupy the area. There was in the village some fear of Russian soldiers and the possible nationalization of private property and land. My big problem, at the moment, was my lice-infested hair and how to remedy it. I knew that with the war's end I would leave the village.

The time had come to do something about my hair. I remembered that kerosene was recommended by the school nurse in Warsaw to the children who had lice. I now used lamp kerosene to douse my hair. The overpowering odor caused questions. The lady of the house was away visiting her children. Vladislav, coming from the barn, asked me what the smell was and ordered me to open the window! I mumbled softly it was the kerosene from the lamp. It was assumed I had spilled the kerosene. I never had lice again.

I never saw German soldiers again. Joining forces and fighting together, the United States, Russia and Great Britain and others had defeated the German army, liberating the many European countries enslaved by Germany between 1939 and 1945. It was a few months before the formal declaration of the end of World War II in Europe, in May 1945, but our world was free. I, cautiously, still remained in the village. But there was a difference. I was not afraid any longer. I did not have to be on constant guard and the threat of death was no longer just a wrong step or the wrong word away. It seemed I even breathed differently. I could now see and hear the birds sing, and could smell the freshly cut grass and the scent of flowering trees. I was free, and the feeling of relief quietly swept over me. Even my angry rash miraculously disappeared. Even though the village did not celebrate the end of the war, I celebrated it in every way, with my body, mind and spirit. I was free.

With the anticipated invasion of the Russian army, Vladislav and Teresa hid in a potato cellar some distance away, leaving me to protect the house against the Russian army. The Russians and their attitudes toward the villagers were still unknown. At night, I went to sleep as usual, unafraid, and was awakened by flashlights shining in the windows. Leaving the house through the back door, I ran through the fields to tell Vladislav and Teresa: *The Russians are here!* I heard shots behind me. Seeing someone running away, they were shooting at me, running through the field.

We walked back to the village together to meet the Russians. We all understood Russian and parted peacefully. There was no looting, raping or any other atrocities in the village by these Russian soldiers.

One morning, as I was drawing water from the well, a Russian soldier approached me, getting far too close. At that time an officer passed by. The soldier left me alone very fast. Evidently, this kind of behavior was not permitted to these soldiers, in this area. I was too naïve even to be afraid. All my fears were gone now.

As the Russian army occupied the village, one of their first acts was to order the village elder to provide a number of girls for compulsory labor. Not surprisingly, I was among those selected. I gathered my few things together and joined the other girls to be brought to the train station. Other girls came with their families. I was alone. During the journey east by train we stopped to sleep in villages, and the local farmers' wives provided breakfast for us. As was the custom, a common bowl of potato soup flavored by fried onions, and a few spoons were placed on the table. None of the girls ate, having their own provisions. I did not eat either, even though I had nothing else to eat. I did not even feel hunger.

It would have been embarrassing to eat. The other girls were showing that they did not need other people's food. Pride, social posturing and position were more important to all of us even than food, and even at that difficult time.

Traveling by train east to an unknown destination in Russia, I was both relieved and anxious. My life was no longer in danger, but where was I going? Working in the Ural mines had been mentioned as our possible destination. I saw visions of dark, underground caves, such as coal mines, and no escape. This, I thought, would be a terrible fate. I was hoping for freedom, education, a new destiny and, especially, for finding my mother. I knew I had to escape, and at one of the stations, quietly and carefully, unnoticed by the other girls, I got off the train and hid in the outhouse, shivering with fear. I expected the guards to notice my absence and search for me. I waited until the train was gone. Breathing easier but still fearful, I quickly boarded another train, going in the opposite direction, traveling west toward Poland.

Chapter 9

Our World in Europe at Peace

Survivors were few and I was one of them. I was now sixteen and totally alone. I remembered the day the Jewish population of Lachowicze, the little village I had last lived in with my father, was rounded up and massacred and my finding shelter in my friend Alicia's house. I thought about my father, two of his brothers, his young sister and other relatives most probably no longer with us. My mother and brother, I assumed, survived in Palestine, and I hoped to find them now.

The world was in motion. Survivors from concentration camps, Siberia, and various hiding places were trying to find other surviving members of their families. Trains carried people, cattle and other cargo. There was some registration for using trains, but tickets were unknown.

Like other survivors in search of families, I returned to the last place I had lived with family, to Lachowicze, in present-day Belarus. If by any stroke of luck my father were alive, he would have looked for me there. My father, of course, was not among the living. I was hoping against hope. I did not really expect to find him.

I came by train and walked the streets I remembered so well. I passed the house I had lived in with my father. It was used as Russian headquarters now. I remembered the months I grieved for my father. I recalled the deep despair and pain. Today, it was alleviated by my survival. It was so long ago. The sun shone warmly and trees sprouted new leaves. Spring was everywhere. There wasn't a single coin in my pocket nor was there a familiar soul. I had no family, no food and no roof over my head, yet I felt wonderful. This was the time I had hoped for so long. I was young, free, and my life was no longer in danger. But there was no one with me to share the joy and relief of liberation or hopes for the future.

My feet carried me to the house of my Christian friend, Alicia. It was she and her mother who had sheltered me in their home during the critical hours, four years ago, while the Germans, assisted by Lithuanian soldiers, had driven almost all the Jews in town out of their homes and executed them.

I knocked on their door. Alicia saw me, smiled and opened her arms. She and her elderly mother calmly asked me to come in. All three of us remembered the soldiers searching Alicia's house for hidden Jews, while I sat on the bed with a cat in my lap. The house looked the same, but now there was no threat of death. The world had changed. Alicia's father, who was then very ill, was no longer with them.

Alicia remarked she knew I was going to survive, her voice quiet and ordinary. It was so self-evident to her. And our entire world was wiped out. Alicia's mother looked at me, saying: *Child, you need a bath*, and immediately and practically went to heat some water. Their simple actions restored me somewhat to the past and to normality. Someone, again, was caring for me. I sat in the steaming water in an aluminum tub, washing my hair and carrying on a casual conversation about hiding from the Germans for five years.

Alicia offered to let me try on some of her clothes, giving me a soft blue angora sweater. She told me that our neighbor's daughter wore some of my dresses after I had left. And a girl in a village nearby was wearing my coat. Alicia gave it to her. The neighbors went into the Jewish homes and took whatever they wanted, Alicia continued her chatting. Did I remember Mr. Katcherginski, the pharmacist? He poisoned his wife, daughter and his five-year-old granddaughter Valia, before the Germans came for them. It was an easier way to die.

Mr. Korygin, a teacher and my father's Polish friend still lived in town. The next day I went to visit him. He and his wife welcomed me warmly and calmly, as if nothing extraordinary had happened to us in the intervening years. His wife offered me something to eat. While I ate, they kept busy, providing me with the privacy I needed and appreciated.

They were not surprised I survived. Jan Korygin remarked that my father used to brag to anybody who would listen that no one had a daughter like his daughter. Some of it must have been true, he continued, because I was the only one who survived the massacre in this town of the Jews who were there at that time.

He revealed that I may not have known it, but my father had given them his valuable gold watch for safekeeping after the Germans occupied the town. The Korygin's house burned down, but they still had the watch, because his wife had sewed it into the hem of her coat. She said she was glad it would finally end up in the right hands. I did not mention that I knew all about the watch, my father's wedding gift from his brother, a prospector for gold in Alaska. The watch, made by Hamilton, had gold covers engraved with my father's initials. Receiving the watch was not an emotional moment for me. I have taught myself to suppress some of my emotions, and survived. I also had little appreciation of the value of money. It did not help me survive. But I thought about my father, especially about his sharing many of his problems with me. We sat in silence, each deeply in our thoughts. I knew my father also hoped the Korygins would help me, should anything happen to him. At a critical time, they did nothing for me, but I understood how difficult it was to help a Jewish child.

And now I had a gold watch, a piece of property, which I knew was of considerable worth. I had survived the Holocaust without any money at all. My life was saved through a combination of luck, circumstances, determination and the help of those who sometimes risked their own lives to save a child. Money had no place in my life.

But this was peace, and the world had changed. I knew I had to travel from eastern to central Poland to get to Palestine, to my mother. I needed provisions for the trip, provisions such as bread. I decided to approach the remnants of a Jewish community in a nearby town, to estimate the value of my gold watch and sell it, if necessary.

I was met by a bearded man who carefully examined my watch and estimated its value, avoiding my eyes. I did not know at that time that this behavior was expected and common to Orthodox Jews. I was sixteen years old, all alone in a devastated land. No one asked if I had food, a place to live, or if I needed help. This was when reality hit me that without something of value, in this case my watch, no one would even speak with me.

Meanwhile transports were going to central Poland by train, but everyone had to be formally registered as a member of the transport. A young couple, Shimon and Miriam, who survived the war fighting the Germans with the local partisans, heard about me, and agreed to add me to their papers.

I was on my way to central Poland by a cattle train. Several families and a cow traveled in the car. The odor was overpowering, but I paid it scant attention. I was going to my mother and a new life, but I had to trade my gold watch for a few loaves of bread. I heard about someone interested in buying my watch. It was a family of Jewish survivors.

The father of that family of survivors told me that it was not for the bread that I was paying them with my watch. He pointed out to me I needed provisions for the trip. Giving up the watch was saving my future. I knew it was not fair, but I thought I had no choice.

Shimon, who with his wife had added me to his papers so I could join the transport to western Poland, was furious about this transaction. He regretted it was too late for him to return the bread to them and get my watch back. He fumed he would spit on them, adding a few obscenities.

In spite of my rude awakening to the need for, and the value of money, it was not a life changing experience. Money did not become the dominating force in my life.

Arriving in Łódź, in central Poland, I turned to the offices of the Jewish community, as all survivors did. Each one of us had a different story to tell. Somehow they had the impression I had survived the war by joining the partisans in the forests. Oblivious of all the implications, especially assumptions of sexual coercion or experiences, since there were few women in the forests, I never corrected them. I thought this was an interesting twist to my story. It was great fun, and I enjoyed their looks of understanding and sympathy.

I was given an address of an apartment I was to share with other Holocaust survivors, young and old. Even though no one looked forward to another person sharing their quarters, I was accepted and allocated a bed in a spacious room. Two young men and a boy and his father occupied the room and slept there. One night, quietly and stealthily one of the young men came up to my bed. I woke up, noticed he was breathing heavily, probably afraid I was going to make noise and raise an alarm. I, just as quietly, sent him packing and never mentioned it to anyone. His pride and reputation remained intact.

I walked the streets of Łódź, a big industrial city, free and unafraid, noticing the sun shining, the wide boulevards, and the beautifully dressed women. I was young, shabbily dressed and alone, but felt safe, secure and hopeful. My future was still to be created and lived.

In the offices of the Jewish community all newcomers were asked to register. I was instructed by a young receptionist to list the names of my parents, my place of birth and other details to identify myself. Everyone was hoping to find remnants of their families. I noticed men and women anxiously searching through the lists of names. Was anyone alive? I was lucky to find Zygmund's name. There he was! Zygmund was the cousin I remembered, who visited us in Warsaw at the war's beginning, the only survivor of our large family. I wrote to him and he came to Łódź to meet me.

Zygmund told me there were groups of young people planning to go to Palestine. Zygmund, who was considerably older than me, promised to help me join them. In Palestine I was certain to find my mother.

Before joining a youth group bound for Palestine I came to live in Częstochowa with Zygmund and his beautiful, dark-haired, slender wife Maryla. The three of us shared one room with another distant relative, Mrs. Ginzburg, who had lost her entire family. She and I shared a wide sofa that opened at night into a bed. At night, she frequently mentioned her teenage daughter, Pearl, who perished, referring to her habits, likes and dislikes, as if Pearl were temporarily away from us. She elaborated on her clothes and food preferences. She talked about Pearl, how she liked her school, how she loved to read. I listened, painfully identifying with Pearl, aware of her mother's need to talk about it. It helped her cope. I was also keenly aware that I was not her child. I knew she would have preferred me not to be there.

Other Jewish survivors in town also shared crowded rooms with distant relatives, friends and strangers. In the war's aftermath substitute families were formed, as if to replace by their presence the lost mothers, fathers, sisters and brothers.

Maryla was movingly kind to me and gave me a black, satin school dress, to be worn with a white collar. Glancing at myself in a mirror, I was surprised to see that I looked … nice. I saw a blue-eyed girl, with a rosy face and blond, curly hair. After years of abuse I began to question some of the negative opinions about myself I had learned to accept on the farm. Perhaps, just perhaps, I could look not so different than others? Perhaps I was not as ugly as they taught me to believe I was? Could I even be considered acceptable? Perhaps there was nothing wrong with my brain? Perhaps I was not as stupid as I had learned to believe I was, and not blind?

One day my cousin Zygmund told Maryla that he was able to recover the factory buildings his family owned before the war from the authorities. All the machinery was gone, but he might be able to sell half of the building. The other half was owned now by a Pole. This should help us to survive for a while. I saw Maryla using her knitting skills to help support the family. I listened, learning some facts about economic survival. Sometimes in the evenings, before going to sleep, Zygmund and Maryla danced to the tune of a phonograph record, frequently a slow, romantic tango. I listened dreamily and saw another image of family life.

I soon joined a group of survivors in Częstochowa. Most of them were young and alone, with only two sets of surviving mothers and their daughters. Children and older people were no longer among us. We ate

9. Our World in Europe at Peace

together and studied Hebrew, preparing for a life in Palestine (present-day Israel), and called ourselves a "kibbutz," meaning a collective settlement in Hebrew. We seldom mentioned our parents or siblings, all dead, except in passing. We all shared a similar past, and our losses were with us, known, present, unseen and unmentioned.

I also heard, about concentration camps, such as Auschwitz. No stranger to horror, such as mass massacres, I was still shocked to hear about gas chambers, the common fate of all their families, and about the public hangings they were forced to witness of girls who tried to escape. I had no words, and words would be useless. I absorbed it all as Jewish destiny at that time. In my innocence, I believed it could never happen again.

The girls shared their clothing with me, being one of the youngest among them. There were also a few young boys and men among us, resulting in some romances. I was not ready for romance and never thought about it. One of the reasons might have been that I did not like any of the boys in our group. And, at sixteen, I saw myself as a student, rather than a young woman, and studied English in addition to Hebrew, not knowing that one day English would become my everyday language. Some people told me that I would never be able to go to school in Palestine, since I knew no Hebrew. I didn't reply. I knew the future would provide answers. And so it did.

The British authorities ruling Palestine in 1946 still did not permit Jewish immigration, even in the aftermath of World War II. In spite of all this, our group embarked on this trip to our Promised Land. Staying in Poland following our Holocaust experiences was unacceptable to any of us. Poland to us was the place of our graves, but we had no other home and no other place on earth to go. And many refugees returning to Poland were killed upon their arrival by a population occupying their homes. Going to Palestine was only a dream, and yet we knew we would achieve it. But trying to get to Palestine was a risky, dangerous proposition.

Well known to the survivors were the stories of the ships like SS *Patria* and later, SS *Exodus*. In 1940, in the midst of the Holocaust, three ships carrying approximately 3,600 passengers, men, women and children, refugees from Nazi Europe, came close to the shores of Palestine. British navy ships, forewarned, surrounded them, refusing permission to land, planning to transfer them to the SS *Patria* and exile them to Mauritius, an island in the Indian Ocean, for the duration of the war. Later, they were to return to their original "homes" in Europe.

The refugees from concentration camps had nowhere else to turn to. No country would admit them, and the Jewish community in Palestine held its breath and continued to negotiate with the British about their permission to land in Palestine, the only place and community on earth that wanted them.

The British were unmoved. Their excuse was the possibility that German spies may be among the refugees. As the deportations date drew near, the Jewish leadership in Palestine, in a desperate attempt to delay their deportation, decided to damage the SS *Patria*, forcing the British to postpone their departure and allow them time for repairs and permission to land.

On November 25, 1940, a strong boom was heard all over Haifa. A bomb, planted in the bowels of the *Patria* exploded. Within fifteen minutes the ship sank. Sirens wailed and rescue operations began. Records vary slightly, but according to some counts, of the 1,904 persons on board of the *Patria*, 260 were missing, 172 were injured, and 209 bodies were found. The rest of the survivors remained in Palestine.

The Jewish leadership did not intend to sink the ship, but the poor condition of the *Patria* might have contributed to the tragedy. It resulted in sorrow and grievous soul-searching by the activists within the Jewish leadership.

The SS *Exodus*, while attempting to land in Palestine in 1947 with 4,515 Holocaust refugee passengers aboard, was shot at and damaged by the British and sent back to Germany, with the refugees to be interned in Displaced Persons camps. Some of the refugees were smuggled to Palestine, and after the founding of the State of Israel in 1948, all reached the desired shores, the only homeland left to them. And among the brave boys, who brought them to this land and carried them on their shoulders from the sea to the shore were also Christian volunteers, among them John Stanley Grauel, a Methodist minister. And many young men among the refugees later joined the Jewish forces in the fight for independence and some fell in battle. The persistence and courage of these remnants of our people might have helped to pave the way to the State of Israel.

The first stage of our own journey was to get out of Poland and to reach Germany.

We knew entering Palestine was considered illegal by the British then in power, and it had to be done in secrecy. Thus Operation Brichah began, the movement of thousands of Jewish Holocaust survivors out of Europe and into Palestine. Brichah (Hebrew for flight or escape) was funded secretly by the Rescue Mission of the Jewish community in Palestine, and aided

9. Our World in Europe at Peace

View of the battered illegal immigrant ship *Exodus 1947* docked in the port of Haifa alongside the British comfort ship *Ocean Vigour*, to which the *Exodus* passengers were being transferred (courtesy U.S. Holocaust Memorial Museum, photograph number 95617).

by other organizations, including the Jewish Brigade, part of the British armed forces. According to estimates, over 150,000 people found their way to Palestine assisted by the Brichah movement.

We were given clear instructions: we will go by train from Poland to Czechoslovakia. No one had tickets. This was a time of upheaval and of great population movement. We will be traveling as Greeks. We were told: do not speak Polish. Since you know no Greek, use the words of the Hebrew songs you know. The Polish and later German conductors know no more Greek than you do. While you pretend to be Greek, the guards may pretend to believe you. Our passage had been arranged, and several countries in Europe cooperated with us. However, if asked for documents and if thrown off the train, we were instructed to immediately board another part of the same train and continue our journey. Just remember the address of our meeting place in Prague, the capital of Czechoslovakia.

In spite of my seriously reciting of the Hebrew song: "Anu banu artza,

Livnot ulhibanot ba..." (We came to our land, To build and be rebuilt...) I was, indeed, thrown off that train. Seeing another girl of our group on the platform, I followed her, we boarded the train again and reached Prague and the rest of our group, where we stayed for a few days, hopeful, anticipating our new, future adventures.

Portrait of John Stanley Grauel, a Methodist minister who was a member of the crew of the *Exodus 1947* (courtesy U.S. Holocaust Memorial Museum, photograph number 95600).

Chapter 10

Displaced Persons (DP) Camp

The next step of our odyssey was a Displaced Persons Camp in Deggendorf, Germany, close to Munich. We lived and worked on a farm, preparing for agricultural work in Palestine and knew little of the town itself. My duties included milking cows every morning. Now an expert, I enjoyed it. I was at peace.

In the camp we were provided with food, shelter and medical facilities. Clothing was received from the United States and distributed among us. It was fun to try on different clothing, and I usually found things fitting me. Once I found a vest made of rabbit skin, very soft and warm. The year was 1946, I was sixteen, and I felt grateful and appreciative for all this. I felt safe from the threat of death after years of suppressed fear.

We were supported by the United Nations Relief and Rehabilitation Administration (UNRRA), but the American Jewish Joint Distribution Committee (AJJDC) was also very active in the Deggendorf camp.

The AJJDC, or the Joint as it was commonly known, originally founded in 1914, was now working together with the Organization Through Rehabilitation and Training (ORT), the Jewish Agency for Palestine, and other Jewish organizations to provide us food, additional rations, clothing and books, and also sent doctors, nurses, teachers and social workers to assist us. I was one of the approximately 420,000 Jewish beneficiaries of the Joint in Eastern Europe between 1945 and 1950. In addition to providing for our physical needs, these organizations also gave us the opportunity to take courses in Hebrew, vocational training and other programs to teach us practical skills, to be independent and an asset to our homeland. Agricultural training was emphasized, but philosophical ideas were not neglected. We learned about and were inspired to understand, value and preserve our history, identity and culture. The ideas inherent in Jewish

At an unidentified children's home after the war (courtesy U.S. Holocaust Memorial Museum, photograph number 25406).

culture were unknown to me. Most of us were young, with our growth and education disrupted by war. Older people and children were no longer with us. I was close to the few surviving older adults.

We did not complain. I thought the conditions were good, especially the freedom from fear of German annihilation, and I was full of hope for a life, which for me was just beginning. After years of starvation for many of us the plentiful food was irresistible. I gained weight and was painfully aware of it, feeling unattractive and unlikable, but unable to change it.

I was sixteen years old at the time, naïve, and preoccupied primarily with my own future, barely aware of the larger issues at stake.

The numbers of displaced persons, or DP's, grew as refugees arrived from Siberia, Poland and from other places in Europe. The American and British governments, then in charge of these areas in Germany, debated on ways and means to resolve the problem of the homeless victims of the Holocaust and war. Following World War II, at one time approximately 75,000 Jewish Holocaust survivors lived in DP camps in Germany, Austria and Italy.

General George Patton, the Military Governor of the American Sector in Germany, was determined to resolve this problem by repatriating the DP's to their countries of origin. This was unthinkable to the Jewish survivors, who as recently as 1946 had experienced new bloody attacks by Poles in several areas of Poland. Attacks occurred sometimes due to the fear that the returning Jews might want their houses back, but the deep-rooted anti–Semitism and the political struggle with the existing communist government in Poland contributed to the violent events.

President Harry Truman dispatched another delegate to investigate the issue and recommend solutions. Meanwhile, the survivors themselves created committees to voice their needs and represent them. The majority wanted to go to Palestine, having no other home or place to go. General Patton was relieved of his command of the area, and with the help and understanding of the Joint, the survivors were assisted to forge their own destiny and reach their homeland. Then again, the Joint, along with other Jewish movements, such as Brichah and Aliyah Bet, were with us and helped us to reach Palestine, and between 1947 and the founding of Israel in 1948, approximately 115,000 Jewish refugees reached Palestine. Those who were interned by the British on the island of Cyprus for trying to reach Palestine underwent much hardship, but were not forgotten by the Jewish organizations.

After many trials and tribulations, after the establishment of the State of Israel in 1948, the policies of the British became null and void, and

A group of young Jewish DPs who are seeking to immigrate to Palestine illegally pose outside in a field with a Zionist flag (courtesy U.S. Holocaust Memorial Museum, photograph number 61178).

most survivors, including those exiled to Cyprus, found their refuge in Israel, and with the help of the Joint, by 1950 more than 440,000 survivors found a haven in Israel, accepted regardless of age, health or work ability. They had come home, and were welcomed, assisted and absorbed into the community. Immigration to Israel continued from many Muslim lands, where persecution increased, including the dangerous escape from Yemen, sentimentally called Operation Magic Carpet.

Meanwhile in 1946 in Deggendorf, our group became a cohesive whole, and many of us remained in contact with each other for years to come. We tried to resume a life as normally as possible. There were marriages and births, and, to my youthful amazement, even conflicts. In my lack of life experience I believed that with the end of the war and the German rule, people would live together without conflicts and stress. I learned otherwise.

While the gates of Palestine continued to be closed even following

10. Displaced Persons (DP) Camp

The wedding of Ibby Neuman and Max Mandel at the Bad Reichenhall DP camp (courtesy U.S. Holocaust Memorial Museum, photograph number 40058).

World War II to Jewish immigration, the British granted a limited number of certificates of entry to children and youths under eighteen. I received one of those certificates, and on a sunny morning in May 1946 some of my friends and I, along with a group of other surviving children and teenagers, reached Haifa, Palestine, on a French ship, *Champollion*, sailing from Marseilles.

Upon reaching the shores of this land our ship raised the Jewish blue and white flag, and we sang the "Hatikvah," or "The Hope," soon to become the Jewish national anthem:

> As long as in the heart
> The Jewish soul is yearning,
> Our eyes turn to the East, Our eyes to Zion.
> Our hope is never lost,
> A hope of two thousand years,
> To be free
> In our land,
> In Zion and Jerusalem.

We could hardly control our tears. Excitedly we walked the gangplank, then stepped in awe and silence upon the soil of this land. We felt we had come home, even though we had never been there before. We felt we were, at last, where we belonged.

We were met and warmly welcomed by the teachers of the agricultural school, Ayanot, near Tel Aviv.

"Shalom!" (Peace) they greeted us. "Welcome home!" The school was not far from the port.

Traveling by bus, we viewed in wonder the new landscape: the palms and orange trees perfuming the air, the Arab villages and cactus plants. As I rode the bus I quietly thought: this was the miracle I dreamt about. This is the future in the Promised Land. I was free to begin a new life.

Upon arrival in Ayanot, they had no room for us, and a tent was erected for us on our first night in Palestine. Exhausted, and very happy, we fell asleep. But in the middle of the night the teacher woke us up. It was raining. Sleepy and confused, we grabbed our things and very quickly were distributed among the girls' dormitories. No one slept that night. The girls from Palestine talked about their life in Ayanot, their work and studies.

A black haired, brown-eyed girl told us her name was Havatzelet, meaning lily. She had come to Palestine from Yemen. I envied her dark beauty. Other girls where named Margalit (pearl), and Vered (rose). I thought these were the most beautiful names in the world.

Margalit worked in the *pardess* (orange grove). They harvested the oranges carefully and packaged them for export. The slightly damaged oranges were called *brara* and were sold locally. Vered worked in the flower garden. They even hoped to export flowers to Europe. This dream came true a few years later. Havatzelet bubbled excitedly that their group worked in the vegetable garden. They planted the seeds, watered them, and weeded them. It was such a pleasure to watch them grow. These girls all had their parents in Palestine. We had lost our parents, but we still felt fortunate to have reached this place and time.

My friends and I, the new arrivals, told the girls about our lives during the war. Renia, blond and pretty, was saved by nuns in a convent. She told us about life in a convent, the strict discipline and time for prayers. I silently wished I had been that lucky. Dark-haired Sarah survived a concentration camp where all her family perished in the gas chambers. We asked no questions. And beautiful Alina survived, hidden in an underground bunker with her mother. During our time in the DP camp I became close to Alina's mother. She served as a mother to all of us, young girls, but I was particularly close to her, telling her about my hopes and feelings. We learned now from Alina that her mother, formerly a pharmacist, hoped to find work in Palestine. Her mother did not come with us—she did not get one of the youth's certificates. She came to Israel later, after the establishment of the Jewish state.

In the morning our teacher, Nurit, told us she was very pleased with our behavior. She told us she was amazed how easily we had adapted to the sudden disturbance in the night. Wordlessly, I thought about sudden deportations to death camps. She was so worried. She thought she would find us in tears at being left in a tent, in the rain, on our first night in our homeland. We could not believe our ears. She was so sincere, but her concern seemed so trifling to us. We laughed: we had survived the war. We were not going to cry because it was raining.

In the morning, our new teacher, Nurit, informed us we would work in the cool mornings in the garden, the cowshed or the nursery, and attend classes in the afternoons. Learning Hebrew was our most important task.

While I was adapting to our new life and new routines, the teachers were trying to find my mother and brother. It was not easy. I knew that finding my mother and Michael would change my life, but I did not permit myself to hope too ardently, not to be devastated in case of failure. All our efforts to find my mother were fruitless, until a notice was placed in the local Hebrew newspaper: "A Girl Looks for Her Mother," which included the names of my family members.

My mother, Dinah, who for weeks after the war had met every ship arriving at the port of Haifa hoping to find me, missed the one that brought me, since it had arrived from France rather than from Poland. Through other, distant family survivors she heard I was alive, but could never reach me, and wondered where I was and in what condition. The day the newspaper notice appeared she received many telegrams from relatives and friends, and even from strangers who knew her. Everyone hoped to be the first messenger of good news: her daughter was alive!

On an afternoon in late summer I was called out of my classroom.

"You have a visitor." I knew who it could be.

Coming to the gate I saw two women. One of them was tall, dark-haired and lovely. But I knew this was not my mother. I learned later that the handsome lady was my aunt, Tova, the wife of my Uncle Kalman about whom I had heard so much years ago. She also saw the notice in the paper and came to meet me.

The other woman at the gate was small, light-haired and pretty. My mother.

I realized I hardly knew her, having been separated for seven years at a young age. Quietly and wordlessly, we greeted each other. We did not hug nor kiss. I had kept so much of my emotions subdued and cautious for so long, never allowing my hopes to fly too high. I did not cry. Neither of us could speak nor express how we felt since we last saw each other. I was nine years old then.

My mother, in a voice I hardly recognized, said quietly that she would have recognized me anywhere. I noticed her voice had changed. I learned later her voice had changed due to smoking and emphysema. I had a birthmark on my hand, but she never looked. It was not needed.

We sat down, talked and soon felt as if we had never parted, and were comfortable and natural with each other, carefully avoiding any mention of the past. The events of the war were known to all, and too painful to recall. Palestine was full of such survivors.

I learned my mother had remarried, and now they lived in Haifa. Now she wanted us to get home as soon as we could.

Carefully and gently, I said that I would prefer to stay here, where I was. I felt that as an adult (I was sixteen) I ought to be able to take care of myself. Mother nodded, comprehending that her daughter was no longer a child and might not wish to be a burden on her. Instead she suggested I come home with her "just for a visit."

Mother continued telling me that my brother Michael was coming from Egypt, on leave from the British army, to meet me. When the Germans were in North Africa, close to Palestine, every man and boy of the Jewish community had joined the British army to defend it. By that time information about some of the persecution and atrocities committed against the Jews in German occupied Europe became known. The Jewish community in Palestine had no illusions about their own fate if the Germans were ever to reach and occupy Palestine.

On our way to Haifa by bus we visited with other members of the family, among them Tova, my aunt. These relatives were warm, informal and friendly. Their clothes were light, and their homes open and uncluttered, with airy terraces and stone floors. I felt comfortable and at ease, and in my inexperience never thought or appreciated the loving acceptance of me into their clan. We spoke Polish, since I did not know Hebrew. This, I thought would be a serious barrier to my future. I felt my identity was closely bound with my choice and use of words and their nuances. I believed I could not be myself until I knew Hebrew as well as I knew Polish. They assured me I would speak Hebrew much sooner than that, even if imperfect.

At home in Haifa, I found roses in a crystal vase to welcome me, and on the wall a portrait of myself, at nine. It was one of the few treasures my mother rescued from her home in Warsaw and took with her on her dangerous journey to Palestine. She had never parted with it. I was speechless. Somebody loved me enough to think about me and my fate. All those lonely years of war and danger were coming to an end. My mother's new husband, Bernard, was waiting with a smile and a comment that I looked like my mother. I began to relax and to feel that perhaps, I belonged.

Now in 1946, my mother welcomed me back to the family, to our homeland and to "normal" life. A few days later Michael arrived from Egypt, on leave from his military unit of the British army. I was shocked to see him: he was a mirror image of our father. Michael brought me a present: a pair of airy sandals on high heels. He lovingly selected them. This was his image of a sixteen year-old girl. He could not have known how inappropriate the gift was: I was a child-woman, and still needed to learn who I was and find my path to adulthood.

Michael brought with him stories of war experiences in the British army and records of his favorite songs of the times. Among the songs I remembered was "Besame Mucho."

"Tiku Tiku" and "Blanca Flor," Latin American love songs, were also among the favorites I played again and again. I was not only a survivor. I was also a young girl at the dawn of her life, with hopes for a future still unknown.

I listened to the music and realized that World War II was fought and won not by the military alone: civilians, musicians, poets and others, all helped to make me free and to give me a chance to create a new life.

I did not think about it at the time, but my life had already changed. Becoming a member of the family was easy and natural for me. My family made it so. I was their daughter and sister. I came and stayed, and the future seemed full of hope, even promise.

Michael Abir, Hava's brother, in a British army uniform, 1942 (family collection).

Chapter 11

Forging a New Future

The war had ended, and a new life had to be forged and lived. It was time to experience what it meant to be a teenager, even though I was now in the middle of my teenage years. Everyday issues, such as life in a pioneering country surrounded by hostile neighbors, high school, learning Hebrew, making friends and becoming, again, a member of a family were taken for granted and expected to be resolved as if the war had not occurred. But it did, and it left its mark.

I remembered acts of savage cruelty. My memory of girls being hanged for trying to escape Auschwitz with all the other inmates watching was always with me. I heard machine guns in backfire sounds of every automobile. A walk in the garden and the smell of grass and trees was lovely, but I saw a mass grave with its earth still moist and moving. Remembrance of my father and other war events remained with me and colored my future experiences. And yet I was young and had no doubts that such terrible atrocities will never occur again. I remembered many other people I had known well and loved, who perished. Could I have helped them? I knew I was helpless, young, alone, and so intent on my own survival!

I understood well I had no right to cry. Israel was full of survivors like me and I could expect no sympathy. They all had to put away their own anguish and grief for their lost children and wives, and focus on creating a new life. I had to remember I was one of the "lucky" ones to survive, and this day, in Palestine, I felt strong enough to overcome any future hardships. Doubts about my abilities seemed to disappear, at that point, like a bad dream.

In September, with the beginning of a new school year, I faced new realities. In the evening as I was washing the dishes, Mother reminded me that the following day would be my first day of school. Mother enrolled me in the Beth Sefer Reali in Haifa. She had sewn for me a blue dress with a white collar, the school's uniform. The dress seemed so ungainly to me, and it was. I knew a prettier dress would help, but this was no time to worry about it. I ironed it. The navy blue badge on the left breast pocket with white embroidery bearing the school motto was a riddle to me. It was a verse from the Biblical prophet Micah: "And walk modestly" (with thy God). I had no idea about the Bible, the Prophets and their message, the core of Jewish values. My lack of formal education was unending.

Mother reminded me that my name was Hava now. I detested the name, but in a Palestine high school in 1946 you could not have a foreign first name. I would have liked to pick a more meaningful name like those of the girls I had met at Ayanot, but I knew I had already been named after my grandmother, Hava. There were more important battles to fight.

Fearful and insecure, I worried that I didn't know a word of Hebrew. Now, without having to focus all my efforts on simple survival, it was possible to feel and admit to fear and anxiety.

I was over a year older than my classmates, and even though I knew my curly, blond hair, clear complexion and perfect teeth were my good features, I considered myself fat and ugly, hoping fervently and silently there would be other girls in the classroom like myself, or perhaps, even uglier. There were. I walked into that unfamiliar, sunny, noisy and happy classroom conscious of my "otherness," quietly looking for an unoccupied desk. All desks were taken. Students knew each other, talked and laughed. No one asked who I was and no one introduced me. I looked for an empty seat and in my hesitant Hebrew asked if anyone was sitting there.

"My friend Miriam sits here," came the quick reply. I found an empty seat at the back of the room, careful not to intrude nor upset any friendships. The teachers were not careless or insensitive. Worried and traumatized by being surrounded by hostile neighbors and an impending war, paying attention to a lonely girl could not be their main concern. We all lived in danger, conscious and aware of the importance of evolving events, such as a battle for a Jewish state. I was, however, so involved and absorbed with my own barriers to cross, I might not have been fully alert to the historical events we all were part of.

In the Hebrew language class, I understood nothing and was totally convinced I would never be able to cope with the curriculum. Math and biology were equally incomprehensible, and, consequently, depressing. But a high school diploma was very important. Without it I could not see any future for myself. Mother suggested a visit to the school's principal, asking for his guidance and advice.

He advised me not to worry. All I needed was to learn Hebrew. All the other subjects will follow. He counseled that I needed some tutoring in Hebrew.

I disagreed, unaware of my nerve to say so. I thought I needed assistance in different subjects, as well as in Hebrew. I knew my survival in the classroom depended on my ability to participate, even in a limited way in the study program.

Mother understood and agreed, and a few weeks later I was able, with difficulty, to read the math and biology textbooks, and to feel that I might, one day, be almost like the other students. I was taught math by one of the teachers who volunteered to teach me and bring me up to date with my class, and an upper grade student tutored me in Hebrew.

I had no friends. I understood it was the inevitable outcome of being a new girl in high school, of knowing no Hebrew, and of being somewhat older than the rest of the students. I knew and understood all this, but it was, nevertheless, painful to endure.

Aliza, sitting in front with her friends, was tall, slender, dark and beautiful, and excelled in sports. She was everything I wanted to be, but wasn't. She and most of the other students, busy with their studies, sports and clubs paid no attention to me. Ruth lived nearby, and after a while we walked home together, somewhat alleviating my loneliness.

A few months went by. I spent long hours in the library, studying the difficult Hebrew texts, and little by little, even the dreaded Hebrew literature became more and more comprehensible.

The teacher announced an upcoming test in Hebrew literature. The subjects will be the modern Hebrew writers and poets, such as Hayim Bialik, Shaul Tschernikhovsky and Yaakov Fichman.

Aliza approached me on the playground at recess, mentioning that she had seen me in the library. She should also be studying for the test, as I was. She asked if she could see my notes. I agreed, of course, and she thanked me. I was glad that someone was paying attention to me at last. On the day of the test Ruth kept glancing at my writing and copied from my sheet. Aliza met me in the corridor, and mentioned she had used my notes. The tests were returned a week later.

"I am afraid we have a problem here," said the teacher. "I have found very similar terms and expressions in the works of Aliza, Ruth and Hava, and I would like an explanation."

The response was total silence. We could almost hear our heartbeats. The teacher waited. And waited. Finally, Aliza stood up and admitted she had used my notes. Ruth remained silent. I said not a word. The teacher's eyes rested thoughtfully on me, for a brief moment. "Let's return to the lesson at hand," she said. Aliza got an "A" on the test, and Ruth a "B." My grade was a "C+," but I did not mind. It was a passing grade. "Well done," wrote the teacher who was familiar with my background and understood my difficulties and efforts.

In my loneliness, friendship was far more important than the grade. I had passed the test, and I felt, at last, able to cope with my studies, and, for the first time, a member of the class. A year later I graduated from high school.

My last high school test was completed on a June day, in 1949. The test was oral and not written. Each one of the students drew a card with three questions pertaining to the Bible. I drew three questions about Isaiah, answered them in my newly acquired Hebrew, and the representative of the Jerusalem Department of Education and Culture, a middle-aged grey-haired, scholarly looking man seemed to be pleased. As soon as I answered the three questions, one of my teachers, Dr. Schechter, trying to prevent any further questions asked of me, stood up, thanking everyone profusely. He knew my knowledge was limited. The ordeal was over.

I walked into the sunshine, my Tanakh, the Hebrew Bible in hand. Elated, I wandered through the now familiar streets of Haifa. I had never experienced before such a feeling of release, achievement and freedom. I felt my yet unknown future was now so full of unlimited possibilities...

Slowly eating falafel, I anticipated no obstacles or difficulties. The world was welcoming me, and I was ready and capable of anything. I thought about my father. I knew he would have been so proud of me.

In later months a letter arrived from my cousins, Zygmund and Maryla. He wrote in Polish:

> We have decided to leave Poland, and have just arrived in Israel along with other survivors of Polish Jewry.
> I may be useful and perhaps even needed here.
> We passed from Czechoslovakia to Munich, Germany, illegally within the framework of "Brichah," or Flight. Organized by the survivors themselves, and aided by the Jewish Brigade, the Jews of Israel and the United States, we traveled across national borders, frequently at night, avoiding detection by the British, who prohibited our entering Palestine. But we had nowhere else to go. While in Munich, waiting to continue our journey, I worked as an instructor in my special field. I taught electroplating in a vocational school sponsored by ORT. This organization for rehabilitation and training re-opened its schools immediately following the war's end. The aim was to teach youths and adults new skills to help them rebuild their lives. We hope to see you soon.

Reading his letter I realized how fortunate I had been to receive a legal certificate of entry to Palestine, granted only to a limited number of youths. Others experienced much hardship to reach this land.

Other survivors, like my cousin, were also busy reconstructing their shattered existences, planning their futures and re-writing their lives.

The seeds of my own future had been sown by my father who had taken me years ago to the local library in Warsaw. I discovered the library was a source of endless joy and pleasure, and was in awe of the vast resources it held. I understood that learning and knowledge was his legacy to me, to love and to follow. Helped by my mother and a scholarship, I continued my education, attended the Teacher's College, and became a teacher and later a librarian, with a special interest in the literature of the Holocaust. This was a very fortunate choice of occupation, and I was to spend many happy years assisting people in using, enjoying and appreciating libraries. But all this was still in the realms of the unknown, faraway goals to be achieved.

I was lonely, working hard and frequently miserable, but I knew that now was the time to build a new reality, to explore new ideas, meet new challenges. A time of optimism, of new aspirations and of hope. I was also growing up, and a new chapter in my life was to begin.

Chapter 12

A New Friend

In 1947 I was still a high school student, recently arrived in Palestine, following the Holocaust in Europe. Mastering the Hebrew language and passing my matriculation exams was not an easy goal, but following the Holocaust we were expected to face and easily resolve such minor problems. All problems seemed minor to me at that time. We were condemned to death no longer. Survival was taken for granted. I spent my time in the library, struggling with the ancient Hebrew Biblical Isaiah and modern Hebrew literature. Even reading was a struggle, considering the Hebrew script and language. But I made progress, and slowly began to participate in some of the lessons. I was hoping to attend the Teacher's College in Haifa.

One Sabbath morning a young man came to visit me. He introduced himself as a friend of my cousin Mardix. He told us they both served in the British army. His name was Ephraim Ben-Zvi. Still in uniform, Mother and I realized he had not been demobilized as yet, even though the war was over.

He told us he was born in Poland, as I was, but far from Warsaw where I was born. His parents called him Rysio. We listened, absorbed in his story.

In the early 1940s, when the Germans were advancing in North Africa, and threatening to reach Palestine, he joined the British armed forces. We knew that thousands of Jewish boys and men, including my brother and cousin, volunteered to serve in the British Army at that time to help defend their land. My mother and I learned that Ephraim came to enroll at the Technion, the technology institute in Haifa. I realized we had so much in common and we instantly understood each other.

I was deeply involved in my own studies and could spare no time for anyone. But this young man, a few years older than me, was attractive, blond, blue-eyed and tall. I was distracted from my studies and was flattered by

Jewish soldiers in the British Armed Forces during World War II. Ephraim is in the second row, first on the left (family collection).

his taking an interest in me. His attention relieved some of my loneliness. I had something to look forward to every Saturday morning. Without noticing it, I became more cheerful, optimistic and hopeful regarding the future.

Ephraim in the uniform of the British Armed Forces, 1947 (family collection).

He and I used to go for walks along the Carmel, the beautiful, still partly wild, hilly area of Haifa. He was handsome, still wearing his khaki-colored British army uniform, and I felt proud to have this man walk beside me, with his protective arm around my shoulders. I was short, and still felt unattractive. I learned later that he considered me nice looking, and attributed to me qualities I never thought I possessed.

We more than understood each other. Having a common Polish background, we instinctively shared each other's hopes, problems and motives. We were both survivors, both of the Holocaust, and he also of the war and of Siberian exile. We comprehended, even then, our needs of education, a new, positive identity and were ready for a long, difficult struggle to build a better future. Between us, few words were needed. It was enough to look into each other's eyes. We both thought we were lucky to have the opportunity to overcome the destruction and cruelties of war, and never expected it to be easy. We became very close, and I wanted to know more about him and his early life as well as something about life in his part of Poland. Slowly, his words evoked an image before my eyes of his family, and of a small Jewish town, its customs and values never known to me before.

In the Beginning

A baby boy opened his blue eyes on November 14, 1922, in Otynia (also spelled Ottynia), a small town in the southeastern corner of Poland, by the Carpathian Mountains, along the banks of the Dniester River. The bigger cities nearby were Stanislawów to the north, Kolomyja to the south, and the larger city of Lvov (present-day Lviv) further to the north. Before World War I this area was part of the Austro-Hungarian Empire. In 1918 it became part of Poland, and following World War II, Ukraine. The little town of Otynia had an atmosphere of peace and remoteness from the outside world, even though there was train transportation, radio and a telephone connection, a party line, where the operator could, and did listen to all the private conversations. She knew everything there was to know about everyone, and used it. This generated much gossip and entertainment in the community.

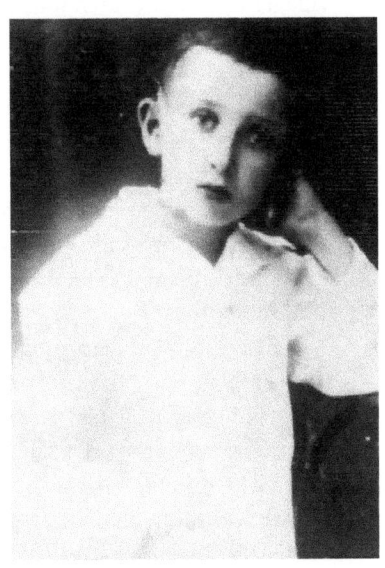

Rysio Sokal (later Ephraim Ben-Zvi) as a young child (family collection).

Occasionally exotic, nomadic, darker-skinned people we called *cyganie* came to the village in covered wagons. Their women, *cyganki*, wore colorful clothes, many gold earrings, rings and bracelets. They were known to be fortune-tellers. Their men played string instruments. Everyone loved their music, sweet and romantic. I, Eva, learned later that this music was similar to the *chardas* that was supposed to have originated in Hungary. The *cyganie*, or Romany people, were also known to be petty thieves and when we children were naughty, our parents threatened us with being stolen by *cyganie*.

I learned about Ephraim's family, warm and close, and so very different from my own. He told me about their house in the center of the little village-town, Otynia. Flowers bloomed around it all summer. Ephraim (then Rysio) lived in one of its apartments with Julek, his brother, and their parents. They were so wealthy, and yet their home was so small. The twin beds of the two teenage boys were side by side by the window, and a double parents' bed near the opposite wall.

The family of Stasia, Ephraim's mother—including Ruzia, Stasia's sister; her two sons, Stasio and Filo; and Stasia's brother Arthur, with his beautiful, eccentric wife Erna and their two sons—lived only a breath away, in separate apartments, sharing one hallway. I thought I could still hear echoes of piano music, Filo practicing. All six cousins grew up, played, fought and ran to school together each day.

Downstairs, their maternal and paternal grandfathers owned two bistros, selling alcohol, bread, salami, cheeses and sweets. Grandfather Schreier also made his own soft drinks. Both bistros were loud and noisy, especially on Tuesdays, market days. People came from all the surrounding villages by horse-drawn wagons or on foot, and set up booths or sold their merchandise from the back of their wagons. Anything was for sale: geese, chickens, grains, fruits and vegetables, eggs and cheeses, and even clothes, pots and pans. Horses whined, dogs barked and vendors loudly praised their wares. The busy, merry market days probably continue, but the Jews, once a third of the population, are gone forever. He gave me his handkerchief. I blew my nose, wiped my tearing eyes and face, and, holding hands we continued our walk, aware of the bonds between us, the chirping birds, the warm sunshine, surrounded by the tall, silent pine trees of Carmel, and remembering.

Every Sabbath morning their paternal Grandfather Shimshon went to the synagogue, faithfully escorted by his cat, who calmly sat on the steps, patiently waiting till the end of the services, then slowly and decorously walked home for a Sabbath meal of *cholent*: a stew of meat, potatoes, onions, beans and barley, put in the oven on Friday and baked overnight. No fire was lit on Sabbath days. Ephraim's mother, following tradition, lit the Sabbath candles every Friday night in their kosher home. However, the family, with the exception of the grandfathers, didn't hesitate to enjoy an occasional meal in a non-kosher pub.

Before the outbreak of World War II the Jews accounted for approximately a third of Otynia's population of 5400, the remaining two-thirds being Poles and Ukrainians. Such small towns, called "shtetls" in Yiddish (the diminutive of *shtot*, a town), have been idealized and romanticized, preserved and enshrined in Jewish memory, literature, music, art and dance.

As we walked and talked, I learned more. The Jews of the shtetls had a clearly defined culture with tzedakah as its cornerstone. The word "tzedakah," meaning good deeds was derived from the word "tzedek," meaning "justice." Sharing with the needy was expected of everyone, even the poorest members of the community. Both individual and communal factors played an important role in their lives, as did learning, both Jewish and secular, hard work and scrupulous observance of Jewish religious traditions. Prestige depended on learning, wealth and good deeds, approximately in that order. I silently thought it was remarkable that education was considered more important than riches. Public opinion was a powerful force, sufficient to preserve and enforce the well-established, seldom varied way of life.

Several Zionist circles were active in Otynia. While all Zionists dreamed about their return to the land of Israel, each circle differed in their ideas about achieving that goal and about future life in this Promised Land. Ephraim was a member of a Zionist circle. His only younger brother, Julek, today in Australia, described himself as a "domesticated animal." He loved to stay at home and listen. And remember.

Social class distinctions were clearly, if informally, delineated. At the very top were professionals, such as rabbis, doctors, lawyers, pharmacists. Below them were the rich, both self-made and those with inherited wealth, and not necessarily educated. Next came the intellectuals, the so-called "intelligentsia": those who completed high school, and perhaps attended university for a few semesters. At the bottom of that social ladder were small shopkeepers, tailors, carpenters, shoemakers, other artisans and servants. And the servants were many, since Otynia had no electricity and no running water or sewage system. Ephraim's mother mentioned the many maids needed to carry out the chamber pots, draw water from the well, clean the many kerosene lamps and care for children. The social distinctions were acknowledged, respected and observed, and the different classes rarely mixed. Many members of the upper classes spoke Polish (and knew Yiddish), while the lower classes spoke Yiddish among themselves, considering Polish an "outside" tongue, used only and imperfectly when necessary, especially in trade transactions. Members of the upper classes with their financial means contributed more to Jewish charities and served as leaders and representatives of the Jewish community to the Polish authorities.

In this social scheme, where did Ephraim's family belong?

Henryk Sokal, Ephraim and Julek's father, completed high school and embarked on studying law at the University of Lvov. He interrupted his studies to marry the beautiful, blond, nineteen-year-old Stasia Schreier, a neighbor's daughter. The marriage was arranged, as was the custom, and their older son, named Frederik, and called sweetly Rysio as a term of endearment, was born a year later, in 1922. In a distant future, in a different world, Rysio Sokal, my future husband, would change his name to Ephraim Ben-Zvi, since his father's Hebrew name was Zvi, and he was indicating, in Hebrew, that he was the "son of Zvi." Julek made his debut a few years later.

Henryk Sokal was a World War I veteran of the Polish army. Being

Ephraim's parents, Henryk Sokal and Stasia Schreier, following their wedding, ca. 1921 (family collection).

12. A New Friend

Ephraim's parents in the 1960s (family collection).

discharged from the army as a lieutenant, a prestigious rank at the time, added considerably to his social standing in the local Polish society in Otynia, as did his education and flawless Polish. It afforded him access to both social circles and commercial enterprises. As a veteran, he soon obtained a license for the wholesale of tobacco products which were under the state monopoly. This meant that all retailers had to buy their supplies from him. This truly distinguished him from the mostly poor Jewish population, and assured his wealth, respect and acceptance into Polish upper classes. He served as a member of the City Council, and for a few years as president of the only Jewish sports organization "Ezra." Henryk resigned when it became "infested" by communists, on the "gentle," friendly advice of the chief of the local police, who one balmy Sunday afternoon stopped by the window of their house engaging in a conversation with Ephraim's father, while standing outside, supporting himself on the window sill. Henryk was also the Registrar of the Jewish population, recording births, deaths and marriages, adding to his income. Ephraim, in later years referred to his father as "the Rothschild of the town," the philanthropist, well known for his wealth. There was one social club in town attended by adults of all religions.

The Sokals had many contacts with both Jewish and non-Jewish communities. The local priest frequented their father's shop to buy tobacco and engage in long conversations. Julek's first piano teacher was the organist at the Catholic church. City mayors, appointed by the state, were never Jewish. The last one, Mr. Bauknecht, was a frequent guest in Henryk's home.

Even though anti-Semitism was deeply embedded in Polish culture, with periodic violent outbreaks, the Sokal family, like my own family, in Warsaw, lived peacefully among its Polish and Ukrainian neighbors.

Ephraim's parents with their younger son, Julek Sokal, 1947 (family collection).

12. A New Friend

All this came to an end a few years before the outbreak of World War II with the rise of nationalism. The open, government-sponsored persecution of Jews across the border, in Germany, awakened and emboldened deep-rooted hatreds. Now the Polish government adopted a policy of institutional anti–Semitism. The attitude and system of granting preference to Poles and rejecting others, especially Jews, permeated all levels of Polish society, from government offices to private enterprises, and was practiced by everyone, from priests to farmers. Henryk's tobacco license was revoked and given to another war veteran, who was Polish. Henryk was left unemployed and distressed, but his Polish loyalty and patriotism were undiminished. On his Underwood typewriter he wrote many letters of protest to influential persons, all to no avail. Increased anti–Semitism took many forms: there were cases of firing Jews from their positions, calls to boycott Jewish businesses, breaking windows in Jewish homes and physical attacks.

In spite of Ephraim's family standing and good relationships with their Polish and Ukrainian neighbors, deep rooted anti–Semitism, endemic to the culture in Poland, found its expression in personal relationships as well.

Otynia had no high school, and Ephraim had to travel to a nearby town, Stanisławów, by train. Ephraim, as a Jew, abused by Polish boys, had to travel first class to avoid harassment, even though there was a discount for students in the regular coaches. Nevertheless, he was approached by a young hooligan who demanded money. This stopped only after his father complained to the stationmaster. In a neighboring village, a Jewish shopkeeper and his family were brutally murdered. The perpetrators were never found. Being unequal, rejected and humiliated as a Jew was taken for granted, and not only accepted, but expected.

There was much poverty among the Jews of Poland, and with rising discrimination against them in many areas, and particularly in employment, emigration to Palestine, their Promised Land, became an attractive, albeit dangerous option. It took courage and determination to leave behind family, property and even relative stability, and only the young and brave left. Even so, emigration, especially to Palestine, increased, and some members of my own family immigrated to Palestine in the 1920s. Others emigrated to the United States and to other lands. The rest of the Jewish population, including my own family in other parts of Poland, and families with young children, elderly parents, or other obligations remained in their homes and familiar surroundings, even though the borders in the 1930s were still open and escape was possible. No one knew or could even imagine the future events, such as the Holocaust.

Chapter 13

The Event That Changed Their Lives

Both boys, Ephraim and his brother Julek, remembered how pleasant the early autumn of 1939 was. They had an Indian summer, still very warm weather late in the season, and were happy to play outdoors with their cousins and friends before the beginning of the new school year in September. Then came the German attack, and when general mobilization was declared on September 1, 1939, their father reported for duty, but returned the next day, rejected. No one ever mentioned the reason for his rejection, but Poland and its army were in disarray. The well-documented Polish defeat was followed by the occupation of this eastern region of Poland shortly after by the Soviet Red Army and led to the event that changed their lives.

Prior to the outbreak of World War II in 1939, Germany signed a secret mutual non-aggression pact with the Soviet Union, dividing Poland approximately in half, along river lines, with eastern Poland to be occupied by the Soviets and western Poland by the Germans. On September 1, 1939, Germany attacked Poland by heavy bombardment of Warsaw and other cities. German planes, flying low, strafed the crowds of refugees, with heavy civilian casualties. Ephraim's uncle Max and his teenage daughter Irena were among the dead. Very soon, on September 17, the Soviet Red Army occupied eastern Poland, including Ephraim's hometown, Otynia. A few of the Jewish inhabitants, traditionally sympathizing with the underdog and naively believing in the Soviet classless society, welcomed them with flowers. This, however, was not at all the sentiment prevailing in the Jewish community. The majority were loyal Polish citizens, many were small shopkeepers, and they were grief-stricken with Polish defeat.

Very soon after the Soviets occupied eastern Poland, they began to arrest and deport those they considered "enemies of the people" to Siberian

13. The Event That Changed Their Lives

Kazakhstan. The enemies of the people were the wealthy, the former Polish government officials and particularly those who previously served as officers in the Polish army. Among the deportees were also refugees from western Poland, who had expressed a desire to return to their homes and families in the western part of Poland, now occupied by the Germans. No one could have known then that being exiled to Siberia would ultimately save Jewish lives. Ephraim's father, as a former Polish army officer, was arrested, deported to the Soviet Union and imprisoned. Then came the fateful night, in April 1940, that changed the course of their lives.

Loud, ominous knocking on their entry door woke Ephraim, Julek and their mother, who were asleep in their beds at 3:00 a.m. on that cold, rainy April morning.

"NKVD!" (the acronym for the People's Commissariat for Internal Affairs, a Soviet police organization, which became the KGB after World War II) A frightened housemaid opened the door. Following the heavy steps of military boots, several uniformed soldiers armed with rifles and an officer with a pistol burst into their bedroom. The boys, in their long, white nightshirts, paralyzed with fear stood by their mother's bed. The soldiers ordered them to dress.

The officer tapped Julek on the shoulder and ordered him to get dressed, fast. The officer informed them that their father confessed to the presence of a gun hidden in their house. Under this pretext the soldiers proceeded to ransack the bedroom and the rest of the house, opening drawers and searching through their contents. Nothing was found.

The officer ordered them to pack their belongings. They would be joining their father in the Soviet Union. They had one hour to get ready, and they were almost frozen with fear. As they had no suitcases and no boxes, they pulled the sheets and covers off the beds, gathered what they could of clothing and bedding and tied the sheets into bundles. They managed to gather a small bundle of food, not knowing what they would need. In their fear and despair, Stasia still had the presence of mind to pack and take with them some valuables, such as her gold watch and silver candlesticks, and even a few family photographs. At a later time in their exile, the gold watch would be traded for a cow and I would inherit the pictures.

It was daylight. Peeking through the Venetian blinds they saw a horse-driven cart waiting. Their grandfather, their aunts and uncles with their families lived only across the corridor in the same building. The loud banging on the door woke everyone up, and they knew their family was being deported, but were not allowed to help them, not even with food.

The officer ordered his subordinates to hoist their belongings into the wagon. Soon they were in the wagon with their bundles. Escorted by soldiers, the cart slowly pulled along the village's main street, toward the railway station. During these early morning hours few friends and neighbors witnessed their deportation into the unknown, their fear and grief, their path of sorrow.

They moved along the bumpy street that had always been the center of the boys' early lives, full of memories of the games and the friends they had played with. Here they learned to ride their small bicycles, played soccer. Would they ever see it or their friends again? They passed a church they knew, and a school they had attended only last fall. Now it seemed so long ago.

Thus came an abrupt, cruel and painful end to their peaceful, sheltered childhood, surrounded by grandparents, aunts and cousins. Sarcastically, the guards bid them goodbye and wished them "a pleasant trip."

At the village's railway station a long train of red cattle cars was waiting. Each car had two wide shelves, one above the other. The top shelve had the advantage of a small, barred window. The three of them were fortunate to occupy an upper shelf. Below one of the lower shelves was a round hole in the flooring that served as a toilet. There was no screening of any kind. Later, one of the older women demonstrated for all its usage by covering her head with the lower part of her apron. This was meant to give her some privacy and anonymity. It lightened the gloomy atmosphere and caused some merriment.

Their provisions were few. Before the train set off later in the day, Ephraim's grandfather succeeded in sneaking through the cordon of armed soldiers and delivered a packet of food. A few minutes later, at dusk, the train departed. They did not know that they would never see neither their grandfather nor any other family member again. The memory of that day, their terror and their grandfather's bravery and love was never forgotten.

Their transport moved east, into the heart of the Soviet Union. At different railway stations they were allowed to disembark, stretch their legs, and breathe some fresh air. They had a chance to meet fellow travelers from different cars of the train. Sometimes they would exchange words with local residents who were friendly and often expressed sympathy with their fate. Their clothing was looked upon and appreciated by the poorly clad Russian locals. Were they jealous? They also met Ukrainians traveling east in conditions similar to theirs. They observed the guards flirting with local girls.

Once Julek was almost left forgotten at a station, when their train

Portrait of a young Jewish boy from Poland in exile in a Soviet gulag in Siberia (courtesy U.S. Holocaust Memorial Museum, photograph number 38178).

started to move—luckily only for a few seconds. Evidently, they needed to move the engine a short distance. In a panic, he ran screaming after their "prison" train. He was eleven years old.

No food was provided. All they had was what their grandfather brought them, and the little they managed to take with them. Sometimes they were able to purchase some food from the locals. At almost every station there was an outdoor tap with boiling water, *kipiatok* in Russian.

During their long travel, as they gazed through the small window of their prison train, they watched people tilling their fields, cattle grazing, streams and forests. After two weeks of travel and of being hungry, one late morning they arrived at their destination: an isolated, deserted railway station. All carriages of the train were opened. They were ordered to get out, not guarded now.

NKVD officers, whose new uniforms contrasted sharply with the shabbily dressed locals, guided them to the station's restaurant where they were served a meal.

Trucks appeared. They were told to mount them with all their belongings. The trucks drove slowly along the uneven roads across wide, flat green steppes, into an unknown future.

They arrived at dusk at a kolkhoz (a collective farm) in Federovka, Kazakhstan (a state in the Soviet Union), and were given a room in a house of an old woman, a widow. She was referred to as Babushka. Her front room served also as a kitchen, with an enormous wood-burning oven, with a flat platform on top used to sleep on cold winter nights. They discovered that the kolkhoz, called Vladykinka, had no toilets, no bathrooms and no running water. Later Babushka welcomed them with a few boiled sweet potatoes. From then on they had to struggle for their own food and survival.

Stasia and the boys were still in a state of shock following that fateful day in April 1940, the day of their deportation to Siberia.

They had lost their father, their family, their home, their security and community, and everything they ever owned and were. Will they always be alone, with no means of support, no home, no family, no community? What would happen to them? But unknown to them, their lives were saved by this deportation.

At approximately the same time, unknown to the family in Siberia, in the German occupied part of Poland, the Holocaust was in its first, dark stages, to take the lives of six million Jewish martyrs: men, women and children.

Chapter 14
In the Kolkhoz

Still in shock, fearful and depressed by their sudden arrest and the change from a comfortable, middle-class existence in their native shtetl, and deportation to this remote village that seemed lost among the steppes, about 500 kilometers (300 miles) east of the Ural mountains, they were far from comprehending and coming to terms with their real situation. Silently they wondered what else was yet to come.

A few days later Stasia, Ephraim, and Julek were awakened by a firm knock on the only little window in the room where they slept. It was already late morning, and a round, slightly smiling face with an untrimmed moustache appeared. The visitor signaled with his hand, indicating for them to come outside, as the window could not be opened. It was mid-May, and the outdoor air, fresh and crisp, contrasted with the stuffy atmosphere in the small room where the three of them slept, and felt refreshing. They were met by a smiling, medium-height young man dressed in long black pants and a long, white, collarless cotton shirt (*rubashka*), tied up at the belt with a black ribbon. The man looked young and fit, but his prematurely aged face mirrored a history of hardship. Without any introduction the man told them in Russian to get ready for a trip to the fields. He informed them that this Sunday there is a need to help with the already late seeding and planting. Everybody, children and women must take part. This said, he disappeared down the road, to knock on the next house. To get ready, Stasia was fortunate to bring with her a pair of old shoes on very low heels. She discovered later, in the fields, that everyone else was barefoot. Having seen this she promptly removed her shoes to save them.

Soon two carts arrived, each pulled by two enormous bulls. Except for the drivers, most passengers were women, with young girls, approximately Julek's age, of eleven and a little older. Older women had their heads covered with traditional scarfs, while the young had their hair exposed, shining from being freshly washed, and tied low in the back of their heads. There was a pleasant commotion with lots of laughter, shouting and enthusiastic voices. They had good reason to be joyful and cheerful, because the previous year the kolkhoz enjoyed an excellent crop which meant an allocation of large quantities of grain to each household. Kolkhozniks (members of the kolkhoz) were never paid ordinary wages. Their main remuneration consisted of a quantity of grain from recent crops that was left after the delivery of the required quota of grain to the state. The state appropriation had to be met irrespective of the size of the crop. As a consequence, a poor crop meant no distribution (no pay) to farmers. Furthermore, the non-fulfillment of the mandatory quota to the state carried a reprimand that had to be tackled by the management of the kolkhoz. The result of this was that poor crops a few years in succession were leaving the kolkhozniks starving. Bread was considered a delicacy. While the alluvial black soil in the region was satisfactory, frequent premature winters buried crops under snow. Some believed that different kinds of grains should have been used.

The remuneration was based on a system of points. The quantity of grains received by each person depended on the number of earned points throughout the year. Different jobs meant different number of points. The best remuneration was given to people in charge of a tractor, the tractorists. This kolkhoz had only one tractor, and during the Sokal family's sojourn there (more than four years) it was always idle for some reason or another. Sometimes it was being repaired, dismantled into bits and pieces on the lawn next to the shabby garage. The tractorist, a massive, tall man with his face blackened by fumes, was seen almost everywhere, all the time alone or with some of his assistants, smoking coarse tobacco wrapped in pieces of newspaper. He was waiting for the supply of parts, and their arrival was as usual delayed in that centrally controlled economy. Once Julek and Ephraim were confronted by the tractorist, as they walked down the main street of the village, a dirt track running at the outskirts of the village. Seeing that big frame of a man standing so close, they feared a humiliating insult, like "You bloody Polish capitalists, serves you right...." However, he calmly asked how they were coping, and without waiting for a reply stormed forward saying: "You will, everybody does." They took it as an expression of sympathy and deduced from it that this must have been representative of the general feeling about them.

The harvested grains were used for baking bread and were also carried to markets for sale in the provincial city. Money from the sale was used to purchase clothing and other commodities. Many transactions were bartered, and to the Sokals' knowledge, taxes were unknown. Each household was allowed to possess one or several milking cows that usually had one calf each year. One of the calves was supposed to be submitted to the state. As far as the boys remembered, that rule was rarely followed by the often starving population. Private vegetable gardens were discouraged because every effort was expected to be spent for the benefit of the kolkhoz community. These collective farming communities were established in the Soviet Union following the communist revolution of 1917. Thousands died of famine following this experiment in nationalization of land and of giving up privately owned property and forced collective living. Now, in 1939, poverty and hunger were still widespread and the boys learned of some cases when children couldn't attend schools in winter because they had no shoes.

After a bumpy ride several kilometers from the village, they arrived at the fields to be worked. The weary bulls were released to graze in the surrounding area, and their family of three was assigned to groups manually working on digging and seeding. Drinking water was supplied in large buckets and everyone drank directly from them, as there was no cup. The almost full buckets were too heavy for Julek to lift, so he found another way. He had to kneel and tilt the bucket slightly to place his mouth

Polish exiles in a sewing workshop, Kniazhpogost, the Komi Autonomous Republic (courtesy U.S. Holocaust Memorial Museum, photograph number 66569).

at the edge. Later meals were brought on two-wheeled carriages pulled by single horses and driven by supervisors. The meal consisted of cabbage soup with rare and small pieces of beef. Locals called it *borscht*. They ate it with wooden spoons, four to seven people dipping their spoons into a single common container placed on the soil. Everyone also received a thick piece of rye bread.

After the meal there was a short siesta when almost everyone, bone-tired, stretched out on the already warm soil. The boys remembered lying on their backs, watching the blue sky and enjoying the surrounding pastoral silence. Then it was back to work for the remaining hours of sunlight.

When the sun began to tilt toward the west an order was given to prepare for return. Bulls were brought back from their wanderings in the steppes and re-harnessed. Julek recalls being seated among young girls that smelled of perspiration and a strong scent, in Julek's opinion, of young women. As the carriage progressed toward the village he found the soft, close contact on both of his sides rather pleasant. Suddenly, as if on command, the girls burst into traditional Russian songs: "Kalinka, kalinka, kalinka maya, V'sadu yagada, malinka, malinka maya…."

Julek remembers this singing and his experiences on the field as being very comforting and healing, and years later he summarized it for me in writing:

> I thought that if these people with so many charming young women who sing these beautiful songs live and survive here, then why shouldn't I? Moreover, I felt as if plunging into a dream created by the combination of warm and mild sunshine, warmth of young female bodies at my sides, and the soft, flat and green landscape around me. With this, I felt an influx of energy in my veins and suddenly all apprehensions and fears disappeared, evaporated, and that strength remained with me for the whole sojourn there, despite extreme hardships and deprivations that we had to endure later, until our return to Poland towards the end of World War II.

Chapter 15

Siberia

At seventeen, seven years older than his brother Julek, Ephraim (at this time known as Rysio) did not wax poetic about the Siberian steppes. He excelled in high school and was his mother's confidant, aide and support. His science teachers could not praise him enough. "He is like a sponge," they told his delighted mother. "*On vsio ponimayet*" (he understands everything) was their opinion of him. It was music to her ears. Entering the last year of high school, he needed help, and some teachers tutored him without any compensation for their labor and kindness. The boys, used to discriminatory, anti–Semitic remarks in their previous Polish schools, were reassured and relaxed by their welcome to school in this area of Siberia. I had heard that in other areas of Soviet exile, the deportees' children were sometimes introduced to their classmates as "Enemies of the People," to indicate their legal status. The boys remembered that in Polish schools the days always began with a long prayer. All Christians, including both Catholics (the Poles) and Eastern Orthodox (Ukrainians) stood up, prayed and crossed themselves many times, while the Jews were expected to stand at attention, feeling isolated and excluded. None of this happened in the Soviet Union schools, and it was a tremendous relief to them. For the first time, they felt equal and "belonging." Julek, the younger of the two brothers, was surprised at being accepted now, by being a "Jew boy" no longer, and even joined a boys' gang to forage some backyards at night, just for fun. For the first time he felt like "one of the boys." One of their teachers was a Jew from Soviet Ukraine, now evacuated to Siberia because of the Germans attack and advance eastward, once came to see their mother to complain about Julek's behavior… in Yiddish! Julek, evidently, was no angel, but they were so happy to see a friendly face and to hear Yiddish again. Stasia, only thirty seven years old at the time of their deportation and not used to serious tasks, now carried the responsibility for her own and her children's survival.

Hunger was pervasive in the Soviet Union at that time. They were always hungry, and getting food became, of course, a priority. Their diet consisted primarily of grains baked into bread, milk and potatoes. There were hardly any vegetables to be had and no fruit at all. They all suffered from scurvy. In this collective society the lack of private enterprise led also to a lack of drive. Private initiative was nonexistent.

Stasia, their mother, obtained permission from the police to leave the kolkhoz. Farmers lived in collective settlements, but the rest of Soviet society led a private existence. In the kolkhoz, illness and lack of sufficient pay for her work were hard to bear but she had another compelling reason to leave the kolkhoz. This village and kolkhoz had only a seven-year elementary school, called in Russian the *semiletka*. To matriculate, Ephraim needed a ten-year school, or high school, in Russian *diesiatiletka*. Stasia rented a *ziemlyanka* (a clay hut, partly buried in earth) in a village near a regional city, where her son could go to school.

Even though far removed from the front, sentimental songs were sung about love, separation and war. In this popular song a soldier, deep in his freezing trench, defending Moscow, sang of his longings:

> From my dark ziemlyanka pours a fire-like song.
> Between us fields and meadows,
> And an accordion sings to me
> about your eyes and your smile.
> About you whisper shrubs and the trees
> in the snow white Moscow fields,
> in my cold trench I am warmed
> by your enduring love.
> A storm is raging over our land,
> No easy way to reach you, but to death—just two steps.

A year later Ephraim graduated, helped by the two teachers who voluntarily assisted him. Stasia, the woman who in her former home in Otynia had not known how to care for her children (the maids and nannies did that), now searched and obtained a job in a state-controlled hairdressing salon. Here, even though the store was owned and controlled by the state, the customers paid for services directly to the store, and only part of the income was sent to the government. Here was an opportunity to withhold some of the money, and they did. I heard this was a common way to generate income. Being very pretty, she attracted male customers who enjoyed this tall, blue-eyed, curly-haired blond shaving them, which was included in the haircut. The boys believed that this helped them survive rather than perish in the prevailing famine.

Stasia and her children were deported to Siberia along with many other Polish families, wives and children of former Polish army officers, the same officers who were now imprisoned, just like Stasia's husband and Ephraim's father. These women's resentment of Jews was appalling, especially in view of their similar circumstances. Stasia, the only Jew, was never accepted as one of them, and described to me their behavior as "animal like." She had held on to a precious gold watch and out of necessity traded it for a cow. Julek was enchanted and never had enough of the warm milk. He described the warm milk he drank straight from a cow as "nectar."

The other Polish women strongly disapproved of having a cow, even though it helped Stasia feed her family and survive. The *korova* (cow) also became an object of their derision. Had they been using the term "*Yevreyskakya korova*" it would merely have meant, in Russian, "a Jewish cow." But this wouldn't have been sufficiently insulting (to the cow). The term "*Żyd*" (Jew, in Polish) conveyed an insult, so the cow was referred to as "*żydovskaya korova*." The care of the korova was delegated to Julek, the youngest member of the family. In summer, the cow was let out every sunrise to join other cows from the same street on their way to pasture on the steppes, and to be brought back at twilight. Stasia milked it twice a day. In winters, when the Siberian steppes were covered with snow, the cow remained in her enclosure and was fed dry hay and watered. Julek also cleaned her and changed her bedding of straw. This bedding served as fertilizer in the spring. And every fall there was an offspring. After a few months, that offspring provided the family with sufficient meat to last almost the entire winter. The cow was an important, contributing member of the family and it is gratefully remembered in their family saga as "the cow in the cellar."

One winter, due to the freezing weather the cow was taken into the *ziemlyanka*, their living area. Under the earthen floor of their *ziemlyanka* was a cellar to store potatoes. One day, that winter, the thin wooden floorboards gave out with a crash. Their cow had fallen into the cellar. She was found there, calmly standing there chewing on the potatoes that had been stored there in the dark. It took great efforts, skill, forceful persuasion and several sheets of lumber to build a ramp to get her out of there. She didn't want to leave that warm and secure place. The cow remained with the family, warmly remembered and enshrined in family stories, and was not sold until the day before they left Siberia to return to Poland.

Stasia's earnings weren't enough to support the family, and the boys also had to find employment. Rather than handling enormous bulls and horses, Ephraim found a job in a noodle factory. Julek, the youngest, worked in a vast green steppe as a lonely shepherd, and stayed at a faraway farm during the summers. The steppes were flat plains, plush green in summer and snow white in winter. Alone with a few hundred cows and bulls and a few thousand sheep following him like an army, he recalled feeling happy and at peace. He also recalled Katherina, a fat, round, rude, big-breasted, big-bottomed woman in charge of milking cows, who threatened him: "If you don't do your work properly, you won't get your ration of fresh milk."

Julek reports: "Fresh milk! Still naturally warm! Unless you tasted it, you have not the slightest idea how good it tastes! It is a real heavenly drink."

In winters he worked on a nearby farm and performed other tasks: breaking ice in a nearby lake to let the cows drink, cleaning the barn, and bringing hay for the cattle. He returned home every day.

In summer, both boys used to take a wheelbarrow that was fortunately available to them, and wandered deep into the steppes, collecting dry or semi-dry cow droppings they used as fuel for cooking in summer and for heating in winter. The cow droppings were ready to be used after being dried in the sun, then cut into bricks. As they had a cow, thanks to their mother's idea at the very start of their sojourn in Siberia, long winters would leave them with a quantity of manure as fuel. With the beginning of summer, they would mix it with dry hay and water from a well and then cut it into bricks and dry it in the sun for winter. The mixing was done by stomping with their bare feet in the overpoweringly stinky mess.

The summer rains would come quietly upon the steppes, without storms and thunder. They would last a few days, and then sunshine would return. They were prisoners, and yet the wide, green steppes seemed to give them some peace and a misleading feeling of freedom.

Chapter 16

Germany, Now a Common Enemy

The Soviets considered the Polish community of deportees as political prisoners and "enemies of the people." They were not guarded, but there was no possibility of escape, surrounded by the endless steppes. All this was about to change due to political developments.

On June 22, 1941, in spite of their non-aggression treaty, Germany attacked the Soviet Union. At this point, Poland and the Soviet Union were in a deathly struggle against a common enemy, the Germans.

As early as 1940 the Polish Government in Exile in London, represented by General Władysław Sikorski, planned to mobilize a Polish army of a hundred thousand men to help the war effort. By July 1941 it became clear that the relationship between the Soviet Union and the Polish prisoners and deportees of which Ephraim's family was a part must change. The former Polish officers were released from prison and allowed to join their families in Siberia, Ephraim's father among them. When he rejoined them in the village of Fedorovka, they could hardly recognize him: a broken man, aged, sick in body and soul. Unable to work outside the home, he peeled potatoes to assist in their fight for survival.

On July 30, 1941, an agreement was reached between the Polish Government in Exile in London and the Russian government. Diplomatic relations were restored, and a Polish army was to be formed in Russia under the command of General Władysław Anders, himself a former Soviet prisoner, who had experienced firsthand the hardships of Russian captivity, starvation and beatings. He was now released from prison, cleaned up and assigned the task of recruiting and organizing this army of former political prisoners and deportees.

Ephraim was nineteen years old. The family discussed what was to be done and the decision was made for him to volunteer and join the

Anders Army in Russia to fight the Germans. It was important to get out of Russia in any way they could.

The night before he left, Stasia baked several loaves of bread to take with him. I can imagine today the feelings and the tears of his mother, sending a nineteen-year-old to war. He packed the bread in his rucksack and in the morning left for Uzbekistan, where the Anders Army had assembled. Waiting for the trains, he was tired, and fell asleep at the railway station, with the rucksack of bread under his head. When he awoke, the bread was gone.

The Anders Army as a rule did not accept Jews, but as a son of a former Polish army officer, he was accepted and assigned to the Polish navy. As to the relationships aboard the ship, the other sailors, his comrades in arms, promised him that after the war, if they had two bullets, one would be for the Germans and the other for the Jew. He never forgot that.

They traveled to England, then through Russia, and in 1942, through Iran, to fight in the Mediterranean, in Italy. While in Tehran, Iran, Ephraim became very ill with malaria. When the orders came to leave, he was unable to carry his heavy gear. Some of his friends among the soldiers carried his gear and took him with them. They did not leave him in Tehran to die. He never told me who these friends were who assisted him, whether they were Jews or Poles, members of the Polish navy or army, but he remembered them. In Italy Ephraim's unit joined the fighting forces and participated in the battle against the Germans.

From Italy his ship was sent to Egypt for further training and, I believe, for rest. But there was no room on the docks to remain in an Egyptian port, and their ship was ordered to the port city of Haifa, at that time Palestine.

Following an orientation by the officers about venereal diseases in the port and the streets, Ephraim stepped onto the soil of the Promised Land. Having had a Jewish education and a Jewish family background, he fully appreciated where he was and what this land meant to the Jews. He made a decision to stay in this ancient Jewish homeland, and, perhaps, transfer to the British Armed Forces, to continue the fight against the Germans. Unknown to him, there were other young men making a similar decision, among them the future prime minister of Israel, Menachem Begin, who also survived in the Soviet Union. Soon these young men would use their military training and experience to fight for Israel, participating in the creation of the first Israel Defense Forces and fighting in its War of Independence.

But now, in Haifa, Ephraim was twenty years old, and alone. He met

16. Germany, Now a Common Enemy

with representatives of the Jewish Agency, at that time the shadow government of the future State of Israel. Many of the Agency's people spoke Polish, and in spite of this new land and environment, he felt he had arrived home. He was sent to a kibbutz near Haifa, Ramat David. Underground immigration to Palestine was very slow during the war years, but continued before and after. As the boats arrived at the shores of their land, boys from Jewish settlements nearby were waiting. The new arrivals were quickly transported to these settlements, their clothes changed, and the British could never tell who was new and who a long time resident. At that time he changed his name to Ephraim Ben-Zvi and retained it for the rest of his life. Changing of first and last names to Hebrew was common and accepted as part of the creation of a new Jewish future, a new national and personal life and identity, rooted in their ancient Biblical, Hebrew heritage.

The war was raging, and the German forces were conquering areas in North Africa. Palestine was in danger of a German invasion. By this time, some information about the fate of the Jews in German-occupied Europe was known. Thousands of Jewish men and boys joined the British Armed Forces intending to avert a potential tragedy, among them my brother Michael, in Palestine since 1939.

Volunteers were needed by the British army, and Ephraim volunteered. He felt he was a youngster among the older men of the kibbutz, who were already husbands and fathers. In this army he joined a Jewish unit, made lifelong friends and remained in the British army even after the war's end in the European theater, in May 1945.

Chapter 17

Return to Poland

And what about their family, left behind in Poland since 1940, at the time of their deportation?

In the coming days, weeks and months following the Siberian exile and the changed alignment of fighting forces against Germany, Stasia and Henryk, her husband, slowly and from different sources learned about the fate of their old parents, her sister Ruzia, Ruzia's husband and their two teenage sons, Filo and Stasio; her brother Arthur and his wife, the beautiful Erna and their two young sons, Jerzyk and Zbysio. Filo, even at 15, was noted as a promising pianist.

I found German records of destruction specifying the numbers of Jewish men, woman and children shot in open-air killings in Russia, parts of Lithuania and in some areas of Eastern Poland, but not in the area of Otynia and its vicinity. Eyewitness reports, survivors' correspondence and testimonies about the dates and manner of annihilation vary, but some of the emerging dates are an unknown day in August 1941; October 5, 1941; and September 25, 1942. The testimonies are alike in some details, and different or contradictory in other important ways.

In one version, the Jews of Otynia were taken by trucks toward Tolmitch, where pits were prepared. They were shot and buried there on October 5, 1941, the first day of Sukkot, a Jewish holiday celebrating the harvest.

In August 1941, under the Nazi occupation, local Ukrainians and Germans carried out bloody pogroms in Otynia. Even though they lasted only a few days, large numbers of Jews were murdered. (See the *Encyclopedia of Jewish Communities—Poland, Volume II*, 1980, pp. 53-54, translated from the Hebrew by Chana Berman and Philip Spiegel and available online at www.shtetlinks.jewishgen.org/Ottynia/ottynia.htm.)

According to Mykhailo Khavalyuk, a Ukrainian source, and based on testimony of a local witness, toward the end of summer 1941 the complete destruction of the Jews began. (For more information on Khavalyuk, see

17. Return to Poland

the acknowledgments of this memoir, as well as the bibliographic essay.) At that time, the Jews of Otynia were driven out of their homes in the temporary ghetto by the Gestapo and transported by trucks which were guarded by an SS soldier with a machine gun to the Szeparowce (in Ukrainian, *Sheparivtsi*) forest. As a Holocaust survivor myself, I can still feel the terror I felt in Warsaw, many years ago and hear the loud, terrible German voices: *Jude, raus!* (Jews, out).

The Szeparowce forest was the place of execution of the Jews of Otynia and the surrounding communities. There, deep pits were waiting. Many women were clutching their young, terrified children to their breasts. A local Ukrainian eyewitness to the execution, born in Rakivchyk, reported scenes of extreme cruelty. An SS soldier tore a baby out of its mother's arms and smashed its head against a tree. The rounded-up Jews were marched to the pits and shot. Many fell into the pits wounded, but still alive, and it was commonly known that the blood-drenched earth across the pits moved for days after. I have no reason to question these reports, as some of them, in addition to Jewish sources, were verified by a Ukrainian source.

The reports of destruction differ in citing different details of torture, not unusual for the Germans, such as forcing the Jews to dig their own graves. But it is recorded in the *Encyclopedia of Jewish Communities* that on September 25, 1942, the entire Jewish population—the remnant survivors of former massacres—was murdered, once again, on the eve of Sukkot. German troops came to Otynia. German and Ukrainian police surrounded the city and put machine guns at street corners, threatening anyone who might have tried to escape. Again, they went from house to house, rounding up the remaining Jews and forcing them into trucks, and, according to one version, all the Jews of Otynia were taken to an unknown place, and only a few escapees arrived the next day in Stanislawów. According to other information, all the Jews of Otynia were sent on that day, September 25, to Stanislawów. At the camp station they were shot on the spot or transported to the Bełżec extermination camp.

In any event, it is clear that the Jews of Otynia, numbering about 1,800 persons, were totally annihilated during the German occupation of that area, by German special forces with the assistance of some of their Ukrainian neighbors. There were few survivors.

At a later date, Stasia heard from an eyewitness that her old mother, Malka, no longer able to walk and wear shoes, was seen, with her feet wrapped in rags, as she and her family were forced into trucks and driven to their place of execution.

While many of the Ukrainians participated in the killings and others abetted and assisted the Germans, the Ukrainian family Lutsenko was an exception. According to Jewish sources, they hid and saved one Jew. The Lutsenkos were later honored with the planting of a tree by Yad Vashem, the Holocaust Martyrs' and Heroes' Remembrance Authority in Jerusalem.

The war in Europe was still raging. The Germans had suffered many decisive losses, but they were not defeated. Heavy fighting continued, with dead and wounded in the hundreds of thousands on both sides, and with the Russians suffering the greatest number of casualties in this area of the war. The fierce battles moved westward, the German forces retreating in defeat, and in January 1944 the Soviet army reached the 1939 Polish borders. Seven months later, in July 1944, the Russians took Lvov. Ephraim's hometown Otynia breathed free.

In 1944, Ephraim's family was free, albeit still in Siberia. The Russian citizenship forced upon them at their imprisonment was no longer valid. Following the Yalta agreement between Roosevelt, Stalin and Churchill, the Soviet Union expected the prisoners to return to Poland. But Otynia wouldn't remain in Poland long; it would soon become officially Ukraine.

Even though the war in Europe was not yet over and battles continued, a massive population movement began. Many former prisoners were on their way to return to their lands and homes. Again, as on their former journey east over four years ago, they traveled by cattle trains. The crowded carriages occasionally carried livestock such as cows, along with their human passengers. The trains often stopped and waited for vacancies in the overworked railroad lines that in addition to being damaged by war were now overloaded with military transports still speeding toward the western front, while many hospital trains carried wounded soldiers back east, as fierce battles continued.

Some former prisoners in Siberia might have nurtured hopes of finding their families. Ephraim's family, however, knew about the fate of the Jews and did not return to Otynia. Nevertheless, Julek visited Otynia, his birthplace. The village was totally destroyed. He found a big crater in the center of town, the area of his former home. In 1941 the town had suffered with the German invasion from the west, and then in late 1944 by the Soviet army, advancing west from the east. The few survivors who returned were not welcomed by the local citizenry, who long ago had occupied their homes and certainly would not have wanted to return them to their owners. In many areas of Poland the returning survivors were met with hostility and violence. Even many years later, when Ephraim and I wished to visit the area of his birth, we were informed we needed a bodyguard.

17. Return to Poland

Ephraim and Julek were both very young in 1939. Their youth might have been helpful in overcoming the ravages of war, and in adjusting to new languages, places and conditions, but the feeling of loss of innocence and security, which, perhaps never truly existed, remained with them for the rest of their lives.

There is no trace of the Jews who once lived in Otynia and of those who died there. Even the cemetery has been destroyed. No Jewish prayers are heard on holidays, no children studying and chanting Jewish religious texts, and no challah or *cholent* is baked in ovens on Fridays.

At the edge of the Szeparowce forest, survivors who emigrated to other lands established a monument in memory of their martyred relatives, with plaques inscribed in Hebrew, Yiddish and Ukrainian. The Hebrew plaque is be translated as: "In eternal memory of the Jews from Kolomyja and surroundings who were murdered here at the hands of the cruel Nazis and their helpers during the years 1941–1944."

Perhaps not wanting to be reminded of their complicity with the Germans, the Ukrainian portion of the monument was vandalized in June 1994 but was later replaced.

I was never more conscious of being a survivor than while writing about these events on a sunny day in California over seventy years later, in 2016. And forever after, while resting in my comfortable bed, my mind revisits the children torn from their mother's arms, my father's last message to me, the mass graves in the Otynia forest and the earth moving after, and the boys I knew digging their own graves. All this will forever be mine.

Chapter 18
Building a New Life

World War II was over at last. It was 1946 and the time had come to think about a new life and a future. I was still in high school. Ephraim was twenty-four years old, in Israel and still in the British army. He thought about his future and a calling. He attempted to work as a watchmaker, but felt he would not succeed. The Technion, the technology institute in Haifa, was something to aspire to and to dream about. The application to enroll, however, was fifty dollars, a sum far beyond his means in 1946. He remembered that in New York there was a society of the former Jewish residents of Otynia (also known as Ottynia). He wrote to them, and to his surprise and relief, the First Ottynier Young Men's Benevolent Society sent him the funds to apply to the Technion. The check might have been authorized by Karl Forseter, one of the society's leaders, who knew his family. It changed his life. Ephraim applied and was accepted, thus beginning his studies in chemical engineering. He later continued with a scholarship from the University of California to earn a Ph.D. in chemistry. Since Ephraim still served in the British army in 1946, he chose guard duty at nights, and attended classes at the Technion in the daytime. He had no other home. His family, recently liberated from Siberia had returned to Poland. Under the circumstances, no one at that time, including himself, considered this daily schedule too much of a hardship. I learned much about it after we met, about a year later.

The Otynia *Landsmannschaft* (the society based on members' former residence in Otynia) was founded in New York in 1900 and later evolved into the First Ottynier Young Men's Benevolent Society. Many such societies were formed in the United States. Their primary function was to bridge the gap between the old life and the new American experience, and to assist Jewish immigrants to America both economically and socially, as well as to assist those still living in Otynia, and later in Israel. They helped new immigrants with jobs, medical care, burial and donations to needy individuals, both in and out of its membership. There were even physicians who helped immigrants by charging modest fees for their services. After World War II they continued their work, helped Holocaust survivors and was still in existence in 1993. But the most important function of these societies was social. In a 1993 essay, brothers Herbert and Norman Latner described the First Ottynier Young Men's Benevolent Society:

> The frequent meetings, once every two weeks with refreshments served, and other gatherings throughout the year provided members with an opportunity to socialize with their childhood friends, to speak in the comfortable and expressive Jewish language, and to reminisce about the good old days in Ottynia. On the occasion of the marriage of any member in good standing, a gift of $10 would be presented, and $5 would be given for the wedding of a daughter or the Bar Mitzvah of a son....
>
> The Ottynia Society is now some 93 years old, and like an elderly Jewish gentleman, has lost the vigor of its youth. But this elderly gentleman, who now walks slowly and wears an out-of-style suit, has much to be proud of—a lifetime of good deeds, of charity and helping the needy, of camaraderie and friendship. While the future may be uncertain, the accomplishments of the First Ottynia Young Men's Society stand as a monument to its glorious past.

For further reading, the Latners' essay is available online at www.shtetlinks.jewishgen.org/Ottynia/ottynia.htm.

Chapter 19

The Rebirth of Israel

While I and other survivors were trying to rebuild our own lives, the struggle for Jewish life in Palestine and for a Jewish state continued. Following a momentous United Nations Partition Resolution on November 29, 1947, to divide Palestine into two states, Arab and Jewish, there was much rejoicing in the Jewish community. It was an acknowledgment of our rights and the intent to establish a Jewish state. I was young, naïve, ignorant of history and totally immersed in restoring my own life, but the general euphoria was contagious. I and many others thought we were at the dawn of an era of peace. The Arabs, however, never accepted the Partition Resolution. While we were dancing in the streets, our Jewish leaders felt like, in their words, mourners at a wedding. They knew a long, costly and uneven struggle lay ahead.

Immediately following the Partition Resolution random violence against Jews erupted again in different parts of Palestine. I remember one of the most brutal massacres of civilians in the oil refineries in Haifa, then administered by the British.

It was on a Tuesday, December 30, 1947, when we were shocked to hear that the Arabs in the refineries attacked their Jewish co-workers, and in the course of a few tragic moments, 41 people were beaten to death and 49 others were wounded. The Arabs came to work with weapons. The Jewish workers were unarmed.

Afterwards, a committee of inquiry by the Jewish community determined that the massacre of the Jews in the refineries was precipitated by and was in retaliation for an attack on Arabs outside the refineries' gates by the Irgun Tzevai Leumi, or National Military Organization. The "Irgun," as it was simply known was an independent Zionist military group, acting on its own, who in turn, had retaliated for a previous attack on the Jewish community. The British police and soldiers arrived an hour after the attack started, but it was too late to stop the carnage.

A general day of mourning was declared. My entire high school class attended the funeral, along with hundreds of others. I remember the burial of the young people, the heartbreaking weeping of their bereaved parents. I noticed one grave with no one around it to mourn. There were no relatives, no friends. The victim was identified only by his given name of "Uriel." No one knew his last name. No tears were shed but mine for this unknown Holocaust survivor, who reached his homeland to rebuild his life.

Months of violence and terror followed. The aim of the Arabs was to kill Jews, anyone, anywhere. Not only did we experience attacks by the Arabs, but the British hindered us further from protecting ourselves by imposing curfews, searches for weapons to disarm the Jewish population and searches for "illegal" immigrants. Immigration by Arabs was, as usual, unlimited, and no attempt was made to disarm the Arab population.

Particularly dangerous were the roads. Over the years my brother Michael became a bus driver. Every day at about 4 p.m., my mother sat by a window waiting for him to return. I saw her fear. Michael was her heart's baby, the one she had rescued from Europe in 1938, just in time, before the war. But I did not fully feel her anguish until I had a child of my own. We were attacked on buses, in market places. No place was safe. I was aware of the danger and I was watchful, but the many years of hiding my identity and self-control had immunized me somewhat from the fear of death. Now, I was not alone and my youthful faith in the power of our leader to protect us was boundless. I knew, as we all did, that we could not fail. I felt I was home.

Many isolated and vulnerable Jewish settlements, on land legally purchased from Arabs, had to fight for their lives, frequently alone. The British were still occupying the country. It was an interim period. The British Mandate for Palestine was still in force, and the State of Israel had not been established as yet. The British, in most cases assisted by the Arabs, held and later turned over to the Arabs many strategically significant areas. The Jewish fighting forces known as the Haganah (Defense) were few and poorly equipped. Under the British Mandate for Palestine, it was illegal for the Jews even to obtain arms, and the British could search for and confiscate weapons.

Not only did we have to cope with the internal attacks by the Arabs, the Syrians attacked from the north, others from the east. In many cases women and children were evacuated from the isolated Jewish settlements in various parts of the country to join with larger towns. The men, even though encouraged to leave with their families—unarmed and outnumbered—refused to give up the battle. They believed they were the outposts of the future State of Israel. I remembered the disdainful phrase I had heard often in the past: *Jews don't fight.* We were fighting now for our survival.

The terror intensified. Particularly dangerous was the road to Jerusalem, and there were many victims. A convoy of seventy-seven doctors and nurses on their way to the Hadassah Hospital on Mount Scopus was ambushed and many were murdered. Ironically, among the dead was Chaim Yassky, an ophthalmologist who had saved the sight of thousands of Arabs suffering from trachoma. The Haganah at that time followed a policy of self-restraint, hoping for and keeping in mind Israel's future relationships with Arab neighbors. We all wept, but were determined to fight back and survive.

On the other hand, the Irgun, the independent military force under the leadership of Menachem Begin, and its splinter group, Lehi, or the Stern Gang, did not believe in limited and controlled responses to attacks and provocation, and carried out acts of terror against the Arabs and against the British military forces. Did they help in our struggle to achieve independence? Perhaps. But in spite of their courage and intentions to fight on behalf of the Jewish people, by acting on their own, they caused the Jewish community much shame and grief, never to be erased. And in the still-unknown future, their leader, Menachem Begin, who like Ephraim survived Siberia, would be elected prime minister of Israel in 1977.

But now, in 1948, the Jewish community in Palestine had suffered heavy losses, and we all mourned with bereaved parents and families. The loss of even one Jew was as if that person had been a member of the family. The burned, ambushed vehicles on the way to Jerusalem remained along the road to remind us of that blood-drenched time. We all knew we could not lose this battle, and knew we had no options but to fight. I was, at that time still so involved in my own determination to overcome my difficulties, graduate from high school and lay the foundation of my life that I did not permit myself to fully feel the mortal danger we lived in. And still, life went on. Schools were open, offices were functioning, and there was no starvation, even though many common products and many foods, such as fresh vegetables and meat, were rationed. We worked, studied, and even sang. I remember a song about the road to Jerusalem and the testimony of those burned vehicles: "Bab-el-Wad" ("The Gate to the Valley"): "*Bab-el-Wad, forever remember our names, Bab-el-Wad, on the way to the City.*"

The entire student body of the Technion was mobilized to fight. I helped Ephraim pack. The year was 1948, and by that time we knew we belonged to each other. I worried about what might happen to him, but kept my thoughts to myself not to burden him further. I didn't think I could bear to lose yet another person I had come to care about. I was also worried: what will happen to my education and future? Never, not for a single moment did I doubt we would defeat the enemy and survive. It was unthinkable to consider the alternative. My mother sighed heavily: "Ephraim's mother is not here even to shed a tear."

The port city of Haifa where we lived was abandoned by its Arab leadership. Even so, there was fighting for control of the city, and in the next morning there was a list of those who fell in battle. I was sure Ephraim had been among those fighting in the battle for Haifa. I was standing at the edge of the crowd of families searching for their sons on this tragic list, afraid to come closer. One of Ephraim's friends saw me standing nervously in the crowd: "Ephraim is OK," he said. I let out a sigh of relief.

The Arab population of Haifa began its exodus from the city. In spite of communication and leaflets asking them to remain in their homes and assurances they were safe, many left. The Jewish Workers' Council of Haifa was clear in their appeal to the Arabs not to abandon their homes, promising a peaceful life and working together in the future, as they did in the

The Liberation of Haifa. Ephraim is in the center at the rear lifting a rifle, ca. late 1940s (family collection).

past. (For more information, see Joan Peters, *From Time Immemorial: The Origins of the Arab-Jewish Conflict Over Palestine*, 1984, listed in the bibliographic essay.) But the Arab leadership encouraged them to leave the city, spreading the news that Haifa would be bombed by Arab forces, and soon be "liberated" by the Arabs, and that they would then return to their homes. For Haifa Arabs, remaining in their homes would have signified treason: an acceptance of the Jewish presence in Palestine.

There is an unfortunate impression and belief that Israel's army had forced many Arab families from their homes. This might have been true is some cases, but in many Arab towns and villages the events of Haifa were repeated, and thousands of Arabs, fearful and uncertain listened to their leaders and tragically, reluctantly left their homes. The Jewish leadership never expected the Arabs to abandon their homes and leave. The Arabs who remained in their homes live in Haifa until this day, and among them are our former good neighbors.

In the midst of all this fighting, there were international suggestions to put Palestine again under the supervision of the United Nations. The British Mandate for Palestine was to end on May 14, 1948, at 9:30 in the morning. A decision had to be made whether to declare the establishment of the State of Israel. It was clear that a life-or-death battle would follow, and that the Jews, outnumbered by tens of millions more Arabs ready to fight, might lose. But numbers did not tell the whole story, and on Friday, May 14, 1948, at 5 p.m., in the Tel-Aviv Museum, David Ben-Gurion, chairman of the Jewish Agency for Palestine, and now, as the prime minister of the new government, in the presence of his peers, read and signed the Declaration of Independence, proclaiming and inaugurating the new country, the State of Israel. The Palestine Symphony Orchestra played the "Hatikvah," now the national anthem. Spellbound, my family and I listened to the radio. A dream of two thousand years had been fulfilled. Such a mixture of emotions, not unlike those at a wedding: tears of joy and sadness for those who were not there any longer to celebrate this historic event with us. Eleven minutes later Harry Truman, the president of the United States, formally recognized the new State of Israel.

The euphoria didn't last long. The next day we were attacked from the north, east and south by five Arab nations: Syria, Egypt, Iraq, Lebanon and Transjordan (present-day Jordan). Still not supportive of the struggling nation, the British left many strategic positions in Arab hands upon leaving the former Palestine. The positive result of the British withdrawal was that Jewish detainees from Cyprus, Holocaust survivors, were freed and then able to come to Israel to join Israel Defense Forces, to fight now

19. The Rebirth of Israel

for the survival of the Jewish state. Sadly, after all that pain and terror, many of them died in battle.

At that time a heartwarming, glorious chapter was written by hundreds of young men from England, South Africa, the United States and Canada, mostly trained army veterans and many of them pilots, who volunteered and risked their lives to help the embattled Jewish state survive. Legend has it that the language spoken in this first Israeli Air Force (of four planes) was English, since these pilots came from English-speaking countries and knew no Hebrew. The fledgling Israel engendered loyalties, generosity and sacrifices. One of the best known of these volunteers was Colonel David "Mickey" Marcus, the commander of the Jerusalem area who lost his life in 1948.

In June 1948, three Egyptian ships appeared on the horizon, coming close to attack Tel Aviv. They were met by three Israeli airplanes from our miniature air force, and following a fierce battle the Egyptians withdrew. However, one plane and two lives were lost: one was David Sprinzak, son of a well-known government official, and the other was Matityahu Sukenik, a younger brother of Yigael Yadin, the area's commander. Yigael wrote to his father, Professor Sukenik, in Jerusalem:

> Don't weep, don't grieve. When Matti took off yesterday to chase away the enemy ships from the shores of Tel Aviv, he knew very well what awaited him. He was not frightened by the risk. He was not terrified or deterred. He fulfilled his duty to his people and his country with bravery.
>
> So don't cry, because the danger did not shake him. With bravery he fulfilled his duty to the people and the homeland.
>
> So don't cry. Just be proud that he was one of us. And let us all cherish his memory with the love and admiration he deserves.

My mother wept. "Our leaders did not hide their children," she sighed, in deep sorrow. This knowledge and feeling was common in Israel those days.

In the midst of celebrating the new State of Israel, the sons and daughters, fathers and brothers who gave their lives to make it possible were not forgotten. They were remembered, eulogized in songs and poetry, and their memory will remain forever in the annals of Israel.

The poet Nathan Alterman felt deeply and was inspired by the words of the first president of Israel, Chaim Weizmann: "A state is not served to a people on a silver platter." Alterman's poem, translated by Esther Raizen, follows.

> ... The land is hushed, a reddening sun
> slowly dims
> over smoking borders.

And a Nation stands—heart-torn yet alive...—
To encounter the miracle
the only miracle...

In preparation for ceremony she rises athwart the moon's crescent
and Stands, before daybreak, swathed in celebration and awe.
—Then from afar come
a maid and a youth
and slowly, slowly they pace towards the Nation.

Clad in ordinary attire but with military harness and heavy-booted,
in the path they proceed,
advancing without speaking.
They have not changed their clothing nor yet laved-away with water
the marks of the day of toil and the night in the line of fire.

Infinitely weary, withdrawn from rest,
dripping with the dew of Hebrew youth—
Quietly the two approach,
then stand motionless,
and there is no sign whether they yet live or have been shot.

Then the Nation asks, flooded by tears and wonderment,
Who are you? And the two softly
answer her: We are the silver platter
upon which was served to you the Jewish state.

Thus they say, and fall at her feet, shrouded with shadow.
And the rest shall be told in the history of Israel.

On June 10, 1948, Syrian forces in the north attacked the settlement Mishmar Ha-Yarden, on the western shore of the Jordan River, to open the road to Galilee. I didn't know it at the time, but Ephraim was among its defenders. The Syrians advanced with tanks and air artillery.

Ephraim wrote to me: "We don't even have rifles. I just hope they will not butcher me with a knife. Every hour sixty minutes, every minute sixty seconds, and in every second you may die a million times."

Women and children were evacuated, and the men fought alone. Mishmar Ha-Yarden fell to enemy forces. Some of the defenders were taken prisoner by the Arabs. Ephraim was fortunate: he was wounded in the chest by shrapnel, rescued by his comrades in the heat of battle, given first aid and rushed to a field hospital. He later credited the first-aid soldier who stopped the bleeding with saving his life.

Notified by the army about Ephraim being wounded, I decided I must visit him and see for myself how he was recuperating. I took a bus from Haifa and during the long bumpy and hot ride into the Golan, I worried about what I would find and see. I found him weak but of good spirit. We talked late into the night, and the lady who owned the house he was stationed in gave us a small white puppy. We thought about the pup as "our son," loved him, kissed him, named him and I brought him home. My mother would have no part of him and I had to face reality. The puppy was very small, cried through the nights, was not house broken and left souvenirs all over our house. We gave him away to what I hoped was to be a good home.

Fierce battles continued even after Ephraim returned to the army. All through the War of Independence we continued our daily life, listening to the radio all day, every day. We knew about many major battles, especially for strategic places, turned over to the Arabs by the British upon their departure, such as Jenin and Latrun and about the fight to open the road to Jerusalem, isolated during the war. We knew our sons and brothers were fighting and dying, even though the radio news, often encouraging, did not report the extent of our losses. We saw around us so many families in deep grief.

Hava's first job as a teacher, ca. 1950 (family collection).

In 1950 Ephraim's parents, liberated from Siberia, came to Israel. I was unexpectedly called out from my classroom in Teacher's College to meet them. I saw a handsome couple, in their 50s and 60s, well dressed and dignified. They heard from a relative I was Ephraim's girlfriend, and asked me to assist them to find him in the Israel Defense Forces. The family was reunited. Ephraim's father, the former Rothschild of his hometown, now settled with his family in a modest wooden hut in the outskirts of Haifa, was helped to find menial jobs, and I never heard anyone complain.

By 1950, as the enemy retreated and the battles ceased, I, always somewhat insulated by my studies, graduated from Teacher's College and was ready for my first job as a teacher. Ephraim and I were married on September 4, 1950, in the home of a rabbi, on the terrace, as required, under the stars, with only the close family in attendance. In total, I don't think we had more than twelve people there. As the rabbi finished the ceremony, Ephraim stepped on the glass, as required by the tradition of remembering the destruction of Jerusalem, lifted the veil, kissed my forehead, and put a ring on my finger. Wine and cake were served. Ephraim was relaxed. I was overcome with the seriousness of our decision.

My mother, stepfather and other relatives escorted us to our new diminutive apartment. Ephraim and I couldn't wait for them to leave. We knew a new chapter of our lives was to begin.

Chapter 20

Newlyweds

Being newlyweds, we were fortunate to have our own apartment of one room with a shower and a tiny kitchen area that measured three square feet just outside of our room. We had a sink, a slab of marble to cook on, a shelf for dishes hung upon a wall and an icebox, which Ephraim kept supplied with fresh ice every day. We thought we had everything we needed.

My Arab neighbor, Anna, felt free to open the door and show off my minuscule, well-organized kitchen to all her friends. She commented, "*jamil*" (Arabic for "nice").

We felt so rich, fortunate and very comfortable in our one room apartment, where of the two trundle beds (one bed under the other) we had, only one could actually be used: there was no room to pull out the other. I tried to cook and ended up becoming the butt of my family's jokes about our complex menu, with foods such as oatmeal.

The day after our wedding, Ephraim received an order to report for his month-long, yearly reserve military service, required of all young men who had already served their full stint in the army. With such a small country without a full standing army, these reserve duties were necessary to keep us alert in case of an attack.

If that were not enough to disturb our nonexistent honeymoon period, within our first days of married life we also received an unexpected letter from Ramat David, the kibbutz which had welcomed Ephraim when he first arrived in Palestine, years earlier, in 1943.

The letter informed him that now he had been accepted as a member of the kibbutz. We knew this was an honor and an expression of trust and approval. To be accepted as a member of a kibbutz you must be considered a suitable and honorable partner in this great enterprise of building a land, a nation and a state. We thanked them but our plans had changed considerably since that time long ago. Now, Ephraim was busy continuing his education and dreaming of professional success and potential fatherhood.

But it would not be easy. Our daily life revealed a Spartan schedule: we still faced two more years of his study to graduate from the Technion. To make ends meet with our expenses, Ephraim also worked part-time as a newspaper carrier and a tutor of mathematics.

As a new teacher, I faced my own difficulties, such as long daily travel to school for about an hour by bus from Haifa to Yokneam, an unconventional classroom of students of different backgrounds and culture, and speaking different languages. Recess time was a challenge: the fourteen-year-old big boys from Iraq carried switchblades to school, and used them to resolve their conflict. But the greatest, most serious problems were my lack of experience, and the absence of resources to engage the children. I needed but hadn't yet prepared or acquired teaching aids, such as sample lesson plans, books, stories to supplement the study program, pictures, songs and games. I searched many libraries, but such aids were not available. My evenings were spent preparing anxiously for the following day's lessons. I learned what all good teachers ultimately learn: the teacher's job is never done.

We were busy every moment of the day and evening, six days a week. We only had a one day weekend, and on the Sabbath, our free day, we walked a considerable distance to visit my mother. After my childhood pastime of curling up with a good book, I dreamt about once again having the time to read a book just for pleasure.

These were hard days and years, but we expected nothing else. At least we were together, we had each other to hold close, love and support and we had our hopes. We knew these years would pass, and life would become easier and better. We had our lives still ahead of us.

I learned Ephraim loved Chopin, Gypsy music. He never passed a beggar without giving him something. I recalled that in Jewish folklore, you never turn a beggar away from your door: it

Ephraim, ca. 1950s (family collection).

Hava and Ephraim following their wedding, 1950 (family collection).

could be the Messiah. One day we heard about an elderly mother who needed help, but was neglected by her children.

"You really should be independent," I commented.

"You should also be young," Ephraim quietly replied. After this lesson in compassion I wondered what he thought about me. I learned, through the years he forgave me and loved me in spite of all my flaws and blunders.

A stray cat adopted us. Suspecting she was pregnant, we fed her a raw egg each day. This was our idea about a nutritious diet for a pregnant cat. Indeed, she gave birth on a pile of my sweaters in the closet.

Two years later Ephraim completed his bachelor's degree in Chemical Engineering and I was expecting our first child. It was the best time of my life. I continued to work as a teacher until the end of my eighth month. These early years of our lives, and of the State of Israel, were also the years of austerity in Israel. Meat, eggs, vegetables, textiles, shoes and many other products were severely rationed. I felt the hardships and longed for potatoes and other simple foods, but no one in the land was hungry, and I was surprised at the complaints I heard from every quarter. But I knew the grumbling was superficial, and that when needed, we will all stand together as one people. Within the rations of every pregnant woman was one coupon for a baby towel, which I still treasure. It was blue, soft and seemed very luxurious to me.

Our son, Igal Henry was born on May 16, 1953. We were exhausted, elated and overwhelmed by love, joy and our new responsibilities. The nurses, citing their long experience, declared he was a beautiful baby. I thought about my father. He would have been so happy, but did not live to see this. Igal's middle name, Henry, was in memory of my father.

By that time the guns of war were silenced, and we had such fervent hopes for peace. Among the many new songs we sang, I remember one in particular:

> I promise you my little girl,
> I promise you once more
> That this will be
> The last of all the wars...

I hoped my child would know no war.

The birth of our son was a life-changing experience. While still in the hospital, Ephraim and I started to keep a diary of our experiences as parents. We both described the baby's progress, but my notes reflected mostly my feelings of love, responsibility and hope, while Ephraim recorded also detailed facts: Igal's weight, size, eyes, and noises, his food, his likes and dislikes.

Ephraim noted in the diary: "We brought Igal home today. Whenever he cries, Hava cries also. We were ordered to feed him every four hours. But he cries more often, and we change him and feed him then. Neither Hava nor I can let the baby cry. Igal eats more than 8 times in 24 hours."

I note: "I am so tired, I can hardly stand on my feet. But it is wonderful to be a mother. We hardly ever call him by his name. We invent all kinds of terms of endearment, frequently in Polish like *kiciula* (small cat). We have to stop it, or he will never know his name."

Neither of us was prepared for this spontaneous outpouring of love and joy. My knowledge of Jewish children's fate during the Holocaust somehow vanished into the recesses of my mind, and did not pertain to my child.

Caring for a newborn was joyful, but very time consuming, especially when it came to ensuring he had clean diapers. Ephraim reported: "Today I washed the diapers." He thought this experience was worth noting.

Diapers were washed by hand, every day, and hung on the line to dry. To boil them, an alcohol-based contraption, or primus, was used, which exploded loudly every time it was lit. It seemed very dangerous and reminded me of the sounds I had heard during the war and the later fighting for Israel. I flatly refused to use it, and my family purchased an electric boiler to wash and disinfect our diapers.

One evening, very shortly after Igal was born, Anna, my Arab neighbor knocked on my door, her hands full of my diapers. She said: "It's going to rain, and I brought in your diapers."

In the course of our conversation I noticed her hands were infected by an angry, red rash. My baby had just been circumcised, and would be very susceptible to infection. How could I use these diapers?

Ephraim came home from work and found me in tears. Following childbirth I wept frequently, for the slightest reason. Without saying a word, he put all our diapers back into the boiler.

Another day, flies appeared in the area of our home, and it was necessary to spray our room with DDT, then a commonly used spray for all kinds of household insects. Ephraim described in the diary how "Hava and Igal sat in the tiny shower area, on the toilet, while I sprayed our room. Then I joined them, and the three of us sat companionably on the toilet and I on the floor, until the room was sufficiently aired."

Igal was four weeks old when we observed the rite of *pidyon ha-ben*—Redemption (or Ransom) of the first-born son. While the family assembled,

Ephraim brought Igal on a silver tray, in a white silk dress, adorned with his grandmother's golden chains, rings and bracelets, and offered him to a Kohen, a Jew of priestly descent, reciting the prescribed formula:

"This is my first born, and the Holy One, blessed be He, commanded us to redeem him."

The priest then replied: "What do you wish to do: Give me your first born, or redeem him for five shekels?"

Ephraim, the father: "I wish to redeem my son for five shekels."

The redemption fee was expected by scripture to be five shekels. In the United States it was usually interpreted as five dollars, and given to charity.

The priest accepted the redemption fee and returned the first born to his father's arms. The father thanked the Lord for the commandment of redemption of his first born son. The priest then blessed the child to grow up to the Torah (scholarship), to his wedding canopy and to good deeds.

The ceremony is of ancient origins. While human sacrifices were still practiced by some of their neighbors in the Middle East, the Jews, since pre-Biblical times were warned against human sacrifices. The commandment to redeem the first-born son is clearly stated in Deuteronomy 12:6. Also in Biblical times, the child could be redeemed by serving God in the temple as a priest.

This drama was acted out at home, while its main participant and star, Igal, was sound asleep.

A year later Igal took his first steps.

My mother breathed in Yiddish: "May you walk long years in good ways."

Igal's first birthday was celebrated by everyone: his mother, grandparents, my brother Michael, who by that time had married Sarah and brought his two children, Shulamit and two-weeks-old Gaby. Following the Holocaust, I was conscious and grateful our Igal had some family around him. Many children his age had lost their grandparents, aunts and uncles in the Holocaust. But Ephraim was absent: he had to serve,

Igal, one year old, 1954 (family collection).

like all other young men, in the Israel Defense Forces for a month every year till their mid-forties, in addition to being called up in times of national emergency. Ephraim's complaint is recorded: "I see Igal every 3 weeks only, and he doesn't recognize me. He cries."

As he grew, I discovered he had an excellent geographic orientation, a very good memory and his own special logic. For instance: Igal liked

Igal and his paternal grandmother, Sarah, 1955 (family collection).

eggs. In the morning he ate an egg for breakfast. I continued to record in my diary.

"I want another egg."

"You will get another egg for supper."

"I want it now." He ate another egg. In the evening, he asked for his egg.

"The doctor said that children should not get three eggs in one day."

"What doctor?"

"Dr. Heller."

"He did not say four. Give me four." Igal, our future lawyer, was four years old.

We were busy. Ephraim had graduated from the Technion by the time our son was born in 1953 and was working in the developing chemical industry. My mother was supportive, and many of our young friends were planning and building their own young families.

The standards, as usual in Israel, were high: a good wife and housewife was expected to be always prepared to receive visitors, even though there were few telephones to warn us about their impending visit.

On a bright Saturday morning in September 1953, I was bathing four-month-old Igal in his bathtub, a laundry washtub. He kicked gleefully splashing water out of the tub until the entire floor of our one room apartment resembled a lake. I was a hot, wet, disheveled, smiling mess. That was when Ephraim's friend, Emanuel, paid us a Sabbath visit with his lovely new bride. On high heels and wearing white gloves she was a portrait of elegance and culture. I was mortified at the state of my home and by my own appearance. The only saving grace was our laughing, shining baby. I certainly must have been a disappointment in not living up to our expected standards of hospitality.

After my leave of absence of one year, in 1954 I returned to my job as a teacher. I returned to the school in Yokneam, about an hour by bus from our home in Haifa.

The school building was in the village, but many of our students and all of my children came from a ma'abara nearby. Ma'abarot, or transition centers for new immigrants, were created as soon as the State of Israel had been established in May 1948. The British authorities were gone, and with them, restrictions on Jewish immigration. Thousands of Jews came to Israel, their new home and haven. Some of these refugees came from Europe like me, survivors of concentration camps, underground bunkers and other hiding places, and from Siberian exile. Others came from many Arab countries, forced by persecution to flee from the lands of their birth.

20. Newlyweds

Now it was our job, as teachers, to assist in their absorption. My fourth grade class consisted of children between the ages of nine and fourteen, born in many lands, including Romania, Yemen and Iraq, speaking different languages, all innocent of Hebrew. Many of them were total strangers to western habits, such as notebooks, pencils, desks, chairs, as well as to listening, raising your hand to speak, or asking for permission to leave the classroom. My position and role in relation to them was also yet to be established. I remember that none of us teachers complained. We had no time to dwell on and appreciate the depth of our problems. We were there to accomplish a task. I thought I was very fortunate to be one of those able to help. And indeed, our students learned Hebrew, acquired western study habits, and, in great measure, we all lived up to our own expectations.

I was young, inexperienced and deeply conscious of my duties and obligations. I began with a song to attract my class's attention. My knowledge of educational methods was limited and our tools were very few, but imbued with enthusiasm, I embarked on my mission to help

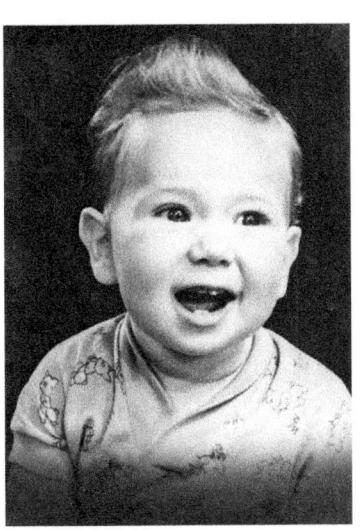

Left: Igal, one year old (family collection). **Right:** Igal, two years old, October 29, 1955 (family collection).

bringing up a new generation of citizens, fighters and heroes for our homeland and our people. My baby was in my thoughts every moment of my life.

On a sunny day I was reading a story to my spellbound class. It was about a young soldier who, during the War of Independence in 1948, with his own body shielded and saved his comrades. As I was reading the story of the youths' sacrifice, I thought about my baby in his crib.

What am I teaching them, I thought. What am I preparing them for?

I continued to teach, aware of our dangerous situation, but stories of heroic deaths always brought me heartbreak and sorrow. I now had a baby boy in his crib, waiting to live his life. I wanted no sacrifices for him. He was growing, and I was growing up as well, and learning.

∽

Ephraim decided at that time that his son must have a father to be proud of, and decided to advance his military training to become an officer. I believe the year was 1954. He was accepted to attend an officer's training course in the Israel Defense Forces. The course was grueling and required much willpower, motivation and endurance. But Ephraim had a

Ephraim is decorated for graduating from an officer's training course with distinction by Itzhak Rabin, then chief of staff of the Israel Defense Forces, June 14, 1954 (family collection).

baby boy to think about and to be a role model for. He graduated with distinction and was decorated by Yitzhak Rabin, then chief of staff, and later the prime minister of Israel. In a few months my son learned to walk, and joyfully laughing, collapsed into my arms. As I held him, I wondered: what did the future hold for him?

Chapter 21

New Horizons

Our child was thriving, and I believed our life was settled, when Ephraim applied for and was granted a scholarship to the graduate school of the University of California in Davis to further his studies in chemistry. Coming to the United States was a new experience and adventure. I knew our lives would change. "America" was synonymous with hope, life, freedom, possibilities and success, and carried no reminders of past horrors. But our home was Israel, and we intended to stay in the United States for a few years only. I was excited about our new plans, and in my naiveté anticipated no problems. We embarked on a new venture, happy, hesitant and curious. Ephraim came to the United States alone in December 1956, soon after serving in the brief and tragic war of 1956, to see if his salary of $250 a month would support us all. Igal and I followed a few months later, in May 1957.

Davis, California, was a small college town dominated by the University of California, especially known for its veterinary school. Students were housed in the Aggie (short for Agriculture) Villa, a series of wooden, two-story, elongated buildings, each of approximately twelve two-bedroom apartments. The rent was very low, and the green in front and in between the buildings were a place for all the children to play. Many students were adults with children, and so were we.

Even though we were graduate students, not immigrants, I was soon to learn about many of the immigrants' experiences, such as loneliness, isolation from family, friends and neighbors, and a language barrier. My high school English helped somewhat.

I remember seeing a group of graduate students, all Americans, sitting at the end of the day together on their doorstep. We did not have such a group. The university sponsored some activities for foreign students, but it was rare, and had an institutional flavor. I appreciated now the most simple human relationships with family and friends I had previously taken

21. New Horizons

for granted. Ephraim was in an easier position. Following his British army "career" he knew English. His studies, research and job as a teaching assistant gave him a goal, many contacts with students, professors and others, and much pleasure.

Ephraim taught me to drive, and I felt elated—I had wings, and now our four-year-old Igal could attend a cooperative pre-school, so-called because of parents' participation. As I watched the setting, the toys and the program, I was tremendously impressed by the attitudes and spirit of the teachers and parents. As a former teacher, I could recognize and appreciate the professionalism and the care. Our children were free to choose their activities. Attention was paid to their behavior, their needs and words. The atmosphere was quiet, relaxed and friendly. I enjoyed and admired it, recalling the atmosphere of tension I often felt in my classroom in Israel and especially the lack of teaching aids. My own inexperience then might have contributed to the difficulties. I looked with wonder at the wealth of books, toys, puzzles, bicycles, and paints. Igal was happy and Ephraim busy, working hard and fully engaged.

It was time to think about myself as well. Anxious, I enrolled in Sacramento City College to fill my time and move me somewhat forward. And my first "A" on an English test proved, to my great surprise, that I knew enough English to go to college. This was a discovery to give me some confidence in my ability to control and improve my life. I always wanted to be a librarian. The goal seemed so far away as to be almost unreachable, but I was determined to take the first steps.

The supermarkets were another wonderland. I purchased some cookbooks and for the first time attempted to learn to cook, remembering the recent years of austerity in Israel. The displays and richness of foods were unbelievable to me.

There were other Israeli graduate students in Davis, and I heard about their preparations, worries and tensions about the oral qualifying tests for a doctorate, something Ephraim never mentioned. I believe today that he evidently anticipated no difficulties at all, or, perhaps, did not want to worry me. Following the qualifying interview, Ephraim reported:

"I was solving an equation on the blackboard. I was so tense that one of the examining faculty members had to say: 'You have resolved the equation. It is done.'" Later, Dr. Allen, his mentor, told him he had passed the orals with flying colors.

We stayed in Davis for approximately three years. I had completed many of the required courses for a B.A. and was ready to continue in a four-year college. Ephraim completed his graduate studies and earned a

Ph.D. in Chemistry. His next step was a postdoctoral fellowship at the California Institute of Technology in Pasadena, and we came to Southern California. South Pasadena seemed all green to me, trees, shrubs and blossoms. We knew no one in this area.

We rented a one-bedroom apartment, part of a duplex, with a huge living-dining room, and a spacious kitchen with a breakfast area. Looking at the enormous hidden Murphy bed in the dining room, I remembered our minuscule apartment in Haifa and I felt like a queen.

One way to start a new life in a new city was to join some organizations whose goals we supported. We met some new friends, and discovered that due to economic need and geographic mobility, some others were also far from their families. We helped one another, celebrated holidays together and little by little, a way of life evolved. While building a new life I was conscious of our freedom, a chance to meet and invite friends to my home, to purchase things I needed, even on a limited budget, and even to care for a cat abandoned by our neighbors. We did not spay her. Remembering my own feelings, I believed that no female should be denied the experience of motherhood, at least once. Her kittens were much appreciated and loved by Igal and his friends.

Our Igal was growing. He was a quiet, bright and observant little boy. We never knew how he learned to read. He evidently understood and applied the system of reading, for even before going to school he was reading.

We thought he was a reliable and responsible child, and believed he would use good judgment to resolve his problems. He always knew where he was and was able to find his way home. I could not get lost with him at my side.

In elementary school he ran for student body president. He lost this election. To make matters worse, his formerly best friend campaigned for the opposing candidate.

I was fearful and worried about his reaction and feelings. Upon coming home, I found him sitting on the floor, watching television.

"Igal, you did not win?" I asked quietly, carefully avoiding the word "losing."

"No, I lost. That is life, Mom," he informed me. I breathed a little easier.

At thirteen we observed his bar mitzvah in Haifa. A bar mitzvah is a ritual of ancient origins, signifying coming of age and being accepted into the Jewish community as an adult male. Today, a boy of thirteen is considered by us little more than a child, but in ancient times, and vastly

Igal and his father at his bar mitzvah in Haifa, 1966 (family collection).

different conditions, maturity depended more on physical development, and children were considered mature at an earlier age. Today, the ceremony of bar mitzvah is considered an act of identity, loyalty and of being a member of the community. We always treated him and spoke to him like an adult, perhaps reflecting our own upbringing and life.

Igal's bar mitzvah was observed in Haifa, in the presence of my mother, Ephraim's parents, my brother Michael and his children and my mother's family who immigrated to Palestine (present-day Israel) before the Holocaust. I thought my child was fortunate to have his family around him. Most children his age had no parents or other family members at all. I thought about my absent father.

Igal, age thirteen (family collection).

In high school he played sports (cross country running). He graduated from Immaculate Heart College *cum laude*, and jokingly commented that, based on his grades, he did not graduate *magna cum laude* only because his father was a professor at the college. Soon after he went to the UCLA School of Law, serving as one of the editors of the student publication, the *UCLA Law Review*. I remember the title of one of his articles: "Mrs. Alice Does Not Work Here Anymore." It dealt with discrimination against woman in the workplace. Today he is an attorney.

Igal married Molly Delaney in 1983, and in a few years we became the grandparents of Sarah, Daniel and Michael. We frequently brought them to our home, full of toys, some of which I still keep, unable to part with. They remember Ephraim baking chocolate-chip bread for them. I was known to make the best pancakes.

When my own child was born all the memories about the fate of Jewish children during the Holocaust retreated into the deepest recesses of my memory. The experience of being a parent was overwhelming, leaving no room for dark thoughts. But the birth of our grandchildren, Sarah, Daniel, and Michael brought back into my consciousness all I knew about the Lost Generation, the more than one million Jewish children between birth

Our son Igal, today Henry, with his wife, Molly, and their daughter, Sarah, seven and a half months old (family collection).

Grandchildren: Michael, the youngest, Daniel and Sarah, 1999 (family collection).

and sixteen who were born, lived and died during World War II under the Germans. Whenever I thought about those lost children, they had faces of Sarah, Daniel and Michael.

~

The postdoctoral fellowship and research at the California Institute of Technology was inspiring. On his first day at Caltech, Ephraim told me about the orientation to the program and the Institute. "They told us we were the top of the nation. I don't know what I am doing there." One day he came home very excited about a newly discovered element which could not be seen, and its existence was known only by its results, a movement. There, with the students, he discovered his interest in teaching, and after a year at Caltech joined the faculty of the Immaculate Heart College (IHC) in Hollywood, California, as a professor of chemistry. IHC was a Catholic college for women, part of a women's religious order. Thus began a long, successful life, full of work, students, grants, chemical research, experiments and friendships. He and Sister Agnes Ann Green, chair of the Chemistry Department, cared much for their students and supported each other. Their chicks were not going to fail, but would go on to success and achievement.

Ephraim teaching a class at the Immaculate Heart College, ca. 1965 (family collection).

21. New Horizons

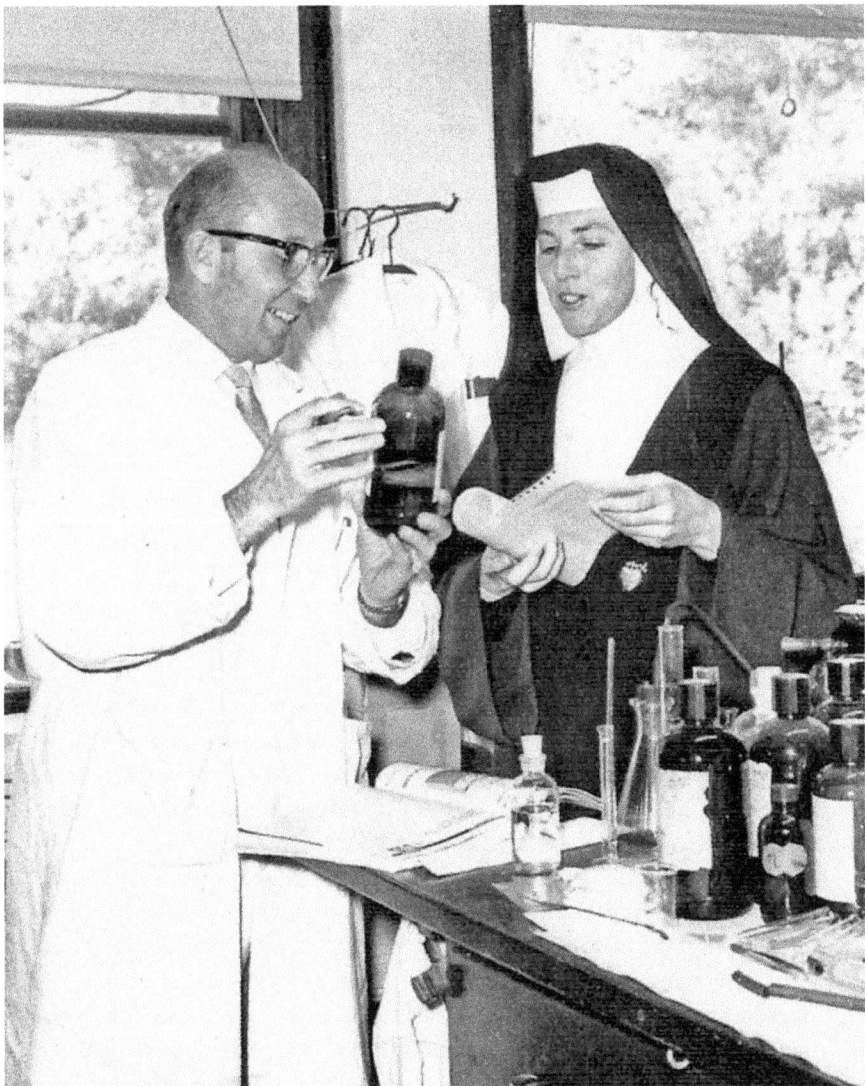

Ephraim and Sister Agnes Ann Green in the laboratory, ca. 1967 (family collection).

From overheard conversations and comments I understood that from the day the students came to college as freshmen, their heads were filled with graduate school and plans for the future. There was an extraordinarily close and warm relationship between the faculty of the Chemistry Department. The chairmanship of the department was rotated and shared. I will never forget that when we flew on our first vacation to Israel, Sister Agnes Ann drove us to the airport and wished us a safe journey. I have learned to appreciate it, but at that time, it seemed just natural to me.

Some things stand out in my memory: I recall attending a Christmas dinner at the Immaculate Heart College for the first time. I was tense. Sister Humiliata, the president, smiling, gracious, greeted us at the door. I remember soon feeling welcome and comfortable, but was too inexperienced to notice that some of the nuns circled around us most of the time, seeing that we were not left alone. I thought there was something exceptional about our presence there, surrounded by habit-clad nuns, and Ephraim was even more aware than I of the meaning and implications of our presence there. We were young, but did not know it. We were a Jewish pair, with a "rich" background and experience in anti-Semitism, the Holocaust, Siberian exile, Israel's resurrection as a Jewish state and in wars. It required even more time and maturity to appreciate our reality, the changes and achievements of our times and the community surrounding us now.

At the time, I took everything for granted, but with time and reflection I came to understand it. And long after retirement, the aging Sister, Ephraim and I used to have breakfast together in a favorite restaurant. She had a sweet tooth (French toast) and we enjoyed being with each other.

I did not forget my dream of being a librarian, and enrolled at California State University in Los Angeles to get a B.A. (with distinction), then a master of library science at the IHC. It was not easy, and I spent many nights studying, and dreaming about a time when I could relax and read a novel, but Ephraim and I supported each other, and on the nights I went to college, he stayed home with Igal. Our goal had been attained, and my first job was as a reference librarian at the White Memorial Hospital Medical Library, and remained in touch with the staff for years to come. I also worked as a reference librarian in public libraries. I advanced swiftly and was promoted to supervisory positions, but I have learned much about human relationships I never knew before. I expected, following the Holocaust and the war years that things would return to "normality." But, having been a child before World War II, I never knew what normality in the workplace could be. Now, I discovered tension and strife. I was learning by experience, hoping to survive. My next and last appointment was as director of the Jewish Community Library of Los Angeles, part of the Bureau of Jewish Education, and I remained in this position for twenty-seven years, ending in 1994 with an award from the Jewish Federation Council for "a significant contribution to Jewish education in the community."

21. New Horizons

Hava, director of the Jewish Community Library of Los Angeles, 1994 (family collection).

Many years have passed swiftly. Both of us worked hard, and were successful in our work, forever finding and aiming at new goals. We bought a house in 1970 and spent many happy years furnishing it. Our goal to return to Israel was not realized, even though Ephraim hoped for it until his life's end.

We joined a synagogue and other organizations, such as Hadassah and Organization for Rehabilitation and Training (ORT), whose goals were close to our hearts, and found new friends and interests.

At IHC, Ephraim was allowed complete freedom to choose his syllabus, texts, and methods of teaching chemistry, as were the other chemistry professors. He continued to support the Immaculate Heart community for the rest of his life. His students valued his patience, care and dedication, and some of their loyalty and sympathy has been bestowed upon me, his widow, even with the passing of years. I am moved, very impressed and touched by his former students' behavior even to this day.

Our lives reflect perfectly, if sadly, Jewish history in our times.

Our story was a journey from childhood to maturity, from a land torn by war to peace, even if interrupted, and from oppression to freedom.

Ephraim and Hava with his former students (left to right) Pat Perez, Carla May Hughes, Maria Alicia Lopez Freeman, Rose Spitt Harris, Sharon August Jones, Carol Galles Grimes, ca. 2008 (family collection).

It was a story of learning and a search for identity, family, a calling, for loyalties and meaning.

I am a grandmother today. I have watched Sarah, Daniel and Michael grow to adulthood and I think about their blessings of freedom, peace, home, parents, grandparents, school, friends, books, sports, food, films and games and everything else they deserve and enjoy. I also write, and often visit schools and libraries, sharing my experiences with students, teachers and parents and many other library patrons. I am careful to pay much attention to young people, believing they hold the promise of our future communities. Often, questions are raised and meaningful and engaging discussions follow. I am glad that we have the freedom to exchange these words and ideas.

I am an author of three other books.

Who is ultimately responsible for the climate and spirit in our com-

Top, left: Hava's first book, 2004 (family collection). *Right:* Second book, published in 2006. Picture of Hava's mother, Dinah.
Bottom: Finalist, National Jewish Book Awards, 2011. Author's family clockwise: grandfather, grandmother, mother, author and brother covered by sticker, husband, brother, and father, 2011.

munities, institutions and schools? Are our leaders, parents, teachers able and expected to bear all responsibilities alone? New terms and phrases come into common use. One of the terms I was intrigued by was "a universe of obligations." What are our obligations? This question usually came up and resonated with all people, young and old.

Perhaps some of the obligations are to be good sons and daughters, good parents to our children, good students, good members of our communities, friends, neighbors, citizens of our country, and even of the world?

Hava Ben-Zvi, 2006.

And my own obligations?

I have been taught well everything I should not be in my relationships with others. I am careful with words I use, knowing their power to wound or heal. Can I live remembering that?

I always knew I had a story to tell, even though similar memoirs have been told before. Each person is a unique and separate universe, and each one of us bears, negotiates and solves the problems of his life alone. I believed that we, the Holocaust survivors, have a duty to tell our stories.

Some of my obligation are to the martyrs, and even more so to the living. I try to meet my obligations, sometimes failing, but always trying.

Chapter 22
End Matters: Love and Loss

Ephraim, my husband of nearly sixty years, passed away in 2009. He is always a presence in my life, not a memory. I weep without tears. Perhaps the pain is too deep to be relieved by tears.

He was my husband, my love, my friend and confidant, supporter and admirer. Of course, I took it all for granted, as if I had deserved it. I always knew he loved me so deeply, and forgave me most of my weaknesses and trespasses.

His memorial service was arranged by our son, Henry (Igal, now using his middle name). I was in a fog of grief and sorrow, and thought I could never live through it. But I did, and hearing some of the eulogies afforded me a measure of comfort, especially some of the words by Carol Grimes, one of his former students at Immaculate Heart College:

> He taught us patience, integrity, rigor, and compassion by his examples as our instructor. And like the ripples from a stone dropped in a pond, his students have carried these qualities into the landscapes of our society and passed them on to students, children, co-workers. His work at IHC has, I think, made our society a better place because of the care he took in nurturing all of us through our degrees.
>
> So I would like us to lift our hearts in a toast to an extraordinary man, one who influenced all of his students profoundly.
>
> To say we loved you, and respected you.
>
> Not just because you taught us about the periodic table (although you did).
>
> Not just because you taught us to go from data A to answer B using a pyrotechnic display of mathematics (although you did that as well).
>
> Certainly not for those open-book physical chemistry exams (because we hated those).
>
> And certainly not because you taught us not to generate stinky gas upwind of Helen Kelley's (the president's) office (because you and Sister Agnes Ann tried to do that, but never succeeded).
>
> We loved you because you took a genuine interest in each of us as individuals. You nurtured our strengths and taught us our weaknesses. You cared about each

one of us, and helped us with whatever we needed. You always believed in us. You rarely lost your temper (and never for long), always had time, and always gave a precise reasoned answer.

Dr. Ben-Zvi, you were a class act, and we will miss you.

In our fifty-eight years together we never had or took time to learn about each other's former life, before we met, shortly after the war, in 1947. We lived in the proverbially "interesting times," but no one in Israel talked about the Holocaust or the experiences of those who survived it. The many survivors were familiar with it, and all energy was and still is needed to build a new life. We were so intensely future oriented: strength was needed to go to college, and to make up for lost time. Life was new and so important, and the past was not to be dwelled upon. I regret it today and try to remember...

Why didn't I ask questions? With the passing of time, maturity and, perhaps, some leisure, I tend to be more forgiving. Not returning to the past might have been a way of coping. Perhaps we could not afford examining the years of death. To start a new life we needed to forge forward.

Ephraim passed away on March 28, 2009. His loving heart stopped beating. I was not prepared for it, and was lost in shock and pain. Our son Henry took over all arrangements and was a source of solace and support. Julek, his brother, now living in Australia, wrote to me.

Sitting numb and silent at the memorial service I heard, as if through a mist, about the family's freedom and return from Siberia in 1950, after the war, Israel then an independent state. I, Ephraim's girlfriend at that time, helped his parents find and contact him. On a leave from Israel Defense Forces, he came to meet them. After years of separation and war, Ephraim was no longer the nineteen-year-old boy but a man, and his once delicate, pale skin was now sun burned, scarred and dry, but his mother's tears were of joy and happiness. The formerly wealthy family, reunited, settled in a little wooden house, hardly more than a shack, in the outskirts of Haifa, worked at menial jobs, but no one had ever complained.

Julek described Ephraim's and my wedding in 1950 and told about the lasting bonds of love between himself and his brother and the fact that they never fought with each other, as brothers often do. Ephraim remains in Julek's memory as a caring brother, always ready to help and advise. Julek, the atheist, tearfully ended his tribute to his brother: "I lost my only brother, and blessed be his noble soul."

I sat at the memorial service, enveloped by the fog of my grief and misery, accepting condolences, unaware of who was or was not there. But I still heard and was moved by Carol's, Julek's and our son Henry's words. He spoke about his father.

Henry had no personal knowledge of army life, yet he knew and understood the hardships, anonymity and sometimes cruel discipline of army life in war his father suffered in his youth, not to mention the dangers of those years. He knew, felt and described the anti-Semitism of his Dad's Polish navy "comrades," the food deprivation and debilitating hunger while, it was discovered later, army bases, full of food were saved by speculators, to sell on the black market.

I remembered all this, but silently wondered: how did he know so much about his Dad's life and character? Henry must have been a very attentive child, knowing far more than we intended to tell him.

He knew about the courage, terror and determination of Israeli soldiers, barely armed, anticipating hordes of Arabs, fully armed, especially with knives. Yet in spite of these hardships, his father was eternally optimistic, entirely upbeat, and totally engaged. He always looked forward: he did not look back, and rarely talked about his past. He did not think what he had gone through was in any way special, much less extraordinary. It just wasn't relevant. His past, and the suffering he experienced, were to him trivial, and therefore not worthy of extended discussion. What was relevant was today and tomorrow.

"Father loved his family and was inordinately proud of his grandchildren. He cherished my mother," I heard Henry say, through my isolation and loneliness.

And he loved teaching. His dedication to his students was as powerful as his insistence that even when people made mistakes, they should get second chances.

Our son recalled the case of a Cal State University student cheating on a test. He did not do what most professors would have done, which would be to flunk the kid. He agonized about this student, and he did not want this student's stupid mistake to have permanent, long-term consequences. So he allowed the kid to retake the test, this time watching him.

"Dad was selfless. I never heard him say a bad word about anyone and he always gave people the benefit of the doubt. He rarely passed a homeless person without stopping and giving him some money. Beyond his family, Dad loved Israel, and hoped to return to what he considered his homeland."

I listened and knew how true all this was. But did Henry know how

Ephraim and Hava, last picture, ca. 2005 (family collection).

deeply his father loved him? I knew Ephraim loved his son far beyond anyone else.

"Dad inspired me," Henry continued. "Not by talking but by doing."

"Dad, I loved you. I will miss you and never forget you."

22. End Matters

The service ended. I say a prayer for you, Ephraim, every morning. *El Malei Rachamim...* (God, full of compassion) and I feel your presence with me at all times.

Thank you for all you were to me, my husband, counselor, supporter and friend. Thank you for putting your life in my hands, for believing in me, for your love, so deep and perceptive. For teaching me, among many other lessons, humility and kindness. I will continue to live, bearing witness to your life, hopes and beliefs. No woman has ever been more loved, protected, encouraged and supported.

Sleep in peace, my dearest. Sleep in peace.

Your Hava.

Aftermath: Martyrs and Survivors

Few were the survivors of our immediate and extended family. I lost my father, Herman Bromberg, in August 1941. I was twelve years old. He influenced my life by his smile, humor, books, patience, by his love and our friendship, and by bringing me to a local library in Warsaw. He will always remain with me, and be a part of me. I became a librarian at the age of eight, with a lifetime addiction and love of books.

I found my mother, Dinah Lewartowska Bromberg, through a newspaper advertisement in Palestine, in 1946. She taught me to be, again, a member of a family, a community and a nation.

Michael Abir, my brother, who left Poland in 1939, grew up in Palestine, lived to serve in the British army during World War II and was fortunate to have a family of three children.

Romek Bromberg, my father's brother, shared the fate of my father.

My father's younger siblings I knew in Warsaw perished: Victor Bromberg and Lusia Bromberg, the youngest, who was a teacher of gymnastics, and recently married.

I remember Zygmund Bromberg, my Częstochowa cousin, who came to Warsaw in September 1939 to say goodbye. He was then about twenty-four years old. I was ten. He remained the only survivor of his family: he lost his father Leib Bromberg, his mother Yetka, and his brother Ignas who was caught by the Germans asleep in his bed, and sister Hanechka.

And our family in Mielec? I remembered their father, Yedidia and my father, Herman, corresponding with each other before the outbreak of World War II, their two daughters, one of whom, Irena, was about my age and wrote poetry. I wondered if she perished, or perhaps found a shelter and survived, as I did.

I soon learned that Irena, today Irene Eber, her mother and sister were the only survivors of their immediate family. Everyone else we both knew and loved perished without a trace in the German machine of destruction, remaining only in our thoughts and memories.

I believe that no one in our family, except Irene Eber and I, recorded our experiences during those years of death.

My book, *We Who Lived*, is dedicated, with love, to my husband Ephraim Ben-Zvi, my father, my family and all the other martyrs of the German occupation.

Irene Eber, true to our family's tradition, never gave up either. Long after World War II Irene wrote a book, *The Choice: Poland 1939–1945* (Schocken Books, 2004), and in 1986 a short memoir of her family's last journey. Reading it, and in spite of being myself a veteran of horrors, I was overcome with grief, sorrow, and again, with despair and anger. I felt that Irene's memoir adds a different and significant chapter to my own story, to the memory of our and many other families who perished without a trace, whose manner of death will never be known, and to the history of the Holocaust. In her own words, Irene Eber tells here about her family's last way and destiny.

Four Days in August: A Family's Last Journey
Memoir by Irene Eber

That August, more than forty years ago, we were in Dąbrowa, a small town with a market surrounded by two- and three-story houses, narrow alleys behind the market. So small was this town that when I later searched for it on a map I could find it only on a large wall map.

We had come to Dąbrowa at the beginning of summer, having made our way back stealthily by train and on foot from the Lublin district to which we were deported in March. I don't know why my family chose to come to Dąbrowa. Perhaps Uncle Ruben thought it was safe. The family often depended on Ruben's judgment. He had been an important man, a member of the Judenrat, before the March deportation. Dąbrowa was out of the way, he might have reasoned, with no railroad nearby; just a small town among rolling hills and yellow wheat fields. He did not know, nobody knew, as I would learn many years later, that the extermination of the Jews was in full swing in the summer of 1942.

The days were sunny and quiet in Dąbrowa that summer. Cousin Esther and I sat on the doorstep in front of the house where our families each had a room, and we watched the people at their busy tasks: fetching water, buying a wedge of bread or bargaining with a peasant for an egg and butter. We no longer quarreled as we had in the past. We were sad and had little to say to one another. Perhaps we were thinking of the friends left behind in the Lublin district that we would never see again.

The adults, too, no longer quarreled. There seemed to be a strange peace in the family; differences and animosities had been suspended. I did not know then, as I know now, that we were waiting, and that for the duration, as if by common consent, we had decided to get along. Mother, Father, Ruben and Feige—the adults—may have known what would happen sooner or later. Or maybe they hoped the Germans would overlook Dąbrowa's existence, forget that it was there, or forget that there were Jews in Dąbrowa. Or maybe they thought of escape, but did not know where to run.

So we waited.

And while we waited, trapped in sleepy, sunny Dąbrowa, I discovered the birds and their magic celebration of freedom.

Each morning I watched the birds in the tall trees around the marketplace. They began to sing and twitter as soon as the first light of the rising sun cast a purple glow over the far end of the square. I would open my eyes and, climbing carefully over the sleeping bodies of Sister and Cousin, tiptoe to the open window. At first the birds were invisible. I only heard the rustle of the leaves and the trills of some master singer. Then, when my eyes adjusted to the twilight, I would see one, two, five, dozens of birds, jumping from branch to branch, calling and answering one another.

Gradually the sky became orange and the birds, obeying a secret signal, ventured out of the trees and gracefully spread their wings in a practice circle over the marketplace. Reassured of their ability to fly, a flock—hundreds, it seemed to me—rose into the orange sky to cruise in the early morning light. The birds flew wondrous patterns, close together and fanning out, separating and coming together, performing a magic airborne dance just for me, watching at the open window. Then, their morning exercise over, the birds settled on the rain drains that ran along the roofs of the houses, chattering to each other while grooming themselves for the coming day.

Meanwhile the orange had changed to pink and in the first bright rays of the sun, the shadows faded from the doorways around the market below. The birds, no longer performers but audience, watched from their high perch as early risers opened and closed doors and went to draw water from the pump. Their delicate chatter became faint. Now there were other noises. Men and women cleared their throats, coughed and spat; pails clanged; babies cried; pots banged; and in the distance peasants' wagons rumbled toward town. The marketplace was waking up, the magic performance had ended, the birds dispersed. I would turn away from the window, suddenly aware of my empty stomach.

The First Day

One morning in August everything was different. I knew it the moment I awoke, not in my customary place next to Sister and Cousin, but in the chair next to the window. I looked around the room. Everyone was sleeping fully dressed. Sheets knotted into bundles lay here and there; Mother's checkered coat was carefully folded at her side.

I shivered in the cool morning air and stood up to look outside. There everything still seemed the same. The birds were beginning their morning song in the purple glow; the leaves rustled and then they flew off. Slowly the shadows melted away and the birds, their flight completed, came to rest on the drains. But this day no doors opened and closed. Pails didn't bang. The market remained as if asleep. Then, as the sun was rising, I heard a sound I had never heard before, a sound so strange I didn't know what to make of it at first. A great wind? Was it like the rising and falling ocean waves Father had once told me about?

"Here they come," said Father, getting up from the mattress on the floor, "get away from the window."

The noise became louder. I could distinguish human voices—wails and cries, the babble of a multitude and the crude shouts of German soldiers; wagon wheels rumbled, there were sounds of motorcycles. The birds' chatter was drowned out by waves of terror-stricken voices that rolled ahead of the people into the marketplace.

"Get up." Father gently pulled Mother to her feet and held the checkered coat for her. She trembled as she put it on.

Father put on his gray coat, he handed me mine, and I thought how hot we would be in the August sun with our winter coats. Then he motioned us together: Mother, Sister, Cousin, and me.

"We must try and stay together. It may be hard because they are bringing in everybody from the villages and towns. Don't take off your coats, we'll need them for blankets at night. We don't know where they'll take us; even Ruben wasn't sure. We might have to march for hours without food or water. But no matter how hot the day, don't take off your coats. When they march us out of here, stay on the inside of the column, don't be at the head or the end. Don't let others push you to the outside. Don't sit down, even when you think you can't take another step. Just keep walking, always on the inside. We must watch and help each other. I'll take care of the child, but if you see anything happen to me, try to take over."

While he was speaking, motorcycles noisily drove into the marketplace and stopped. The people were coming through the narrow alley to the right of the square and the cries of the women and children were now very distinct. The noise became louder as the multitude poured into the marketplace. Then the soldiers began to bang on the doors, shouting for the people to come out.

Father bent down to adjust my backpack, in which I carried the previous winter's shoes. "All right," he said, placing his hands briefly on each of our heads, "let's leave now. They mustn't come after us and beat us. Let's be careful and see the end of this day." He took my hand, the three women picked up their bundles, and we walked out of the room. Father touched the mezuzah on the doorpost.

It was in August 1942, the day of the deportation from Dąbrowa.

The moment we stepped out of the doorway, I forgot the familiar room upstairs where the five of us had lived since the beginning of summer. I forgot everything, as if my mind had been wiped clean of everything I ever knew. The sight that met my eyes made me clutch Father's hand, and terrible fear cramped my bowels. Dark-clad women and men and their children were milling in the marketplace; more were pouring in through the alley, pushing and stumbling as the throng behind them surged forward. Sobs, cries, "God in heaven have mercy," together with the shouts of the Germans, filled the air. The soldiers banged with their rifles at doors and, when a Jew got in their way, they brought the rifle crashing on his head or back. Some people had already stumbled and fallen. Others sat on the cobblestones with dazed eyes, blood running down their faces. And still more people pushed through the narrow alley.

The sun that day was strong and golden in the cloudless, blue sky. I looked up at the drains that ran along the roofs, hoping to see the birds, but not one was in the customary place. They must have fled and hidden, I thought, as frightened as I by the terrifying sight.

Led by Father, we slowly inched our way into the dark multitude, into the knotted mass of crazed humanity. The periphery was dangerous. The Germans started pushing the crowd toward one side of the market. They pushed the people so close together that it was hard to breathe or to keep one's balance. Small children fell, having let go of the hands that helped them, and were stepped on by the heavy boots of the men. There was no room in the dense dark mass to bend down and pick them up. Their pain-filled sobs were muffled by the men's long coats and the women's heavy shirts. At last there was no more room to move back. The people stood still and tried to straighten out in the tiny space they had gained. Now the Germans began to arrange this crowd in straight lines.

"Bad," said Father, holding my hand very tight in his, "we're too close to the front. I hope we don't get pushed into the first row."

We could not move back. We had to stay where we were. I could not even crane my neck to look for Mother or the birds. Then, somewhere in front of us, shots rang out.

Screams. Like the cries of wounded animals. And in the sudden hush that fell over the crowd I heard the startled twitter of the birds.

The morning wore on and the sun rose higher. Gradually lines formed and straightened in accordance with some German design unknown to us, "Now you must stand very still," Father said to me, "you mustn't move. You mustn't let your knees buckle, or God forbid, sit down. Don't look around. Don't talk."

The crowd grew quieter. Children continued to cry, but otherwise the dark men and women stood very still in straight rows as the hot sun, now high in the sky, shone on them. And then the searches began. The soldiers disappeared into the houses that ringed the square and fanned out in the alleys behind. Another kind of noise began, the sounds of walls and furniture being smashed. Windows broke and pots and pans, chairs and dishes came crashing down on the cobblestones and the people below. Then a white, fluffy bundle sailed through the air from a second-story window; a baby, I realized, when its thin cries hovered above the market. I thought I still heard the pitiful "wa, wa" even after it had crashed with a terrible thud. Somewhere inside the house a woman screamed, long and shrill. Then two shots, and she was quiet. A tall man ran out of an alley. I heard his short, piercing shriek while the laughing soldiers shot at him. He ran here and there, and in crazy circles; fresh, bright blood covered him and the gray cobblestones, until he finally fell and did not move again.

"Close your eyes," Father whispered hoarsely above me. "Don't look. Close your eyes." But I couldn't force them shut. My sweaty hand shook in his, and he tried to get a tighter grip on my slippery fingers.

Something was happening in front. Although we were only a few rows away, I could not see. A German soldier shouted something incomprehensible, while the lines seemed to ripple as if moved by a sudden wind. "Every tenth person," said a thick voice behind me, "they'll take out every tenth person to shoot."

Every tenth person? Would I be the tenth? Father? Mother? How many people to the end of the row to the right? To the left. No, I mustn't look, Father had said. Now a silence so great, a stillness so vast, as I had never heard before, fell over the multitude. No one spoke. The counting began. Quietly, sometimes with only a gasp, the tenth person stepped out of the line in front of us. Sometimes it was a woman alone, a man, sometimes a mother and child, a boy, an old man and his wife. Quietly they walked away. There were suppressed sobs among those left behind, no time to mourn, for the count went on relentlessly, methodically. I finally closed my eyes when the count seemed close, not wanting to know whether I would live or die. Much, much later, when I dared open them again, it had passed Father and me. A sudden feeling of relief made my knees buckle, and I might have sunk down had Mother's quick hand not steadied me. I recognized her touch without turning my head. So she was alive, too. I longed to see her face, but knew that I mustn't turn around. Father had warned me.

The moment I realized that we would live a little longer, sensations returned. I was thirsty, terribly thirsty, hungry and tired. My legs ached unbearably, my tongue felt thick and swollen in my dry mouth. I did not think it possible to stand still another minute. I smelled the stench of urine and feces, of fear and death. How had I not noticed it before? When a breeze caressed my hot face, I thought that it must have been getting toward afternoon.

A horse-drawn wagon rolled into the market. After a day's hard work, the tired soldiers climbed onto it, carrying their guns. The motorcycles started up. Slowly a column of dark people formed, shuffling along, heads bowed, bodies weary in heavy clothing. Slowly the column crawled out of town. When we entered the alley that led out of the market, I briefly glanced back for a last look. I did not see the birds. Nor did I hear them. Formless, dark shapes were lying in the square among the broken furniture and dishes, their blood already dry on the gray cobblestones.

We walked out of town, past the church, past the low huts that stood in green gardens where tomatoes and sunflowers ripened. The peasants' watchdogs strained at their leashes but did not bark. They crouched on their hind legs and, barring their teeth, growled at the strange and terrible sight. Cows in the pasture left off eating and raised their heads, watching the column trudge by. Then, indifferent, they returned to chewing the green grass. There wasn't a soul to be seen on the dusty road. Nor were the peasants at work in the fields. The countryside was still and silent in the afternoon sun. Only sometimes a lace curtain moved behind a tiny window of a hut.

We walked along the road raising clouds of dust that settled on our hot, sweaty faces and seeped into our clothing. Before long, old men or women with babies began to drop out of the slowly moving column, sat down at the roadside. Soon thereafter, a shot or two would ring out. Father still held my hand in his. When I stumbled, he supported me. When I slowed down, he pulled me along. He was breathing hard, but he walked on steadily. Once I heard him say, half to himself, "They're taking us to Mielec," and later, "No, it must be Dębica." Mother walked behind us with sister and cousin.

The shadows began to lengthen; the day was nearing its end. Now, the soldiers, having rested a few hours on the wagon, began to hurry us on, afraid that people would try to escape in the dark. More and more fell out, sitting quietly at the roadside waiting for death. A cooling evening breeze carried the sound of church bells from a distant village. The peaceful chimes mingled with the burst of guns. I no longer averted my eyes from the slumped and sprawling dark shapes. Killers and killed and the mass of stumbling, shuffling humanity had become a part of the green meadows ripening yellow grain and the dusty road leading into the distance.

The Second Day

"Out of the barracks," shouted harsh voices, "everybody out."

"Hurry," I heard Father's urging somewhere far away, "we must go outside."

I opened my eyes, and in the gray light that filtered through a grimy window, tried to understand where I was.

"Hurry!" Father's voice was louder now. It seemed to come from below. I sat up, not knowing what to do. "Hurry, and climb down," Father said again.

Still half asleep, I did as he told me. Once down, I saw that we were in a barrack with two tiers of long wooden platforms. At one end was the high window, at the other end the door. We had slept on these platforms, crowded close together, though I couldn't remember how and when we got here.

The narrow passage was filled with pushing, cursing people, all trying to get to the door as quickly as possible. The five of us were swept up and carried outside by the crowd. I saw a line of barracks to the left and right, and a clear space in front with aimlessly milling people.

"Go a little forward into the crowd," Father advised. "I'll try to find food and water. Don't worry, I won't lose you." His voice was thick and I thought that he must be as thirsty as I. Father soon returned and led us to a long line of people waiting their turn at the water pump. He looked pleased with himself. "We'll wash and drink, then we'll see if there is food. It will be all right." He looked at Mother as if trying to get her agreement. But Mother said nothing. She did not look at Father, but stared off into the distance. She seemed strange and remote. I thought her eyes had become very large and dark, and I tried to remember what she looked like before we left Dąbrowa.

Father grew full of energy that day, as he discovered where we were and what seemed to be happening. While the four of us huddled in silence, he repeatedly disappeared into the crowd, returning each time with another piece of news.

"We're in Dębica, just as I thought," he reported. Or, "This business is not yet over. The Germans are rounding up everyone. There'll be selections, they'll send people away. They won't keep everyone here. We must be careful." Another time he came back almost smiling and put his hand on mother's shoulder. "I found Ruben, it'll be fine, you'll see. Ruben has some kind of position again, and he'll take care of us. He promised. The family is together, that's the main thing. As long as we make it through the selections...."

For the first time Mother raised her head and some life seemed to return to her face. "Ruben and Feige? Esther and Malke too? Take me to them."

Patiently, Father explained that Ruben was outside. There was something about a ghetto; Ruben would bring us to it, Father said. Ruben said to be patient and careful. They were bringing in more people from the villages. Then there'd be the selection. "Here, he even gave me food." Father pulled a large slab of black bread from his pocket and gave it to Mother. "We must trust Ruben."

Mother hid the bread under her coat and said nothing. I wanted her to believe Father and Uncle Ruben because then, I thought, I could also believe that we would somehow live. But Mother looked so frightened, as frightened as Sister and Cousin, who clung to each other, not speaking to Mother or me. I wanted Mother to be strong, as she had been in March when we were driven out of Mielec and had to march in deep snow and ice-cold weather. She took care of us then. She held me tight when I thought we'd all die in the cattle car and she comforted me when the pain in my frozen feet seemed impossible to bear. Now, I thought, she no longer managed at all. I looked up at Father, wanting to feel reassured; his kindly face seemed unchanged. Yes, I wanted to believe him, even if Mother didn't; Uncle Ruben would save us. And Father would watch over us and not let anything happen.

We sat down in the dust, there was no place else to sit. We were not allowed in the barracks during the day. There were no trees, no shade, and when I looked up at the sky, I saw only vast emptiness. The hot sun, hunger, and the noise of many frightened people crowded into a small space made me dizzy. I wanted this day to end, yet I also wanted it to go on. Today, at least, we were alive. Who knew what would happen tomorrow?

Knowing himself protected by Uncle Ruben, Father grew more daring. At noon, when the sun beat down mercilessly; when the stench of sweat and waste became unbearable; when swarms of evil-looking green flies descended on the penned-up people, he told me to slip into the barrack for a brief rest.

I climbed up on the platform and lay down in our spot, which was at the far end of the barrack near the window. I squeezed into the corner, pulling up my legs. No one could see me, I was sure. I did not sleep, although I was very tired. My feet hurt terribly; they were covered with dirty festering sores from the long march. I was hungry and afraid. I knew all about selections. Where did the trains take the people? To Majdanek? To Bełżec? Where had I heard about Bełżec? Is that where they had taken my friend, Toska, and her family? I wished Mother would speak to me, and if not Mother, at least Sister, who was older and should know more. But the three just huddled together, their eyes large and frightened. They had not even combed their hair, or helped me with my wounded feet. They left everything to Father, I thought, and he tried so hard to find reassuring things to say to them.

"The great lady in a fine coat, how shameless can you get?" I suddenly heard a woman's hoarse voice below.

"Wearing pants like a man. You tell me, Malke, is that how a Jewish daughter behaves at a time like this?" answered another.

So someone else had decided to sneak inside, I thought. Who would they be talking about? Mother wears a coat. No, it couldn't be Mother. She is wearing a dress, and she is not shameless. I lay very still, wanting to hear more of their low conversation.

The woman with the hoarse voice continued. "How can a woman her age carry on like this? He could be her son; why, he must be half her age. Is that what Jews do in cities? Where's she from?"

"Kraków, I think, I heard her say she was deported more than a year ago. I don't know where he is from. A nice-looking boy, so young. Maybe a student. And the way she is hanging on to him. It's disgusting. She's a whore, that's what she is. Gray hair and all. Did you see the fine soap she uses? Shameless, washing herself with perfumed soap at a time like this."

"They sleep next to each other like an old married couple. Last night while everybody was groaning and farting with hunger, they played their little games. She, a woman with gray hair, and he, a mere boy. Just wait until the selection starts. Nothing will help her. Not her pants, not her fine coat, not a young lover. They'll take her away with the rest of the old women. Shameless whore."

The voices stopped for a while. Then the hoarse voice began again. "What's going to happen to us? Oh, Lord of the universe, have mercy. My mother is worn out, finished. She won't make it. I thought I'd bring her inside, but I'm afraid. She barely got up this morning. They drove us here like cattle. Merciful God, how will I save my mother?"

"Don't carry on like this, Malke," said the other, "we're still alive. The All Merciful will send help. Don't give up."

"Ha, it's easy for you to say," the hoarse one said venomously, "you have your Yossel. But me, a widow with no money and an old mother...?"

Then all was quiet. The women had left as noiselessly as they had come.

For the rest of the day, in spite of hunger and fear, I continued to think about the conversation I had overheard. I was not curious about the women, who had sounded coarse and vulgar. No one I knew talked like they did, or ever said such things about other people. It was the old woman with gray hair and coat and the young boy that I wondered about. Who could they be? Had I seen them in the crowd? And what were they doing that made the women go on so about her? I had heard the word "whore" before; sometimes my older cousins had said it, under their breath, and then they giggled. They never explained, but I knew it was a bad word, said of women who did bad things.

In the evening, after we were herded inside, I tried to have a look at everyone who climbed onto the upper platform. Sister wanted me to lie down; sitting up I took up too much room, she complained. Father pleaded for me, "Let her sit for a little while, the child is restless. It's hard for her to fall asleep in the tight space."

I sat, leaning against the wall and, in the twilight, watched the stout women in their dark skirts and wool shawls heave themselves up. The men were helping, sometimes one from below and one from above. First I saw their heads and shoulders, hands grasping for something to hold onto, then a heave from below and one and then the other knee, until finally, crouching on hands and knees, they were on top, breathing hard, sweat running down their faces. The younger women had an easier time of it. But there was much complaining and arguing as each crawled toward her little space. Some women wept and begged to be allowed to sleep on the lower platform. But the people wouldn't give up their little spaces. It was as if, after having lost everything, each person now clung to this last piece of board in order to feel that he or she belonged somewhere.

Finally I thought I saw the woman they had been talking about. I was quite sure. She was tall and slim and wore long pants like a man. She threw her coat over the top and pulled herself easily up onto the platform. She was not at all old, and nothing like I had pictured her. Her hair was short and gray, though she seemed only a little older than Sister or Cousin. She wore a white blouse, open at the neck. Directly behind her came the young man. He certainly was not a boy, I thought. He too was tall and slim, with brown curly hair. He smiled at the woman when she held out her hand to pull him up, and said something I could not hear.

I watched them arrange themselves for the night. Quietly talking to each other, and seemingly oblivious of the harsh voices and crude curses, as if they were in their private bedroom, the two pulled off their shoes and put them at their heads. The young man removed his shirt and she helped him fold it neatly, first one side, then the other, and next in half. Sometimes their hands touched and they looked at one another without as much as a glance at their surroundings. He put the shirt over his shoes and she emptied her coat pockets, carefully dropping the things inside the shoes. Then she straightened the coat and covered him and herself with it. Finally they lay down, her head resting on his arm. I too slipped down. They have neither bundles nor suitcases, I thought, everything she owns is in her coat pockets. Who are they and why have they no belongings? They are so different from everyone else, no wonder the women gossip about them. But why pity him and call her bad names? Thinking about the couple helped shut out for a time the fear of tomorrow and the hunger.

The Third Day

Mother seemed to be feeling better. Perhaps Father's attempts to cheer her had worked. In the morning she took us to the pump. We filled a pot with water and, moving to the side, washed as best we could. Mother sent me back for more water to clean the sores on my feet. Waiting in line, I saw the woman ahead of me. She stood tall and erect, so different from the squat broad-hipped women around us. Her gray hair was short and thick. When she glanced over her shoulder, I noticed her smooth, clear skin. I thought she was very beautiful. She looked as I imagined ladies did.

When her turn came, she moved the pump handle smoothly up and down and filled her pot with three spurts of water. She too carried the water a little distance and set it on the ground. I watched her pull out a pink bar of soap from her pocket. She rolled up the sleeves of her coat, carefully soaped her arms, hands, neck and face, returned the soap to the coat pocket, and rinsed herself. Last, she pulled out a handkerchief and dried her face. By then I had returned to Mother with the water, and I continued to watch while she cleaned my feet. The woman must have seen me stare; she briefly looked in my direction and seemed to smile. From one pocket she took a small comb, from the other a hand mirror, and combed her hair. All this she did naturally and unhurriedly, as if that was the way she had washed all her life. Her face was calm and, except for that brief smile in my direction, she paid no attention to the squabbling crowd at the pump, or to the despondent men and women in front of the barracks. As she slowly walked away with long swinging strides, one hand in her coat pocket, the other holding the small enamel pot, she seemed like someone from another world.

Again the hot sun rose and shone on the sweating, penned-in crowd. They got tired of milling and walking in circles. Families dropped into the dust, not talking to each other, eyes dulled by heat and hunger. Mothers held small children in their arms, too tired even to rock them to sleep. Great clouds of poisonous flies swarmed over the motionless people, who only troubled to brush them away when they crawled into their mouths or up their noses.

A tree, I thought, a tree to give shade, and green grass. I remembered the birds in the Dąbrowa square. Had they returned to their nests in the trees? If only one bird were to appear, I would consider it a good sign, I said to myself; only one bird. But none came.

On this day too, Father casually walked with me toward the barrack and, when he thought no one was watching, motioned me to run inside and hide. I quickly climbed up on the platform and crept behind our bundle. The effort had made me dizzy, and it seemed a long time before I caught my breath. The barrack was cool after the heat and dust outside. Exhausted, I dozed off.

And somewhere in my strange and disconnected dreams of cool forests and blueberries, a woman's voice, soft and full; "Shimon," it said, "don't be sad. Come, look at me, my love. We have each other for another day. You mustn't want more than that. We're beggars living on the dole of time. Beggars can't be greedy. A minute here, a minute there, my Shimon, don't waste the precious minutes."

"Don't talk like that, Halka. I love you. From the moment I saw you. Halinka, we mustn't lose each other. Not yet. I don't know how it is possible, this feeling between us when we're in such danger. Who knows what they're planning to do with us, tomorrow, the day after? Our love seems like a flame whose final flickers dazzle before it is extinguished and dies."

"Just like a poet. But why think of the future, foolish Shimon? Why argue with fate? There is no future. No tomorrow. Only now, this moment and the next. Maybe the rest of this day. Maybe the night. How long since we met? Three days? Three days ago, and yet it seems like I always knew you. What is time, Shimon? What meaning has it for us? Years, days, hours, they're all the same now. Listen to me, Shimon, I'll tell you a story, the story of our life together, how it might have been."

"Let's pretend we're back in Kraków. I have stopped on Floriańska Street, at Jama Michalika for a cup of coffee. It is spring, yes, late spring, maybe May, and I'm wearing my blue dress with the white collar, and white patent leather shoes. I have chosen a table next to the window; I want to watch the pigeons circling overhead. Suddenly a handsome young man, with eyes as deep as the sea, comes to my table. We look at each other for a long time, he takes my hand in his and asks me to marry him. I nod my head, too happy to speak. That was many years ago. We married and loved each other; with each passing day our love grew stronger. You became a famous lawyer, and I a children's doctor. You helped fight injustice, and I cured sick children. In time we had a lovely boy, with deep blue eyes like yours, and later a girl with thick black braids down to her waist. Our children grew up and married. Like us, they too knew how to love well. Grandchildren were born. Six. Yes, we wanted many grandchildren to fill the large apartment with their games and laughter. And we grew old, you and I, and whenever we went to Jama Michalika, we held hands and watched the pigeons circle overhead. Your brown hair turned gray, and my black head became white. There were wrinkles around our eyes; we said they were wrinkles of laughter, not of age. Sometimes our bones were a bit stiff, perhaps a touch of rheumatism. You even used a cane when we walked up Floriańska to the Main Market. One day, we knew, Shimon, we had to die. Were we afraid? Of course, everyone is afraid of dying. You and I feared most of all the loneliness of the one left behind. Only when one has loved and been loved, does one know that the black hole of loneliness is the absence of love. We prayed for strength, Shimon, strength for the one who remained to live out the allotment of days. After all, hadn't we.... Shimon, don't cry, my love."

The woman stopped speaking and I heard the man's heartbreaking sobs. Tears came to my eyes as well. I had not understood everything she said. Her voice had been low and gentle, as if she were telling a story to a child. A beautiful and sad story. I knew, of course, who it was that had been speaking so. I wished I could let them know that I was behind the bundle. I did not like eavesdropping, yet they must not know that I had been listening.

"Get out of here, you shameless whore," a hoarse voice suddenly hissed below, "you want to get us all killed?"

The sobs ceased. No one answered. It must be the one called Malke, the one I had heard the day before. "In broad daylight, they carry on like they're in Warsaw or Łódź. The fine miss, who thinks she is better than the rest of us with her soap and mirror. Get down here at once, and get out of this barrack. Better start counting the gold and diamonds you have in your coat seams. We'll see how the fine miss will manage tomorrow. Get moving," I heard the woman spit resoundingly.

Late that afternoon more people started pouring into the enclosure. They came, as we had two days earlier, exhausted and dusty, with bleeding wounds, and children more dead than alive. There were hurried exchanges with the newcomers. Where did they come from? Which villages and towns? Many dead? Had there been selections? The newcomers were not talkative. They dropped to the ground where they stood, too worn out to take any interest in their surroundings. Mother's face, which had seemed a little less frightened during the day, again became tense and worried. Her terrified eyes swept over the newly arrived men and women. Was she looking for a familiar face?

"You won't find anyone from home," said Father, his hand on her arm. "There are no Mielec people here, they remained in the Lublin area after the deportation. Only a few lucky ones made it back."

"What's so lucky about this?" said Mother.

"Did I hear you say you're from Mielec?" a young man, standing near Father, interrupted. "Don't you know what happened to the Mielec people? It's a miracle you're still alive, if you're from Mielec."

"What happened to them?" Mother's voice was nearly inaudible.

"How come you don't know, if you're from Mielec?" he asked suspiciously.

"The transport was split up when we got to the Lublin district, and some families were sent to Sosnowice. We completely lost touch with the others. We stayed there until after Pesach, when we paid a Pole to bring us one by one to Dąbrowa. Three days ago Dąbrowa was liquidated," Father explained.

"Sosnowice, eh," the man spoke rapidly as if he were in a great hurry. "I didn't know about Sosnowice. I was told everyone was killed, except for the people sent to Pustków. Listen to me," he said urgently, his face close to Father's. "No one believes me when I tell what's happening. But I know, I've had word; they're using gas. They're killing thousands each day. They used gas in Bełżec on the Mielec people; they're using it in Sobibór. You think if you work for them, they'll let you live? No, they want to kill every Jew. Save yourself if you can, believe me, I know, save yourself.... Jump off the train, if you're taken, don't stay on the train...."

Father listened intently and I thought I saw a look of disbelief in his face.

"They've brought the trains already," Mother whispered, and while Father turned to her the man disappeared in the tightly packed crowd.

That night the barrack was filled with the stench of fear and death.

The Fourth Day

"Would you like to wash yourself with my soap?" The gray-haired lady—Halka, the man had called her—handed me the pink bar of soap, when once more we had gone to wash ourselves, carefully picking our way through the excrement that was now everywhere.

"May I? Thank you," I said, forcing out the words. Fear had closed my throat and, every time I wanted to speak, I had to swallow hard. I carefully took the sweet-smelling soap from her hand. It was smoother than any soap I had ever held, delicate and luxurious, not at all like the rough, homemade soap we had used in Dąbrowa, and in the end forgot to take along. She stood next to me, tall and straight, in her wide coat, gently stroking my hair. I washed my hands, arms, neck and face, as I had seen her do the previous day, smelling the sweet perfume. For a moment, the stink of excrement and urine was less strong. I stared at my flea-bitten arms and hands, at the little red circles with a darker point in the middle, then I looked up at her. She was sad, and her deep gray eyes seemed focused on some distant point beyond the barracks and beyond the enclosure with its suffocating crowds.

"You may keep the soap," she said. "Somehow I feel that I won't have any use for it after today."

I wanted to say something encouraging. No words came. Today the selections would begin. The cattle cars stood on the siding, I had heard people say. Why was she so sure she'd be on the train? It must have been those nasty women and their ugly talk who put the thought in her head.

"Please," I started, but she stopped me and bent down. She put both hands on my shoulders. "Keep the soap," she repeated, "Make sure you live. Wash yourself every day, make yourself smell good as girls should."

She walked away and I soon lost sight of her in the crowd of people.

Our small group huddled together in the crush. All color had drained from Sister's pretty face. She held on to Cousin, whose glasses were so grimy I could barely see her eyes. They looked at each other every so often without saying a word and held hands more tightly. Mother seemed shrunken in her large checkered coat, and even Father sounded half-hearted as he tried to reassure us.

"Everything will be all right, Ruben promised. But we must be careful. It will pass, this day. You'll see. They won't take us." Mother was shaking uncontrollably and Father held her arm.

I touched the pink bar of soap in my coat pocket and felt its smooth, cool texture.

Rain clouds covered the sky and obscured the sun. The air became heavy and still, crushing the people beneath its gray weight. The people's shoulders sagged and their feet were rooted to the spot, clinging to the earth as if that would save them from being taken away. Men, women and children stood motionless in front of the barracks. The men's lips moved in silent prayer, and deep moans were heard in the crowd. As if the souls were pleading wordlessly for life this day. Children whimpered in their mothers' skirts, staring with big frightened eyes at the shiny boots of the German soldiers moving back and forth among the people.

A light drizzle began to fall on the standing multitude, covering heads, clothes and faces with fine gray droplets. And still the people stood hour after hour, all through that long day, the crowd thinning out as time went on. Old, bearded, bent-over men vanished, mothers with flocks of tiny children, old women, their faces hidden by dark shawls. Young boys and girls in the prime of life were suddenly gone. Families disappeared as if they had never been. And still the others stood, the groans now louder, the weeping greater, and the shouts of the Germans more brutal. Here a woman was clubbed with a rifle and fell into the wet dust, there a man staggered under the blows of a young soldier. Others dropped exhausted to the ground and didn't get up again. In the distance we heard shooting.

We stood together, and whenever I saw a pair of German soldiers approach I closed my eyes, pretending that I didn't exist. The drizzle turned to rain and, as we stood in the enclosure, the dust became mud, mud that squished through our toes and rose above our ankles. Waves of nauseating fear swept over me and in between each wave incoherent thoughts surfaced, only to disappear in the next wave. The shooting went on.

Finally this day ended and once again we were herded back into the barrack. It was much emptier. Now there was enough room for everyone to spread out. Bundles, suitcases, their owners no longer here, were lying all over the platforms. Father helped us climb up. We were weak, legs shaking uncontrollably. When was the last time we had eaten? I couldn't remember.

"It's over," Father said. "We are saved."

"Saved? Ha!" a man laughed eerily next to us. "For how long? Soon they'll take us too. Another week? Another month? Don't you know what's going on?" The man was covered with mud, his wet pants and shirt clung to his body. He leaned toward Father, swaying this way and that. His face was twisted and his eyes gleamed feverishly. "I was down there," he spoke rapidly in disconnected sentences, "at the trains. Thousands of people. A rabbi, don't know from where. With a long beard, beautiful man. They put a nightpot on his head, tore the clothes from his body. Paraded him up and down. Then shot him dead. Threw babies around. Smashed them. Dead everywhere. The end of the world. My God."

He put his head in his hands. "Listen, a hell. I was there. Stuffed Jews in the cattle cars, even the doors didn't close. They'll be dead before they get there. Where are they taking them, where?" He shook Father's arm as if Father had the answer.

"How did you get back here?" Mother asked.

"I crawled away in the rain, up the hillside. Crawled through the barbed wire, and stood again with the rest like I was never taken away. Left Sheine-Dvora and the baby down there."

The man stopped, his wide-open eyes staring blindly. "Sheine-Dvora," he mumbled. "Wait, I'm coming for you, Sheine-Dvora...." He moved his arms as if trying to get hold of something in order to stand up.

I moved away, frightened by the man's crazy behavior, while Father tried to quiet him. "Now, my friend," he said, taking hold of his hands, "don't lose hope. You may find your wife and child again. Tomorrow, yes, tomorrow perhaps."

For a moment the man looked at Father, then he threw back his head and howled, "Hope … tomorrow … that's a good one … the crazy Jew says hope…." He doubled over in a fit of coughing and Father patted him on the back.

I remembered the soap.

I carefully took it out of my pocket and held it in my hand. It was soft and slippery. Why did she leave me this gift? Was it perhaps a sign to me that I would live? Whoever had the soap would live, was that it? I should give it to the man, then he would know he'd live. But he is crazy and might not recognize how precious the soap is. I glanced at the man; he was mumbling to himself, spittle dribbling from his mouth. No, the soap was mine, at least for the time being. I gently stroked it and smelled the sweet perfume on my fingers. What had happened to the gray-haired lady? Had she really been taken away? I looked around the platform. Where she and the young man had been the night before, there was now someone else. Maybe they had moved to another place. I remembered that they had no possessions, and needn't come back here. Or was she already dead? I shouldn't have taken the soap from her. If she still had the soap she'd be alive. I so wanted her to live, even for a week, even for a month.

Darkness filled the barrack. Nearby, men were talking; their voices were toneless, brittle as if their bodies did not belong to them. In the far-off corner a woman was softly weeping. On the lower platform people were restlessly moving about. The man was still now, his black shape swaying back and forth. In the night, first one and then another long whistle of the locomotive was heard. The train was starting. A deadly stillness fell over the barrack. It was the end of the fourth day.

That August, more than 40 years ago….

⁓

Ephraim, my husband, was another teenager caught in the hurricane of World War II, facing other challenges in a world suddenly changed and unknown. I could not but compare Irene Eber's family deportation by the Germans with Ephraim's family deportation by the Soviet authorities to Siberia. Ephraim's father suffered imprisonment and fear of death. His family, in Siberia experienced fear, hunger, insecurity, and hardship, but were not sent to their death, and survived.

Irene's family, driven by foot under threat of death, under inhuman conditions, was sent to concentration camps, and, ultimately to their death. Only Irene, her mother and sister survived.

The European theater of World War II ended on May 8, 1945.

Postscript

The years 1939 through 1945 of World War II are known as the Holocaust period.

All wars are destructive, but this war surpassed all others in the numbers of its victims, and especially in the speed and mass methods of their annihilation.

Estimates vary as to the number of people who lost their lives during World War II, but according to many sources approximately 50 million people perished.

For the Jews, World War II had a special significance. Every Jewish man, woman and child was automatically condemned to death simply because they were Jews, and of the murdered people, authorities agree, 6 million were Jews. Of those, 3 million were the Jews of Poland alone.

The destruction of the Jews was not a by-product of the war. It was one of the major German objectives, planned and mercilessly implemented. Even as the German army was advancing and occupying the European lands, especially established units, the Einsatzkommandos, or German mobile killing squads, followed the army and carried out massive and widespread "actions," a Nazi euphemism for the immediate massacres of Jewish communities and deportation to death camps and ghettos. I was an eyewitness to the mass murder of the Jews in one such town in Eastern Poland. And even during the German defeat and retreat from Russia and other areas, the deportation of the Jews to the death camps by cattle trains continued.

But destroying the Jews was not sufficient.

The diabolical cruelty of the Germans has been well documented even by the Germans throughout the lands they had conquered. Humiliation, starvation, beatings, hangings, and forcing Jews dig their own graves were widespread and common.

How could this have happened?

A new leader, Adolf Hitler, who came to power in Germany in 1933, blamed the Jews for all of Germany's problems, such as unemployment, poverty and hunger. At that time, many other countries, such as the United States, experienced deep economic depression. Adolf Hitler promised the Germans full employment, prosperity, and rule over others, claiming the Germans were the "Master Race." According to the Nazi ideology, the Jews were an inferior race, and had to be destroyed as enemies of Germany. Hitler had many followers ready and willing to implement his plans. Others, fearing for their lives, kept silent, or had no power or courage to resist.

Scapegoating, or blaming a defenseless minority for national problems, was not new. It has been and still is practiced today by politicians to divert public attention from real causes of crises, and to gain popularity and power. While the Holocaust was, in steps, unfolding, even some politicians believed that by lack of resistance they bought "peace in our time." Anti-Semitism, or prejudice and an unfounded hatred of the Jews were well known, accepted, tolerated and practiced for centuries across Europe and in other areas of the world, and still are. Robbery was a significant motive for the destruction of the Jews during the Holocaust and at other times as well. Their properties were confiscated, and Jewish slave labor helped and contributed to the German economy and war effort.

Until September 1, 1939, the day World War II began, Poland was the greatest center of Jewish life and culture in the world. Approximately 3,400,000 Jews resided in Poland. Nearly three million of them perished during the Holocaust years at the hands of the Germans. My father was one of their victims. In contrast, never to be forgotten, Sweden, Finland, Denmark and Bulgaria helped their condemned Jewish brothers by evacuating them to safety or accepting the refugees in spite of the risks involved, or by evading German orders. In Poland, however, there was no outcry and no outrage against the total destruction of the Jews on Polish soil. Many Poles cooperated with the Germans, and even the mainstream Polish underground newspapers, *Narod* among them, opined that the Germans were helpful in solving their "Jewish Question": "'The Jewish Question' is now a burning issue. We must tell ourselves that the Jews cannot regain the political rights and the property they have lost. Moreover, they must entirely leave the territories of our country" (quoted from *Narod*).

Particularly poignant was the fate of children and even babies, who shared the fate of their parents. Well over one million Jewish children were murdered in the areas of German occupation, an entire generation of youth.

The Jews of Germany were in a "privileged" position. As Hitler came to power, the Nuremberg Laws of 1935 deprived Jews of their citizenship rights and dehumanized Jews by caricatures, depicting them as ugly, blood- and money-hungry monsters. The ensuing persecution served as fore- runners of things to come and a warning to some. Many escaped. Others hoped that their lack of resistance would prevent further evil.

Some had foresight of things to come. Groups of Jewish children were sent to what was then Palestine, today Israel, and were cared for by the Jewish community.

Prior to the actual outbreak of the war, during the last months of 1938, Great Britain, to its eternal credit, rescued 10,000 children from Germany, Czechoslovakia, Austria and the Free City of Danzig. With lightning speed arrangements were made, laws passed and funds obtained, and the Kindertransport children, sent by their weeping parents "into the arms of strangers" were admitted, received and distributed to children's homes, farms and foster families. All of them survived, grew up to become members of their communities, formed long-term friendships and loyalties to England and some lived to tell their stories. Most of them never saw their parents again. It was one of the finest chapters in the multi-layered history of Jewish-British relations.

Children's identification card issued by the German police to Igne Engelhard, in which she has been given the middle name of "Sara" and declared stateless. She was one of the lucky children of the Kindertransport who were reunited with their parents after the war. Most Kindertransport children never saw their parents again.

In Poland, a brave and righteous minority helped the Jews at a risk to their own lives, since sheltering a Jew was punishable by death. Convents saved many Jewish children, mostly girls, but also boys. I personally knew Hanka and Renia, who were saved in convents.

Other children, smuggled out of the ghettos were hidden in underground bunkers, bathrooms, attics and closets, or in plain sight as Christians, sheltered or adopted by Christian families. Some survived. Each one of the survivors has a different story to tell. Eva's story is mine, but some names have been changed and some locations omitted to protect the privacy of the people involved who may still be living and subjected to suffering for sheltering a Jew, as had happened in some cases following World War II.

I hope this story will help young people and all others to learn about the Holocaust from a personal perspective, through the eyes of a young girl, and the role, power and obligations of individuals who played a role in determining her destiny. Their help during a critical day, hour, minute or year made the difference between life and death. I hope the readers will recognize the evil effects or results of discrimination, and be inspired to become members of a different generation, rejecting prejudice of any kind, before it erupts into another Holocaust. To help prevent it, read and remember.

Appendix
Chronology, 1933–1945
Major Events of World War II with Emphasis on the Holocaust and the Events in Our Lives

January 30, 1933—Adolf Hitler is appointed chancellor of Germany.

March 1933—One of the first concentration camp opens in Dachau, Germany.

April 1, 1933—Boycott of Jewish stores and other businesses.

May 10, 1933—Burning of books written by Jews, political opponents and others rejected by the Nazi regime.

September 15, 1935—The Nuremberg Laws are passed in Germany denying Jews German citizenship and citizenship rights.

October 25, 1936—Hitler and Mussolini sign a treaty, forming the Berlin-Rome Axis.

1937—Eva's parents separate. Eva comes to live with Father, while Michael remains with Mother. Michael leaves for Palestine.

March 12, 1938—*Anschluss*: Germany incorporates Austria into the Third Reich.

Summer, 1938—Mother leaves illegally for Palestine.

October 28, 1938—Germany expels Jews born in Poland. Eva's father helps the refugees.

November 9–10, 1938—*Kristallnacht*, the Night of Broken Glass. Jewish stores and homes are invaded and vandalized. Synagogues are burned. Jews are brutalized in the streets.

Approximately 30,000 Jews are deported to concentration camps.

March 1939—Germany occupies Czechoslovakia.

August 23, 1939—Germany and the Soviet Union sign a mutual non-aggression pact, and agree to divide Poland between them.

September 1, 1939—Germany invades Poland. World War II begins. Bombing of Warsaw. Eva survives with father.

September 3, 1939—Britain and France declare war on Germany.

September 17, 1939—The Soviet Union invades and occupies the eastern part of Poland, including Ephraim's hometown, Otynia. The river Bug is part of the dividing borders.

September 27, 1939—Warsaw surrenders to Germany. Soon German forces occupy Warsaw. Jews are singled out for abuse.

September–December 1939—Persecution of Jews in Poland continues. Economic sanctions are imposed. First ghetto established. Jews are forced to wear an identifying mark, such as a yellow star or a white armband with a blue Star of David. Eva and father escape across the river Bug to the Soviet Union (USSR) zone.

November 1939—Eva is admitted to the orphanage.

The 1940s—Michael, Eva's brother, joins the British Armed Forces to protect Palestine.

April 1940—Ephraim and his family are deported to Siberia by the Soviet authorities, following the imprisonment of his father.

April 9, 1940—Germany invades Denmark.

May 10, 1940—Germany invades Belgium, France, Luxembourg, and Holland.

July–August 1940—Massive bombing of British targets. The Battle of Britain begins.

September 27, 1940—The Tripartite Pact: Japan joins Germany and Italy, expanding the Axis Powers and promising to assist each other, including offering military help.

November 15, 1940—Warsaw Ghetto is surrounded by walls and sealed.

June 22, 1941—Germany attacks and invades the Soviet Union (Operation Barbarossa). Eva and father find themselves under German rule again. Soon after, the systematic mass murder of Jews in Eastern Poland and Russia begins.

July 31, 1941—Reinhard Heydrich is appointed to carry out the annihilation of the Jews in German-occupied territories.

July–August 1941—Many thousands of Jews are murdered by the Einsatzgruppen (extermination units) in the German-occupied, formerly Polish and Russian territories.

Beginning of August 1941—Eva's father is ordered by the Germans to report for a day of compulsory labor. He never returns.

Summer, 1941—Towards the end of summer, the total annihilation of the Jews of Otynia begins.

Mass murder of the Jews of Otynia in the Szeparowce forest. A plaque in memory of the murdered Jewish victims at the edge of the Szeparowce forest was vandalized in June 1944 and replaced.

September 29, 1941—Over 33,000 Jews murdered at Babi Yar, near Kiev. The annihilation of Jews in Russian territories continues.

December 7, 1941—Japan attacks the U.S. naval base at Pearl Harbor, Hawaii.

December 8, 1941—The United States declares war on Japan.

December 11, 1941—The United States declares war on Germany.

1942—Partisan movement in forests, especially in Byelorussia, eastern Poland, and Jewish armed resistance organized in many ghettos.

January 20, 1942—The Wannsee Conference in Berlin on the destruction of the Jews of Europe and the solution to the Jewish Question: "The Final Solution."

April 1942—Mass extermination of Jews begins in the Bełżec and Sobibór death camps.

Spring, 1942—Eva arrives at the farm.

July 1942—Treblinka II extermination camp established.

August 23, 1942—The battle for Stalingrad begins, ending on February 2, 1943, with German defeat and surrender.

September 25, 1942—The remnants of the Jews of Otynia murdered by Germans and Ukrainian police.

April 19, 1943—The Warsaw Ghetto Uprising begins.

October 1943—The rescue of Danish Jewry. Expulsion of Danish Jews planned by Germans. The Danes help over 7,000 Jews escape to Sweden. Few are captured.

October 14, 1943—Revolt in the Sobibór death camp.

June 6, 1944—D-Day: The invasion of Europe by the Allied forces begins in Normandy, France.

November 1944—Ephraim's family returns to Poland from Siberia.

July 1944—Majdanek concentration camp liberated by Soviet troops.

October 7, 1944—Uprising in Auschwitz.

January 1945—Soviet troops liberate Auschwitz.

January 1945—Soviet troops liberate Warsaw following a revolt by Poles.

April 1945—Buchenwald and Dachau concentration camps liberated by American forces. Bergen-Belsen liberated by British forces.

April 30, 1945—Hitler commits suicide.

May 7, 1945—Germany surrenders to the Allies.

May 8, 1945—V-E Day: The war in Europe ends.

June 1945—Eva returns to Poland.

August 6 and 9, 1945—Atomic bombs dropped on Hiroshima and Nagasaki.

September 2, 1945—Japan formally surrenders. World War II ends.

November 20, 1945—Nuremberg trials of German leaders begin.

May 1946—Eva arrives in Palestine and is reunited with her mother.

Spring, 1947—Hava meets a new friend, her husband-to-be, Ephraim Ben-Zvi.

November 29, 1947—The United Nations Partition Resolution to divide Palestine into two states: Arab and Jewish.

December 30, 1947—Attack on Jews in the Haifa Oil Refinery.

May 14, 1948—The State of Israel, the Jewish National Homeland is proclaimed.

June 4, 1948—Arab airplanes attack Tel Aviv.

June 10, 1948—Ephraim wounded at Mishmar Ha-Jarden, in the Galilee.

Academic year 1950-51—Hava's first job as a teacher in Yokneam.

September 4, 1950—Hava and Ephraim married.

May 16, 1953—A son, Igal Henry Ben-Zvi, is born.

1954—Ephraim graduates with distinction from an officer training course and is decorated by Yitzhak Rabin, then chief of staff of the Israel Defense Forces, and later the prime minister of Israel.

1956—Ephraim comes to the United States on a scholarship from the University of California.

May 1957—Hava and Igal arrive in the United States, joining Ephraim in Davis, California.

1961—Ephraim joins the faculty of the Immaculate Heart College.

March 28, 2009—Ephraim's life ends.

Bibliographic Essay

This bibliographic essay is different from many others. It is rather a conversation between us, the author and the reader, about the selected resources I have used in my work to fill in the missing pieces of information, to broaden my own horizons by learning about the period, and about other survivors' experiences through memoirs and diaries; to hear the voices of those who did not survive; to shed light upon rescue operations, heroism and sacrifice, upon postwar events; and to illuminate contrasting perspectives on historical events. I thought some readers may find these notes interesting and informative.

For example: Consider the differences in perspectives between *The Black Book of Polish Jewry* and Raul Hilberg's *Documents of Destruction: Germany and Jewry 1933–1945*.

Apenszlak, Jacob, Jacob Kenner, Isaac Lewin, and Moses Polakiewicz, eds. *The Black Book of Polish Jewry: An Account of the Martyrdom of Polish Jewry Under the Nazi Occupation*. New York: The American Federation for Polish Jews in cooperation with the Association of Jewish Refugees and Immigrants from Poland, 1943.
These grim, unvarnished accounts of unspeakable cruelties and atrocities, fully described and p9+p9 documented from the Jewish perspective, provide a stark contrast with parts of Hilberg's *Documents of Destruction*, public documents from the German point of view.

Appleman-Jurman, Alicia. *Alicia: My Story*. New York: Bantam Books, 1988.
A heartbreaking young girl's memoir of the Holocaust in Poland. Alicia describes the death of each member of her loving family, and the different faces of human cruelty. In spite of this, she selflessly, heroically helped others.

Bascomb, Neal. *Nazi Hunters: How a Team of Spies and Survivors Captured the World's Most Notorious Nazi*. New York: Arthur R. Levine Books, 2013.
A riveting, powerful and suspenseful spy thriller documenting the historical facts of the capture and trial in Jerusalem of Adolf Eichmann, who organized the seizure and delivery to their death of eleven million people, six million of them Jews. Detailed documentation, notes, index.

Bitton-Jackson, Livia. *I Have Lived A Thousand Years*. New York: Simon & Schuster, 1997.

Elli was thirteen in 1944, happy, carefree and looking forward to attending a new school in Budapest. Her life changes without warning with the German invasion of Hungary. Deported to concentration camps, she fights for survival and tells her story in all its pain and horror, including her hope and will to live. Chronology, glossary.

Boas, Jacob. *We Are Witnesses: Diaries of Five Teenagers Who Died in the Holocaust*. New York: Henry Holt, 1995.

David, Yitzhak, Moshe, Eva and Anne (Frank) lived in different places in German-occupied Europe. Their stories, while different, all reflect their strength and ability to face the unspeakable, their struggle to live and to grow, and their hope, until the very end. Index.

Buergenthal, Thomas. *A Lucky Child: A Memoir of Surviving Auschwitz as a Young Boy*. Foreword by Elie Wiesel. New York: Little, Brown, 2009. First English-language edition published in Great Britain by Profile Books, 2009. First American edition, April 2009. Originally published in Germany by Fischer Verlag, as Ein Glückskind, 2007.

Ten-year-old Thomas arrived at Auschwitz with his parents and by a stroke of luck avoided the initial selection of who will live and who will die. Separated from his parents, he learned to survive Auschwitz, and then Sachsenhausen, aided by his luck, instincts, non-Jewish looks, perfect German and Polish language skills, and the sheer force of his will to live. Today a judge at the International Court of Justice in The Hague, he tells his story of horrors simply and calmly, from the distance of more than fifty years. Family photographs.

Churchill, W. S. *The Second World War*. Boston: Houghton Mifflin in Association with the Cooperation Publishing Company, 1948–1953. Copyright 1948 by the Houghton Mifflin. 6 vols.

A detailed history of World War II, written in clear and readable language, including strategies, names, dates and places. Index to each volume.

Eisenberg, Azriel. *The Lost Generation*. New York: The Pilgrim Press, 1982.

A most impressive collection of authentic, primary documents: first-hand accounts by survivors, witnesses and others, in historical context. Parts especially recommended: "We will Not Hand Over the Children Alive" by Fredka Mazia; "Janusz Korczak Marches to Death With His Children." Selections reprinted also in Ben-Zvi, H., ed., *Portraits in Literature: The Jews of Poland. An Anthology*. London: Vallentine Mitchell, 2011.

Eisenberg, Azriel. *Witness to the Holocaust*. New York: The Pilgrim Press, 1981.

Testimony of the Holocaust based on heartbreaking primary documents from diaries, memoirs, letters and other sources, focusing on the fate of the Jews.

Fox, Anne L., and Eva Abraham-Podietz. *Ten Thousand Children: True Stories Told by Children Who Escaped the Holocaust with Kindertransport*. West Orange, N.J.: Berhrman House, 1999.

Excellent historical background and photographs. Told in personal, moving terms. The reader's involvement is reinforced by up-to-date information about the children as adults.

Gilbert, Martin. *The Holocaust: A History of the Jews of Europe During the Second World War*. New York: Holt, Rinehart and Winston, 1985.

An authoritative, well researched and fully documented account of a devastating time in history.

Greenfeld, Howard. *The Hidden Children.* New York: Ticknor & Fields, 1993.
Between one and one and a half million Jewish children were killed by the Germans during World War II. Helping a Jew or hiding a Jewish child was punishable by death in Poland. And yet thousands of children survived, hidden by people who risked their own lives to save them. This is the story of thirteen boys and girls who were hidden and saved under different circumstances.

Gruber, Ruth. *Destination Palestine: The Story of the Haganah Ship Exodus 1947.* New York: Current Books, 1948.
The dramatic story of the attempt by S.S. *Exodus 1947* to bring its passengers, 1,600 men, 1,282 women, and 1,672 children, all Holocaust survivors, to the only place on earth that wanted them, Palestine, their Promised Land. It describes the unequal battle between the British Government and the desperate survivors. The British refused to allow them to land in Palestine, and following a painful sojourn in Port De Bouc, France, the refugees were returned to camps in Germany. Jewish organizations smuggled some of them to Palestine, and after the establishment of the State of Israel in May 1948, all the refugees reached Palestine.

Gut Opdyke, Irene, with Jennifer Armstrong. *In My Hands: Memories of a Holocaust Rescuer.* New York: Dell Laurel-Leaf, 1999.
"When forced to work as a housekeeper of a Nazi major, she hid twelve Jews in the basement of his home until the German defeat." Irene Gut was seventeen, a student nurse, a Polish patriot, a good Catholic girl. A story of courage, sacrifice, strength and moral conviction. Irene was granted the Israel Medal of Honor, Israel's highest honor and the Vatican honored her with a special commendation.

Harris, Mark Jonathan, and Deborah Oppenheimer. *Into the Arms of Strangers: Stories of the Kindertransport.* Preface by Lord Richard Attenborough. Introduction by David Cesarani. New York: Bloomsbury, 2000.
The story of Britain's extraordinary rescue mission of ten thousand children from Germany, Austria, and Czechoslovakia within the Kindertransport. In the words of the rescued children, parents, foster parents and rescuers, we hear about the agony and hope of sending their children "into the arms of strangers" to save them. Most of those saved never saw their parents again. The book is based on the feature-length documentary film *Into the Arms of Strangers: Stories of the Kindertransport.*

Hilberg, Raul, ed. *Documents of Destruction: Germany and Jewry 1933–1945.* Chicago: Quadrangle Books, 1971.
The documents, complete with sources, have been derived from German public records, while Jewish records are mostly personal and autobiographical. Jewish public records were frequently destroyed, along with the burning ghettos. The perspectives are, accordingly, those of perpetrators rather than victims. Hilberg presents details of German actions recorded in small villages and cities, which together add up to a wide panorama of destruction. Even a Holocaust veteran such as I was still shocked by some of the reports of the facts and attitudes of the soldiers, signed by their commander. For example:

> Open Air Killings in Russia.
> On June 27, 1942.
> In the course of this action we cleared the Jewish ghetto in Slonim. About 4000 Jews were laid to rest that day.
> From July 25 to 27, new pits are dug.

On July 28, major action in Minsk Russian ghetto: 6000 Jews are brought to the pits.
On July 29, 3000, Jews are brought to the pits.
The following days were filled with cleaning weapons and repair again.
The behavior of the men, on and off duty is good and gives rise to no complaints.

Arlt
SS-Sergeant

Kacer, Kathy. *Hiding Edith: A True Story*. Toronto: Second Story Press, 2006.

The remarkable true story of Edith, born in Vienna in 1932, who survived the Holocaust in a children's home in Moissac, southern France, run by a young French couple. The home was heroically protected by an entire town. Written from a child's perspective.

Khavlyuk, Mykhailo. *Otyniya: Historical Essays*. Trans. Philip Spiegel. Los Altos, CA: P. Siegel, 2000.

Mr. Khavlyuk "has done considerable research on the history of this town and its surroundings." This work traces the history of Otyniya from ancient times through 1991. The annihilation of the Jewish population is described on pages 56–57. Mr. Khavlyuk was the mayor of Otyniya.

Kramer, Clara, with Stephen Glantz. *Clara's War: One Girl's Story of Survival*. New York: HarperCollins, 2009. Originally published in Great Britain by Ebury Press, 2008.

Based on a diary of fifteen-year-old Clara Kramer, who was hidden for twenty months in an underground bunker, writing the details of her life during those terrifying months. Eighteen people lived in the bunker. The original diary is in the U.S. Holocaust Memorial Museum in Washington, D.C.

Laskier, Rutka. *Rutka's Notebook: A Voice from the Holocaust*. Jerusalem: Yad Vashem, The Holocaust Martyrs' and Heroes' Memorial Authority, and Time, Inc. Home Entertainment, 2008.

Rutka, a fourteen-year-old girl in Będzin, Poland, describes her inner life, within her community of friends, her complex and difficult relationship with parents, and the horrors of the reality around her. She is a witness to unspeakable cruelty and fully aware of her own approaching deportation and death. A primary document testifying to the life of youth under the threat of certain death. In August 1943, Rutka and her family were deported to Auschwitz and perished. Included are an Introduction by Zahava (Laskier) Scherz, Rutka's half-sister; a biography of Yaakov Laskier, Rutka's father; "My Search for Rutka's Family" by Menachem Lior; "The Holocaust in Będzin" by Bella Gutterman; "'Something Has Broken in Me': The Diary of Rutka Laskier and the Writings of Jewish Youth in the Holocaust" by Havi (Ben-Sasson) Dreifuss; "Adolescent Holocaust Diaries: A Selected Bibliography" by Havi (Ben-Sasson) Dreifuss. Photographs.

Ligocka, Roma, with Iris von Finckenstein. *The Girl in the Red Coat: A Memoir*. Trans. Margot Bettauer Dembo. New York: St. Martin's Press, 2002.

Roma Ligocka was born in Kraków, Poland, in 1938. The author relates experiencing German searches and massacres from a very young child's perspective. As Roma grows up, she describes her later life.

Lobel, Anita. *No Pretty Pictures: A Child of War*. New York: Greenwillow Books, 1998.

The author, saved by her nanny, today a distinguished, award-winning illustrator of children's books, tells her story as a Jewish child in German occupied Poland. Five years old at the start of the war in 1939, she experienced a life in hiding, in the ghetto and in concentration camps. After the war, she was fortunate to find refuge in Sweden. A powerful tale, told with sincerity and feeling. A sentence not to be forgotten: "Nanny, are they going to kill us tonight?" Lobel lives in the U.S.

Meltzer, Milton. *Never to Forget: The Jews of the Holocaust.* New York: Harper & Row, 1976.
    A comprehensive yet concise history of the destruction of the Jews of Europe, including poetry, songs, letters, statistics, chronology, bibliography, index.

Meltzer, Milton. *Rescue: The Story of How Gentiles Saved Jews in the Holocaust.* New York: Harper & Row, 1988.
    Using diaries, letters, eyewitness accounts, interviews and memoirs, the author records and describes the decency of ordinary people who, risking their own lives, saved many Jews during the Holocaust. Maps, bibliography, index.

Muller, Melissa. *Anne Frank: The Biography.* With a note by Miep Gies. Trans. Rita and Robert Kimber. New York: Henry Holt, 1998.
    An impressive, readable, multi-layered biography of Anne Frank, utilizing interviews with many remaining family members and friends, revealing information unknown until this time and shedding much light on Anne's character, background, beliefs and hopes. In the end, we are taken back to Anne's own words.

Nieuwsma, Milton, ed. *Kinderlager: An Oral History of Young Holocaust Survivors.* New York: Holiday House, 1998.
    Personal stories of the young children imprisoned in the Kinderlager, a section of the Auschwitz-Birkenau concentration camp. Detailed descriptions of the camp and life before, during and after the war. Photographs, maps.

Novac, Ana. *The Beautiful Days of My Youth: My Six Months in Auschwitz and Plaszow.* Trans. from the French by George L. Newman. New York: Henry Holt, 1992.
    A primary document, written in Auschwitz by a fifteen-year-old girl, sobering and unsparing. And yet, Ana is able to describe these horror-filled days with an author's perspective and even a touch of humor. Index.

Oren, Ram. *Gertruda's Oath: A Child, a Promise and a Heroic Escape During World War II.* New York: Doubleday, 2009.
    Michael was only three years old when the war broke out, in 1939, in Poland. Michael's father left for France to settle his business interests, leaving Michael with his mother and Gertruda, his Catholic nanny. Michael's mother died of a stroke. Nanny, who loved Michael as her own, promised his mother she would save Michael and bring him to Israel. The story recreates Gertruda and Michael's journey, the dangers and the people who helped them, including an SS officer. A tale of courage and moral strength. Family pictures.

Peters, Joan. *From Time Immemorial: The Origins of the Arab-Jewish Conflict Over Palestine.* New York: Harper & Row, 1984.

Rabinovici, Schoschana. *Thanks to My Mother.* New York: Dial Books, 1998.
    A heartbreaking report of the day-by-day destruction of the Jews of Vilnius, Lithuania, through the eyes of Susie, eight years old in 1941. Susie survived life in the ghetto, several concentration camps and a death march, thanks to the love, courage and ingenuity of her mother, who at one point hid her in a backpack.

Reinhartz, Henia. *Bits and Pieces: Memoirs.* Toronto: The Azrieli Foundation, 2007. Azrieli Series of Holocaust Survivors Memoirs.

An award-winning, exceptionally vivid and detailed memoir, describing facts and feelings by teenaged Henia, born in Łódź, Poland. Through ghettos, deportations, concentration and death camps, Henia survived to build a new life in Canada. Glossary, index, bibliographical references.

Rochman, Hazel. *Bearing Witness: Stories of the Holocaust.* New York: Orchard Books, 1995.

An anthology of stories from children's and adult literature, reflecting the conditions and feelings of the victims, the rescuers and the bystanders. Index. Note: An annotated bibliography is available in a special issue of *Booklist*, June 1, 1989, "Remembering the Holocaust." In this case I wished to see books published earlier, and closer to the described events.

Rosenberg, Blanca. *To Tell at Last: Survival Under False Identity, 1941–45.* Urbana: University of Illinois Press, 1993.

Blanca, born in Poland shortly before World War I, was a young mother when the effects of World War II reached her in 1941, in Eastern Poland. She tells her story of hiding from the Germans, losing her child and landing in Heidelberg, Germany, where she survived, working as a maid until liberation. Blanca tells her story, sparing no details. Today, Blanca Rosenberg is a retired associate professor of social work at Columbia University and has a private practice as a psychotherapist. Photographs, index.

Rosenberg, Göran. *A Brief Stop on the Road from Auschwitz.* Trans. from the Swedish by Sarah Death. Ed. John Cullen. New York: Other Press, 2012.

A young journalist describes his father's life and struggle to survive the aftermath of Auschwitz and to build a new life in an industrial city in Sweden. Originally published in Sweden. Winner of the August Prize, 2012.

Wiesel, Elie. *Night.* Trans. from the French by Marion Wiesel. New York: Hill and Wang, 2006. Originally published in French by Les Editions de Minuit, 1958.

"If in my lifetime I was to write only one book, this would be the one." In simple, everyday words Elie Wiesel describes the unspeakable. We see the young boy in his small town, Sighet in Transylvania, his family, his synagogue, we feel his deep faith, and follow him through death and horrors, to Buchenwald and liberation. The book today is in the curriculum of high schools and many colleges. Includes Wiesel's Nobel Prize acceptance speech, delivered in Oslo on December 10, 1986.

Wiesenthal, Simon. *Every Day Remembrance Day: A Chronicle of Jewish Martyrdom.* New York: Henry Holt, 1987. Originally published in French by Editions Robert Laffont, 1986.

"Simon Wiesenthal has compiled a chronology that shows how easily prejudice can descend into barbarism." Following the calendar, this Book of Days, January 1 through December 31, records Jewish suffering, using existing documents, through World War II. This heartbreaking calendar of events is preceded by a narrative history of Jewish martyrdom and followed by a detailed index of places.

Wood, Angela. *Holocaust: The Events and Their Impact on Real People.* Foreword by Steven Spielberg. New York: DK Publishing, 2007.

A magnificent, oversized 190-page volume, presenting the history of the Holocaust, combining text and images, facts, maps, and statistics. The chapters are: The Jews of Europe, The Nazi Rule, The Ghettos, The Murder of the Victims, Clinging to Life, The

End of the War, and The Aftermath. Accompanied by a DVD of survivors' testimonies from the University of Southern California Shoah Foundation Institute of Visual History and Education.

See also online: "The Trial of Adolf Eichmann."

Zapruder, Alexandra, ed. *Salvaged Pages: Young Writers' Diaries of the Holocaust.* New Haven: Yale University Press, 2002.

Voices of young writers, many of whom perished, speak to us directly, in their words. Zapruder comments and interprets the authors' feelings and conditions, using psychological, sociological and historical insights. A film and companion study guide based on *Salvaged Pages* is available: *I'm Still Here: Real Diaries of Young People During the Holocaust,* Brookline, MA: Facing History and Ourselves.

Index

Numbers in ***bold italics*** indicate pages with illustrations

Abir, Michael Bromberg (brother) *12*, 14–*17*, 20, *21*, *23*, 24, 52, 107–*110*, 139, 147, 160, 169, 184, 205–206, 213
Aliyah Bet 103
Alterman, Nathan x, 151
American Jewish Joint Distribution Committee (AJJDC) 101
Anders, General Wladyslaw 137
Anders army 138
anti-Semitism 7, 19, 43, 46, 67, 103, 122, 123, 133, 174, 181, 201
Arabs 146–150, 152–153, 181
Auschwitz 8, 97, 110, 207, 210, 212–214

Balfour, Lord Arthur James 24
bar mitzvah 145, 168–*169*
Begin, Menachem 138, 148
Belzek 141
Ben-Gurion, David 150
Ben-Zvi, Daniel (grandson) 170, *171*
Ben-Zvi, Ephraim (husband) 1–8, 115, *116–117*, 118–120, *120–122*, 122–126, 129–130, 133–139, 142–144, 148–*149*, 152, *156–157*, 158–*164*, 166–171, *172–173*, 174–175, *176*, 179–*181*, 183; see also Sokal, Rysio
Ben-Zvi, Hava, books by 177
Ben-Zvi, Henry Igal (son) xi, 158, *170*, 179–183, 208
Ben-Zvi, Michael (grandson) 170, *171*, 172, 176
Ben-Zvi, Sarah (granddaughter) x, *170–171*
Bonaparte, Napoleon 29–30
Brichah 98–99, 103, 113
Bromberg, Dinah Lewartowska (mother) 11, *12–13*, 17, 19, *21*–22, 24–25, *32*–33, *34*–*35*, 38, 42, 56, 94, 107–108, 111, 114, 147, 160, *177*, *184*
Bromberg, Herman (father) *12–13*, 17–*18*,
19–20, 24, 26–28, *30*–31, 34, 42, 48, 50–53, 59, 60, 62–64, 66, 72, 86, 114, 184
Bromberg, Leib (uncle) 184
Bromberg, Lusia (aunt) 26, 184
Bromberg, Maryla (cousin by marriage) xi, 96, 113
Bromberg, Michael see Abir, Michael Bromberg (brother)
Bromberg, Romek (uncle) 26, 184
Bromberg, Victor (uncle) 26, 184
Bromberg, Zygmund (cousin) xi, 27, 50, 55, 95–96, 113, 184

California Institute of Technology see Caltech
Caltech 168, 171–172
camp, German 88–89
The Choice: Poland, 1939-1945 185–198
compulsory labor 62, 64, 90, 106, 202, 207
convents 61, *62*, 63, 106, 202
The Cow in the Cellar 7, 135
Czechoslovakia 39, 99, 113, 202, 206, 211
Częstochowa 27, 50, 55, 96, 184

Dąbrowa 185–187, 190, 194, 196
Danish Jewry 207
dates of annihilation 140–141, 206–207
Davis, California 166–167, 208
Debica 189–190
Deggendorf 101, 104
Delaney, Molly (daughter-in-law) *170*
displaced persons (DP) 2, 98, 101, 103

eating days 29
Eber, Irene (Irena) ix, 27, 85, 184–185, 198–199
Egypt 108–109, 138, 150
Einsatzkommandos 200
Encyclopedia of Jewish Communities—Poland x, 140, 141

Index

SS *Exodus* 97–98, **99–100**, 211
Facing History and Ourselves x, 215
family relationships, farm 85–88
Feiga Zisl (grandmother) 28–31
First Ottynier Young Men's Benevolent Society x, 144–145

German records of destruction 140
Gestapo 141
ghetto 53, **54–57**, 61, 76–77, 141, 191, 200, 202, 206–207, 211–214
Great Britain 90, 202, 206, 210–212; army 108–**109**, 115–**116**, 139, 144, 167, 184, 206; kindertransport 202, 210–211; mandate 24
Green, Sister Agnes Ann 172, **173**, 174, 179
Grimes, Carol x, **176**, 179

Haifa 105, 107–108, 110, 113, 115–116, 138–139, 144, 146, 152, 154, 156, 162, 168–**169**, 180, 208; liberation 98–**99**, 149–**150**
Hatikvah 105, 150
Heydrich, Reinhard 206
Hitler, Adolf 40, 43, **44**, 45, 59, 201, 205, 208
Holocaust 1–3, 5–6, 8, 60, 94, 97–98, 103, 114–116, 124, 128, 141, 145, 147, 150, 159–160, 169–170, 180, 185, 201–203, 205, 209–215
The Holocaust Martyrs and Heroes Remembrance Authority *see* Yad Vashem

Ilienkowa, Nina Luszczyk ix, 34–36
Immaculate Heart College 170, **172**, 174–175, 179, 208
Irgun Tzevai Leumi 146, 148
Isenberg, Madeleine x
Israel 98, 103, 139, 150–151, 158, 208, 211; declaration of independence 150; defense forces 138, 150, 153, 161, **164**

Jerusalem 19, 105, 113, 142, 148, 151, 154, 209, 212
Jewish Agency 101, 139, 150
Jewish-British relations 24, 25, 202
Jewish Community Library of Los Angeles 174–**175**
Jewish Council *see* Judenrat
Jewish National Fund **22**
Jews, annilation of 140, 141, 142, 143, 144
Judenrat (Jewish Council) 49–50, 64, 185
Julek *see* Sokal, Julek

Khavlyuk, Mykhailo x 140–141, 212
kibbutz **24**–25, 97, 139, 155, 216
King Matia the First 39
Kohen 160
kolkhoz 128–131, 134
Korczak, Janusz 39, **40**, 57–58
kosher 64, 83, 118

Kraków 192, 194, 212
Kristallnacht 45, 46, 205

Lachowicze 60, 92, 65–68
Latner, Herbert and Norman x, 145
League of Nations 24
Lewartowska, Chawa (grandmother) *31*
Lewartowska, Dinah Bromberg (mother) *see* Bromberg, Dinah Lewartowska (mother)
Lewartowski, Akiba (grandfather) **28**
liberation **62**, 89, 90–92, 214
Łódź 95, 195, 214
Lost Generation 170, 210
Lublin 185, 195
Lutsenko 142
Lvov 117, 120, 142

Majdanek 191, 207
Marcus, Colonel David 151
McDermott, Irene x
Medem Sanatorium 37–38
the Mediterranean 138
Mielec 27, 184, 189, 191, 195–196
Mishmar Ha-Yarden 152, 208
money 7, 35–36, 50, 55, 60, 94–95, 123, 130, 134, 181, 192, 202
Murphy, Marti Tippens x

name change 120, 139
nanny *see* Niania
Niania 14–15, 74
North Africa 108, 139
Nuremberg Laws 43, 202, 205

officers training course 208
open air killings 140–143, 211
Organization for Rehabilitation and Training (ORT) 101, 113, 175
Otynia x, 117, 118, 119, 121, 123, 124, 134, 206, 207; Jews x, 140; landsmannschaft 144

Palestine 16, 20–25, 38, 43, 52, 56, 63–63, 92, 94, 96–99, 101, 103–111, 113–115, 123, 138, 139, 146–148, 150–151, 155, 170, 184, 202, 205–206, 208, 211, 214; immigration 23–26, 43, 52, 63, 92, 94, 96–99, 101, 103–111, 113, 115, 123, 138–139, 146–148, 150, 155, 169, 205–206, 216
Pas, Justine x, 1, 4
SS *Patria* 97–98
Patton, General George 103
Pidyon ha-Ben 159
Polish: history 29, 37, 47–49, 59, 124, 128, 137–138, 140, 142, 200–202, 205; life 2, 6, 9, 11, 14, 20, 25, 34, 37–38, 40, 43, 47, 50–51, 61–**62**, 71, 76, 94, 117, 123, 185; refugees 1, 52–53, 55–56, 67–68, 91, 94–95, 97–99, 103, 107, 113, 115, 117, 125, **127**, 132, 135, 144, 184, 208–214

population movement 99, 142
priest **62-63**, 67, 74, 122, 123, 160
Promised Land 97, 106, 123, 211
Pustków 196

Rabbi Joshua, princess story 27
Rabin, Itzhak **164**-165, 208
Raizen, Esther x, 151
Ramat, David 139, 155
refineries 146
Reichman family 27
Russia: history 29, 48-51, 59, 90, 137-138, 140, 200, 206-207, 212; language 2, 55, 68, 72-73, 77, 84-85, 89, 127, 129, 132, 134-135; life 51-53, 59-60, 65, 70, 75, 90-92, 126, 137, 142; partisans 61, 82, 88; soldiers 48, 50; see also Soviet Union

Sacramento City College 167
Schreier, Grandfather 118
Schreier, Stasia (Sarah) (mother-in-law) 7, 118, **120-122**, 125, 128-129, 133-135, 138, 140-141
self image 96
Shelburne, Jeanette x
Sheparivtsi Forest 141, 143, 207
Siberia 2, 7, 92, 103, 116, 124-125, **127**-128, 133-137, 140, 142, 144, 148, 153, 162, 174, 180, 198-199, 206-207
Sikorski, General Władysław 137
Sobibór 196, 207
Sokal, Henryk (father-in-law) 7, **120-122**, 123, 140
Sokal, Julek x, 6-7, 113, 118-120, **122**, 124-126, 129-133, 135-136, 142-143, 180-181
Sokal, Rysio 7, 115, 118, 120, 133; see also Ben-Zvi, Ephraim (husband)
Sosnowice 195, 196
Soviet Union: deportation to 125; history 48-49, 124, 142, 206; life in 131, 133, 137; regime of 52; see also Russia

Spiegel, Philip x, 140, 212
Stanislawów 117, 141
Star of David 61, 206
Stern Gang 148
Szeparowce forest 141, 143, 207

Teachers College 153-154
Technion 115, 144, 148, 156, 162
Tel-Aviv Museum 150
Toledano, Shulamit x, 160
Treblinka 58, 207
Tripartite Pact 206
Truman, Harry (president of the U.S.) 103, 150

UCLA: *Law Review* 170; School of Law 170
Ukraine 117, 133, 142; people 119, 127, 133, 140, 142
United Nations 101, 146, 150; Partition Resolution 146, 208; Relief and Rehabilitation Administration (UNRRA) 101
University of California at Davis 166

Wannsee Conference 207
War of Independence 138, 153, 164
Warsaw: attacked by Germans 47-48, 124, 206; ghetto 53, **54-57**, 206-207; life 2, 11-12, **13**-14, 17-**18**, **21**, 26-28, 31, 34, 37, 39-40, 43, 49-50, 57, 70-71, 74, 90, 95, 109, 114-115, 122, 141, 184

Yad Vashem x, 142, 212
Yadin, Yigael ix, 151
Yalta 142
Yokneam 156, 162, 208

Ziemlyanka 134-135
Zieselman of Honchavska Street 34-36
Zionism 20, 104-106, 119, 146
Zyd 43

www.ingramcontent.com/pod-product-compliance
Ingram Content Group UK Ltd.
Pitfield, Milton Keynes, MK11 3LW, UK
UKHW041952140426
5217IPUK00015B/764